# WORKERS AND THE NEW DEPRESSION

Robert Taylor

MACMILLAN PRESS
LONDON

*First edition 1982*
*Reprinted 1983*

*Published by*
THE MACMILLAN PRESS LTD
*London and Basingstoke*
*Companies and representatives throughout the world*

ISBN 0 333 19295 8 (hardcover)
ISBN 0 333 33411 6 (paperback)

Printed and bound in Hong Kong

# Contents

*Introduction* vii

1 The Unemployment Crisis 1

2 The Wages Jungle 46

3 The Productivity Problem 79

4 The Training Scandal 100

5 Inequalities at the Workplace 119

6 Britain's Strike 'Problem' 150

7 The Myths of Trade Union Power 171

*Postscript:* In the Depths of the Slump 198

*Index* 203

# Introduction

Britain is suffering from its worst economic slump since the years between the two world wars of this century. Many forecasters do not expect the country to stage a major recovery for the rest of the eighties. Our own troubles are by no means unique. Most of the world has been plagued with inflation, high unemployment, rocketing energy costs and international monetary instabilities that worsened from the last few months of 1973, with the first shock waves of the quadrupling of oil prices by the world's oil exporting countries. We are already looking back to the early seventies, above all to the fifties and sixties as a golden age of successful achievement, even though such sentiments may have been hard to find at the time. With the new depression came a major philosophical assault on the main assumptions that produced levels of individual prosperity unprecedented in human history. Both social welfare spending by governments and the use of demand management in running the modified market economy are now denounced by an influential chorus of opinion-formers as dangerously inflationary and therefore mistaken. Many politicians (even some on the left of the spectrum) have gone back to older so-called economic truths of probity, self-reliance, thrift and in doing so they have been more ready than at any moment since the thirties to risk the dangers of social division and conflict within industrial societies that result from such views. It is the old, the poor, the sick, the racial minorities, above all the unemployed, who have become the victims in the battle to defeat inflation and destroy Britain's post-war consensus. We are witnessing a similar, depressing trend in President Reagan's America.

This book is not concerned primarily with either a description or analysis of Britain's new depression. Its aim is more exact – to look at the impact of our hard times on the condition of the British labour market, above all on the position of the country's manual workers. The basic argument contends that it is those men and women, without skills or qualifications, who are the overwhelming casualties. Of course, by the standards of the thirties, the condition of manual workers hardly looks desperate. The rhetoric of the 1936 Jarrow march seems out of place today. Despite its inadequacies, the welfare state has taken much of the sting from the pain of social deprivation. Nor if we look at the horrors of the Third World can the position of any of Britain's workers appear desperate. It is always useful to keep reminding ourselves that every complaint and criticism is relative. But this should not encourage complacency, even if it might start to modify the unappealing insularity and griping that bedevils so much thought and action in the Labour 'movement', where solidarity at home or abroad is in sadly short supply and appeals to sectionalist self-interest and economic nationalism hold sway.

Britain's manual workers are no longer having their grievances and fears articulated in our political system. The middle class revolutionaries who have taken over so many constituency Labour parties display little interest in 'piecemeal social engineering', in the gradual improvement of conditions for workers through patient reform. Manual workers are invariably seen as cannon fodder in a bogus class war, people whose votes can be used to pursue the politics of affirmation.

The British Labour 'movement' must stand condemned for its inability to either change or represent attitudes of mind among manual workers in our society. Elsewhere in western democratic Europe, Social Democracy has achieved social justice and economic growth in market economies. Here, for all its radical language and grandiose programmes, Labour has proved more accommodating to the conflicting external pressures that hamper progress on the one hand, and yet more dogmatic about such nonsenses as state ownership of industry (all power to the bureaucrats) on the other. The party and the trade unions who dominate its extra-parliamentary activities have failed to make Britain more egalitarian and socially mobile. Words like fellowship and fraternity are merely engravings on old banners. Solidarity between workers in Britain has become a rarity. A self-regarding sectionalism dominates today's Labour movement, the pursuit of individual gratification through the collective power of the workgroup. Union bosses and the politicians must bow to their demands and thus support and reinforce existing inequalities, where the survival of the fittest remains uppermost. Workers are left to the harsh, unforgiving, arbitrary ups and downs of the labour market. Those with muscle look after themselves and do so at the expense of everybody else. Others are priced out of their jobs or compelled to take low paid dead-end work.

We continue to live in the age of *laissez-faire* liberalism in the labour market, whose chief defenders are trade unions. The Labour party has become – more than ever before – the voice of the middle class protester and the union *apparatchik*. It speaks primarily for public service monopolies, for the powerful producer groups in our unequal society, who wax strong in the jungle of free collective bargaining. While Labour leaders mouth the slogans of Socialism more fervently than ever to curry favour with the tiny oligarchies who control the party at the grass roots, that once noble word has lost all meaning. The world of manual work is known only from books, not experience for a growing number of Labour party activists, while the Social Democrats are essentially a middle-class party.

By 1985 – for the first time in our history – Britain will have more white-collar than blue-collar jobs in the labour market, but the overwhelming majority of the massive flow of unemployed during this decade will come from the ranks of the manual workers. In the age of the micro-chip and robot, it is hard to see what the future holds for those millions of manual workers who were once the mighty collective labour power in our basic industries of motor cars and engineering, shipbuilding, coal and textiles. The Conservative government of Mrs Thatcher has brought a virtual halt to the onward expansion of the public service job boom, so there will be far fewer job opportunities for manual workers in that sector, even if they could become qualified and flexible enough to adapt to such an occupational change. The prospect of turning Tyneside shipyard workers into bank clerks and computer operators in Milton Keynes looks unreal.

The problem stems in part from the persistence of the voluntarist philosophy in Britain's labour market. Over the past twenty years there have been some important modifications, particularly with the introduction of redundancy provisions by law in 1965 and the creation of the tripartite Manpower Services Commission in 1974, to give a higher priority and coherence to manpower planning. But in essence, the old habits of mind remain very strong. The state is seen as a second-best substitute for the provisions of worker or union rights in the wider industrial relations area, compared to the hit and miss of collective bargaining where capital and labour wrestle for supremacy. As a result, we retain the worst industrial training system in the west. We neglect the manpower needs of our society and allow up to 300 000 young boys and girls to leave school each summer to sink or swim in an unfriendly, chancy, often brutish adult world for which they are ill-prepared by the schools. Our manpower practices, with their traditional emphasis on job restrictions and controls on skill entry, hamper efficiency and productivity and thus impoverish workers. Britain's workers (manual and non-manual) lack any sense of common purpose. The power of the workgroup predominates, far more than the muscle of the union, which is usually illusory. Our manual workers remain the most socially degraded, relative to white-collar staff, of any in western Europe. The 'them' and 'us' divide may not stimulate a clear-cut class conflict, but it remains tenacious, a social stigma in the market place that has hardly changed, despite superficial post-war material affluence.

Yet all is not gloom. The fluidity, the aversion to authority in most forms, the irreverance or cynicism, sheer bloodymindedness, makes our manual workers more unpredictable, much less passive than those of many other countries. They are not revolutionary proletariat, far from it. Yet nor are they submissive or mere aspirers to a so-called middle class life style. Owning a car, a colour television set, even a home, has modified but not overcome more fundamental traits and attitudes.

Conflict at work is a necessary consequence of living in a democratic society. Collective bargaining can lay down intricate ground rules that shape the demands of employers, union negotiators and workers, but it is unable to eradicate the dynamic of action and reaction on the shop-floor that reflects the divided interests of capital and labour. Marxists and business consultants alike may dream of a Utopia without strife, but industrial relations remains an endless dialectic, a constantly shifting pattern of unequally balanced forces, where capital not labour dominates.

This book is not concerned with the production of blueprints or 'solutions'. It remains an understandable but nevertheless exasperating habit of the British mind to assume that every human problem must have a sensible, all-embracing answer to which everybody can agree, if only they are given the facts. My purpose has been to highlight a vital part of the wider national problem. It is an examination of our labour market – unemployment; wages; productivity; training; workplace inequalities; strikes; the so-called power of the unions; the political realities of the workplace. If you take those issues together they represent an important reason why Britain has suffered a relative economic decline during the past twenty years that has speeded up under the conditions of the new depression.

This book owes an enormous intellectual debt to many writers on the labour market, as you will see from my notes. There is one particular inspiration, who would be saddened by our continuing inadequacies if he were still alive – Santosh Mukherjee, a brilliant labour market economist, who died tragically young. He helped me to understand and appreciate the wider, underlying problems of our labour market in my early days as a labour correspondent.

*May 1982*

# 1 The Unemployment Crisis

## THE NEW SLUMP

Mass unemployment has returned to haunt and bewilder the western industrialised world during the past few years for the first time since the great depression between the wars. In the countries of the Organisation for Economic Co-operation and Development (OECD) in the winter of 1981–2 more than 28 million people were jobless, compared with around 10 million in 1973. Across the world the International Labour Office in Geneva has estimated that over 300 million people have no work to do and many more remain underemployed. In the United Kingdom over one in twelve was unemployed by the winter of 1981–2. The Manpower Services Commission has projected that the numbers out of work in this country will continue to rise and fail to fall very dramatically at least before the late eighties. There seems very little prospect of any return to 'full' employment for the rest of this century.

The optimistic commitment of Winston Churchill's coalition government in 1944 to make 'the maintenance of a high and stable level of employment after the war' one of the primary aims and objectives of domestic policy-making was regarded at the time as wildly improbable of achievement. Whitehall poured scorn on Lord Beveridge's hope of 1942 in his famous social insurance plan that the registered unemployed could be kept down to no more than 3.5 per cent of the labour force. In the event, from 1948 until 1966 the average monthly total for unemployment in Britain was a mere 1.7 per cent. As late as July 1966 it stood at 1.1 per cent.[1] In 1947 the Attlee cabinet was so worried about labour shortages rather than unemployment that it even considered the abolition of football pools to release desperately needed women workers for what was deemed to be more useful and productive work.

Now those post-war years already look like a lost golden age, a fond memory that has gone forever.

The British people became concerned about the return of mass unemployment only in 1980–1, but the upward trend in the dole queues first began with the July 1966 economic measures. Thereafter, even during the boom periods, the level of unemployment never dropped again to the lowly figures of the early and middle sixties. During the seventies successive governments from Heath to Callaghan worried over how many jobless the country would tolerate without protest. In the winter of 1971–2, Mr Heath's Conservative cabinet decided to change the whole course of their economic strategy, in part because of the deepening anxiety in Whitehall about the level of registered unemployment which threatened to break through the psychological shock barrier of one million. When the actual total reached that figure under a Labour government in October 1975, there was much public hand-wringing, particularly from union leaders, but few obvious signs of awareness that the unemployment problem was going to turn rapidly into a national tragedy. It was not really until the summer of 1980 that public opinion polls began to record greater anxiety among people about unemployment than about inflation. Suddenly Britain's recession quickened pace, more savagely than in any other western industrialised country.

Between October 1979 and October 1980 the numbers out of work rose by 48 per cent in Britain, compared with a rise of 31 per cent in the United States over the same period, 15 per cent in West Germany and 7 per cent in France. In September 1980 the seasonally adjusted unemployment rate in Britain was 8.0 per cent, compared with 3.5 per cent in West Germany, 6.8 per cent in France and 7.5 per cent in the United States. Only Belgium and Ireland experienced a higher proportion of jobless workers through the winter of 1981–2 and into the spring of 1982.

## WHY NO REVOLT?

The outbreak of riots in many inner city areas of Britain during July 1981 suggested that the limits of social tolerance about unemployment were being reached. No doubt, there was a complexity of reasons behind the rioting mainly on the streets of Brixton and Southall in London and Toxteth in Liverpool, but lack of work combined with poor housing, widespread poverty, the collapse of the family network, and clumsy police behaviour produced some of the most savage scenes of mob violence witnessed in Britain since the eighteenth century. It took a long time to reach that disintegration of authority and social control. There seemed to be an almost complacent belief among politicians that the country's social fabric was strong enough to withstand mass unemployment.[2]

Why did the return of worklessness fail to generate so little genuine protest for so long? It is true there were large Labour party organised demonstrations in Liverpool and Glasgow in the winter of 1980–1 and a People's March from Liverpool to London in May 1981 under the auspices of the unions. Union leaders warned the government *ad nauseam* about the dangers of conflict as the dole queues lengthened. Ultra Left groups like the Socialist Workers party and the Militant Tendency (a Marxist organisation within Labour's ranks) sought to mobilise unemployed youngsters through marches and demonstrations, but they made no lasting impact. The National Front launched a big effort to recruit among the ranks of the white young unemployed with a racist appeal. Yet none of this could really be described as central to Britain's unemployment crisis. For the most part, we moved almost stoically into an unhealthy acceptance of the inevitability of mass unemployment, for which there was no alternative.

Members of Parliament – Labour as well as Conservative – were not inundated with letters from their unemployed constituents, angry and frustrated because of lack of work. Union officials, Labour party politicians, even the so-called Tory 'Wets', talked in a rather vague and abstract manner about contemporary unemployment. Their fondness for flamboyant rhetoric which conjured up a vision of a return to the conditions of the thirties betrayed the failure of their imagination to understand that worklessness in the eighties was quite different. Very few union activists spoke at union conferences with any recent, personal knowledge of what it was like to be without a job in Britain in 1980–2. We saw nothing really to compare with the Jarrow hunger march of 1936 or Wal Hannington's National Unemployed Workman's Movement of the inter-war years.

The trade unions were rather slow to gird themselves into protest against the high level of unemployment, perhaps in part because the dole queues lengthened with speed during the period of the 'social contract' between the Labour government and the Trades Union Congress from 1975 to 1978, when union leaders were being treated by ministers as partners in the management of an economy in crisis.

But there is a more fundamental explanation for the apparent union indifference and inertia about unemployment, at least until the winter of 1980–1. Most workers who lost their jobs in the early years of the new depression during the late seventies were not in trade unions. A survey carried out by the Policy Studies Institute in May 1980 found that as many as 61 per cent of the jobless had not been union members.[3] A total of 69 per cent of those who had been in a union in their last job lapsed their membership when they became unemployed. A mere quarter of the unskilled male whites had been union members in another PSI study.[4] A clear fracture exists between a worker without a job and the trade union. Once unemployed, workers often see little point in belonging to a union anymore.

A TUC survey of union facilities for the unemployed carried out in 1980 brought only 27 responses from 110 affiliate unions representing five out of eleven million trade unionists. While 23 said they allowed workers to stay in the union if they lost their job, most were found to provide no special benefits or service for their unemployed.[5] The average union unemployment benefit amounted to 4 pence a year per member, but only six unions told the TUC they provided any such benefit to their jobless members, although there was a readiness to reduce the membership subscription for those who lost work. In 1981 the TUC began to encourage the development of special centres for unemployed workers, where they could hope to find help with their personal and practical problems such as social security and job search. By the summer of that year ten full-time such union centres had started up, with a further 20 part-time advice bureaux in the unemployment blackspots. The most effective one was at Newcastle-upon-Tyne with four full-time workers under the special employment programme of the Manpower Services Commission.

It could be argued that most union leaders only started to wake up to the magnitude of the unemployment crisis when their own organisations began to suffer a net decline of members in the winter of 1980–1. Too often union officials found themselves having to bargain against their own better judgement over generous severance pay for their members in doomed plants rather than providing an effective resistance to compulsory redundancies and factory closures. Certainly there was no consistent and obvious outside pressure on the Labour government during the late seventies to even accept a modest measure of reform that would have given a measure of belated justice for many of the unemployed – by putting those without work for more than a year onto long-term security benefits such as the sick and disabled enjoy. David Donnison, then chairman of the now defunct Supplementary Benefits Commission, fought an almost single-handed battle, alongside the Child Poverty Action Group, to achieve that laudable objective with little overt support from either Labour cabinet ministers or union leaders.

The minister in charge of welfare benefits at the Department of Health and Social Security, the left-winger Stan Orme, recognised it was a sensible, long overdue reform which would have helped to pull a growing number of adult workers out of acute deprivation, but he admitted that few voices were raised in its support in the political system to ensure it became an urgent priority on the Labour cabinet's agenda. Union leaders seemed more preoccupied with using what little influence they had in protecting the value of old age pensions and pressing for the introduction of child benefit. Yet the cost of putting the long-term jobless on long-term benefits would have been no more than two fifths of the £45 million a year (at 1976 value) by which Denis Healey, the Chanceller of the Exchequer, cut the tax on company cars in 1976–7 in response to pleading from business pressure groups.

To an alarming extent, Britain's unemployed in the late seventies and early eighties failed to constitute an effective, organised lobby of protest. They did not mobilise themselves into a mass movement which Whitehall policy-makers were compelled to heed. It was only with the eruption of violence on the streets in the deprived inner city areas in the summer of 1981 that the government began to recognise the size of the catastrophe. Nor did the jobless exercise much influence over the ranks of the Labour 'movement', where the producer interests of public service white and blue collar militants grew more dominant. The unemployed do not enjoy immediate or easy access to the power elites of our society. The experience of unemployment for a lengthy period of time falls on a relatively small minority of workers on the outer fringes of the labour market. For most workers, the early years of the slump did not produce cuts in living standards, genuine hardship and the loss of their job. There was an obvious lack of solidarity, of comprehension between those in employment and those without any work. Once the champion of the underdog, the Labour 'movement' became much more the powerful voice of the producer groups with proven muscle power. Unemployment was a useful propaganda weapon with which to attack the Conservatives, but far too often the issue appeared to generate indifference, resignation, inertia, rather than anger and disgust, leading on to radical action.

Certainly the mood appeared to change in 1981–2, but observers of the slump would suggest the new concern was long overdue. Why did it take so long for mass unemployment to arouse wider anxiety and eventual protest?

## A FLOW NOT A POOL

In part, it is due to the main characteristic of today's unemployment. The overall monthly total of the registered jobless provides the shock-horror headlines in our daily newspapers, but that figure conveys a misleading picture of the nature of the crisis. It gives the impression that the unemployed are somehow set apart from the rest of the country's working population, a stagnant pool of unwanted labour, surplus to the needs of an economy where domestic demand is being kept down as a deliberate government policy to defeat inflation. But Britain's jobless are not a standing army, ready for action and growing larger all the time, but a changing crowd of individual workers who are moving in and out of the labour market (see Table 1.1). The monthly aggregate figure remains only a hurried snap-shot taken on one day each month of the constant flow of people who move at varying speeds through the experience of unemployment. A better image of the reality is not of a pool but a bath of water where the taps are running at an increasing volume and the plug hole at the other end of the bath has become gradually blocked up. More than four million people a year found

TABLE 1.1 The unemployment flow, July 1975–December 1981

| | *Joining register* | *Leaving register* | *Excess of inflow over outflow* |
|---|---|---|---|
| *1975* | | | |
| July | 326 000 | 282 000 | 44 000 |
| December | 318 000 | 280 000 | 38 000 |
| *1976* | | | |
| July | 313 000 | 300 000 | 13 000 |
| *1977* | | | |
| July | 290 000 | 277 000 | 14 000 |
| December | 290 000 | 290 000 | – |
| *1978* | | | |
| July | 279 000 | 286 000 | –7 000 |
| December | 277 000 | 287 000 | –10 000 |
| *1979* | | | |
| July | 263 000 | 276 000 | –13 000 |
| December | 279 000 | 267 000 | 12 000 |
| *1980* | | | |
| July | 317 000 | 263 000 | 54 000 |
| December | 368 000 | 274 000 | 94 000 |
| *1981* | | | |
| July | 320 000 | 273 000 | 47 000 |
| December | 340 000 | 315 000 | 25 000 |

SOURCE Unemployment statistics (monthly press release).

themselves on the unemployment register by 1980–1, nearly one in six of the workforce, but for many of them the experience of being workless was a relatively short-lived one. Just over a third of the unemployed who registered in a month found a new job within three months in October 1980 and a quarter received fresh employment within eight days. These are the people the economists call the 'frictional' unemployed, the mobile workers required in any free market economy. Even in a slump those men and women provide the necessary lubricant to ensure the match of supply with demand. In January 1981 about 283 000 of the jobless had been without work for less than four weeks, but we just do not know how many of them will stay on the register longer than this.

The unemployment picture began to worsen dramatically after the summer of 1980 as it took longer than it used to do for workers to find a new job. The actual duration of unemployment is what should stimulate public concern rather than the overall aggregate total. In 1973 at the height of the Heath leap for growth it took a worker an average eleven weeks to find a new job. By 1978 the length of time rose to 17 weeks. In the autumn of 1980 it reached more than 20 weeks. By the winter of 1981–2 the average period out of work was over six months.

The numbers of workers joining the register climbed during the 1975–6 period, but fell back a little during the late seventies as the economy enjoyed a brief recovery. From the summer of 1980 the monthly flow onto the dole queues began to rise sharply again. At the same time, the numbers leaving the register each month fell. As the figures opposite demonstrate during 1978 and the early months of 1979 there was actually an excess of outflow over inflow on the register, a clear sign of a marked improvement in the unemployment position that brought a fall in the overall figures. But from the autumn of 1979 there was a dramatic reversal in the flow data, which accounts for the frightening jump in the jobless totals in 1980–1. 'The small changes between monthly totals arises not from small movements on and off a largely unchanged register but from the difference between two very large flows on to and off the register each month. So while there are many long-term unemployed, a feature of the register is its constantly changing composition', argued the *Employment Gazette*.[6]

The ratio of the registered unemployed to the vacancy figures also provides an important indication of the magnitude of the unemployment crisis. The job vacancy statistics cover the number of jobs notified each month to the state employment service between the dates of each unemployment count and the number of vacancies that are either filled or withdrawn. These give a rough impression of the vacancy position in

TABLE 1.2 The job prospects since August 1979

| | *Average level of vacancies* | *Change* |
|---|---|---|
| *1979* | | |
| August | 253 400 | −2 000 |
| September | 249 100 | −4 300 |
| October | 244 300 | −4 800 |
| November | 239 600 | −4 700 |
| December | 231 800 | −7 900 |
| *1980* | | |
| January | 221 300 | −10 500 |
| February | 206 900 | −14 400 |
| March | 193 000 | −13 800 |
| April | 180 200 | −12 800 |
| May | 170 800 | −9 500 |
| June | 159 400 | −11 400 |
| July | 145 200 | −14 200 |
| August | 131 000 | −14 200 |
| September | 119 700 | −11 300 |
| October | 111 200 | −8 500 |
| November | 103 500 | −7 700 |
| December | 99 900 | −3 600 |
| *1981* | | |
| January | 99 500 | −4 000 |
| February | 100 200 | +700 |
| March | 99 600 | −800 |
| April | 93 400 | −6 200 |
| May | 90 100 | −3 300 |
| June | 84 700 | −5 400 |
| July | 92 900 | +8 200 |
| August | 98 500 | +5 400 |
| September | 97 800 | −700 |
| October | 100 600 | +3 200 |
| November | 104 300 | +3 700 |
| December | 107 500 | +3 200 |

SOURCE Department of Employment press release.

the economy, for only as estimated one in every three jobs is actually notified to the state employment service.

But the official vacancy data, as shown in Table 1.2 and Figure 1.1, provide a graphic illustration of the sharp decline in the economy during 1980.

## WHO ARE THE JOBLESS?

The official monthly statistics cover those people who have registered at the employment office as 'seeking employment' and accepted by the staff

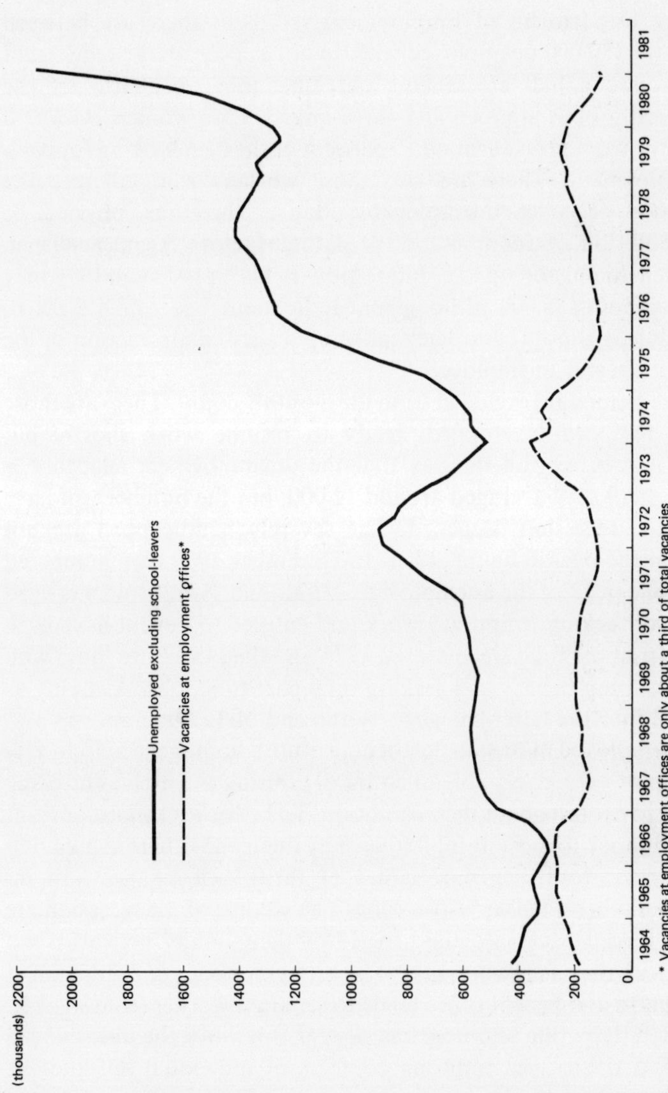


FIGURE 1.1 Unemployed and vacancies in the United Kingdom 1964–81(three-month moving average, seasonally adusted)

SOURCE Department of Employment press release.

as being 'capable of and available for work, whether they are entitled to unemployment benefit or not'. This has been the definition since 1922. Not everybody without work is included in the monthly unemployment total. The Department of Employment estimates there are between 300 000 and 350 000 unemployed who do not appear on the register, of whom around a half are seeking part-time jobs. A quarter of the unregistered jobless are men and three quarters are women, with two thirds of the women and around 10 per cent of the men looking for part-time employment. There are also those workers who fall into the classification of being 'unemployable' due to their age, physical or mental condition, or a combination of all three factors. Again, such men and women do not add up to a static figure. Between 1973 and 1976 they numbered about 135 000, although unemployment rose from 453 000 to 888 000 during those years. They make up a very small fraction of the overall number of unemployed.

Various groups are excluded from the monthly count. There are those who are temporarily stopped, ready to resume work shortly but available for benefit on the day that the unemployment snapshot is taken. In 1979 they averaged around 12 000, but the number will have risen as the recession deepened. The severely handicapped are not counted in the overall figure either. In December 1979 they numbered 120 000, one in 12 of the unemployed at that time. Adult students aged 18 and over seeking temporary work and entitled to benefit have been dropped from the total since March 1976 and then there are those who are not claiming benefit and seeking only part-time jobs. As many as 35 000 fell into the latter category by the end of 1979.

The unemployed in Britain do not constitute a homogeneous, closely-knit group of people, capable of either organising themselves or being mobilised to protest about their condition. To be without a job comes as a personal shock to most. It is often seen by them and others as a kind of moral stigma. Mid-Victorian values of thrift, self-reliance and individualism remain tenaciously strong. The victims of the recession are generally forced back into the privacy of their family networks and isolated from their fellow workers. The very experience of signing on at the job centre and benefit office tends to separate worker from worker. In the often desperate and hopeless struggle for work the unemployed usually find themselves enduring conflicts of individual self-interest, where the divisive character of the competition for a limited number of jobs discourages the growth of much sense of collective solidarity, a recognition among the unemployed themselves that they suffer from common problems. Words such as alienation, boredom, passivity, emptiness summarise the daily condition of many unemployed workers. Such a condition seems hardly conducive to the organisation of a protest movement.

The unequalising impact of unemployment on the labour market (perhaps even more startling than it was between the wars) is a major reason for the lack of public anger about the return of mass unemployment.

The 1978 Department of Health and Social Services cohort survey of the unemployed emphasised the fact that the majority of the jobless are manual workers, many of whom have suffered some previous experience of being without work.[7] As many as 78 per cent of the sample had suffered at least one spell of registered unemployment between 1973 and 1978, while more than two in five had at least two spells and a quarter three or more. Only 8 per cent of the sample had last worked as a manager, employer or in a professional occupation, compared with 23 per cent of the general population and 40 per cent who had worked in semi-skilled or unskilled manual jobs, compared with 19 per cent of the general population. Similar findings were also reported in the PSI survey in 1980. A total of 40 per cent of the male jobless stock is made up of the manual unskilled, while only 7 per cent of the labour force is in this category. Around 15 per cent of men entering unemployment are unskilled. Nearly two thirds of young males aged under 25 had been out of work on two or more occasions in the previous two years, while one in eight had been unemployed three or more times. Indeed, it seems that unemployment is still suffered by a limited proportion of the workforce. The typical member of the dole queue of 1982 was a youngish male unskilled, unqualified manual worker, who was not in a union in his previous job, which was with a small manufacturing firm in an assisted area of the country.

The main victims of the slump are male manual workers without any skills or qualifications. In October 1980 as many as 40.4 per cent of the male unemployed were classified as 'general labourers' (473 400). This compared with 25.7 per cent from other manual occupations; 15.5 per cent from craft and other manual occupations; 8.2 per cent from managerial and professional jobs; 7.5 per cent from clerical and related and 2.8 per cent from other non-manual occupations. Just under one in five were from the stagnant construction industry (267 996), compared with 8.1 per cent from manufacturing and the same proportion from mining and quarrying. A mere 34 449 of the jobless were previously employed in the government service and 60 336 in local government.

If you are an unskilled manual worker you are more than six times more likely to be without a job than if you are a white-collar worker, relative to the working population. The more a worker is disadvantaged, the greater the probability that he or she will find it hard to get a new job. Even now, when the scourge of unemployment has begun to hit a much wider cross-section of the country's workforce, the overwhelming majority come from the ranks of manual labour. Many of those workers often found themselves in and out of a job, even during the relatively affluent years of the fifties and early sixties. Now they have become the most dispensable for employers who are trying desperately to maintain their businesses through cost cutting and higher productivity.

## THE HARD CORE JOBLESS

The long-term unemployed have become almost the forgotten men and women of the depression, but Table 1.3 shows that they make up an increasingly large proportion of the overall jobless. In October 1981 the number of those unemployed for more than 12 months reached 747 000, just over one in four of those without work. That figure is expected to stay at more than one million, near to one in three, even if the general level of unemployment begins to stabilise or fall by 1983–4. The Manpower Services Commission noted in its 1981–5 corporate plan:

> The number would go still higher but for the tendency of many of the long-term unemployed to move off the register into sickness benefit or retirement: if more long-term unemployed did leave the labour force because of poor employment prospects this would represent a change in the balance between registered and unregistered unemployment rather than a diminution of the problem.[8]

The long-term unemployed are still likely to be older workers. In January 1982 as many as 168 300 out of the 398 200 male jobless over the age of 55 had been without a job for more than a year, compared with 97 900 who had been unemployed from 26 weeks to a year and 132 000 without work for under 26 weeks. This compares with the duration of the under 25-year old males, where a total of 162 800 out of the 708 000 unemployed had been jobless for over a year, compared with 156 600 in the 26 week to one year category and 388 600 in the under 26 week position.

TABLE 1.3 The rise of the long-term unemployed, 1975–81

| *July* | *Number* | *% of all unemployed* | *Males* | | *Females* | |
|---|---|---|---|---|---|---|
| | | | *Number* | *%* | *Number* | *%* |
| 1975 | 143 000 | 14 | 129 000 | 16 | 14 000 | 6 |
| 1976 | 230 000 | 16 | 202 000 | 20 | 28 000 | 8 |
| 1977 | 307 000 | 20 | 254 000 | 23 | 53 000 | 11 |
| 1978 | 328 000 | 22 | 264 000 | 25 | 64 000 | 14 |
| 1979 | 341 000 | 25 | 269 000 | 29 | 72 000 | 16 |
| 1980 | 343 000 | 19 | 268 700 | 29 | 74 000 | 12 |
| 1981 | 627 000 | 22 | 490 600 | 24 | 136 000 | 16 |

SOURCE Manpower Services Commission annual reviews.

Studies carried out for the Manpower Services Commission in 1979 by Research Surveys of Great Britain and Cragg Ross and Associates provide graphic evidence of the long-term unemployment problem, which has grown much more serious since the middle seventies.[9] It was found that nearly a half of the long-term unemployed were over the age of 54. While the impact of unemployment remains harder on younger people, once unemployed an older person finds it much more difficult to find a new job. A quarter of those interviewed in the RSGB survey who had gone for work said they had failed to obtain it because of their age. But this is not to play down the spread of long-term unemployment to younger workers. In 1970 only 21 per cent of the long-term jobless were aged 25 to 44; by 1979 that proportion had risen to 33 per cent. Among the 20 to 24-year olds the figure went up from 3 to 11 per cent over the same time period.

For those who had worked, most had enjoyed a reasonably stable employment history. Just over half (53 per cent) had been in their last job for at least two years and 20 per cent had spent a decade or longer in their last job. However, one in five had more erratic work experience. A quarter of the semi-skilled and unskilled workers and two fifths of the general labourers had had 10 or more jobs in their lives.

Redundancy was the main reason most of the long-term unemployed gave for losing their previous job. This was especially true of manual workers in construction and the basic manufacturing industries. Poor health was a major factor affecting the employability of some of the long-term jobless (see Table 1.4). Less than two thirds of those in the RSGB survey rated their general state of health as good, while 30 per cent rated it fair and 8 per cent poor. Just over a third (37 per cent) of the

RSGB survey interviewees said they did suffer from some handicap or illness which affected their activities. As many as a third of these people were actually registered as disabled. Just over half the 45 to 59-year olds and 44 per cent of the 60 to 64-year olds said they were affected in some way by ill health.

TABLE 1.4 Health and unemployment

| *State of health* % | *1 year– 18 months* | *18 months– 2 years* | *2 years– 3 years* | *Over 3 years* |
|---|---|---|---|---|
| Good | 74 | 66 | 59 | 47 |
| Fair | 21 | 29 | 32 | 39 |
| Poor | 4 | 5 | 8 | 13 |

SOURCE 'A Study of the Long-term Unemployed', Manpower Services Commission, 1979, 4.28.

The long-term unemployed are caught in a vicious spiral of decline. As the MSC's own study in 1978 argued:

> Boredom leads to loss of drive, laziness and inertia; skills decline and the individual feels less and less capable of taking up work again; at the same time he is less likely to secure work because his social contacts decline and because, insofar as employers regard a long period of unemployment as indicating unfitness for work, they will tend to look to more economically active recruits. Moreover, because the long-term unemployed risk being rejected out of hand by prospective employers, they stand less chance of being submitted for vacancies by local Job Centre staff of the employment service.[10]

Less than half the respondents to the RSGB survey enjoyed any formal training either for or during their working lives. Only 19 per cent had ever been apprenticed. As many as 77 per cent had no educational qualifications at all. A total of 16 per cent suffered from literacy problems, while as many as 36 per cent thought it would be personally important to them if they were given a chance under a government scheme to improve their reading and writing. Half the respondents in the CR study thought their lack of skills and/or qualifications was an obstacle to them finding work.

But the accusation that the long-term unemployed are work-shy is misplaced. Only 8 per cent of those interviewed for either survey, who registered in order to obtain benefit, were not looking for work. But as time goes by more and more of the unemployed cease to visit the job centre. Less than two thirds of those unemployed for more than two years were still doing so. A total of 60 per cent of those unemployed for a year to 18 months were still actively job seeking, but only 35 per cent of those without work for more than three years were doing so. Nearly a quarter of the RSGB survey sample said that they were not currently looking for work, while a further 29 per cent said they were job-seeking in only a desultory way. Only 12 per cent said they were still taking a great deal of their time in the search for work.

The long-term unemployed face much more serious difficulties than other people in finding new work, but they receive less help from the Manpower Services Commission, mainly as a result of government indifference. On 1 April 1978 the special temporary employment programme (STEP) was launched by the MSC, directed at helping long-term unemployed adults over the age of 18. The original intention was to provide for 25 000 people to be in the programme by the end of 1979. As the MSC explained: 'The work provided by the sponsors of the projects has to be work which would not otherwise be carried out, so that the jobs provided genuinely add to the numbers of jobs available to the unemployed.[11] The employment provided was to last up to a maximum of one year. Two priority groups were defined at the start – those aged from 19 to 24 who had been without work for more than six months and those aged over 25 who lacked continuous employment for more than a year. The aim was to ensure two thirds of the STEP participants came from those particular categories. After a slow start as many as 13 400 people were on STEP schemes by March 1979, with 44 per cent of them from the two priority groups, far below target. In 1978–79 only 26 per cent of STEP entrants had been jobless for more than a year. Three quarters of the participants were men, with 54 per cent aged between 19 and 24.

Undoubtedly a major restraint on developments lay in the decision not to allow any private sector sponsors to gain commercial advantage out of participation in STEP. The incoming Conservative government left no time in cutting back STEP. In June 1979 the 1979/80 STEP budget was slashed from £84 million to £54 million and STEP was confined as a result to special development and development areas and designated inner city areas. The original target of places was also cut from a planned 30–35 000 to only 12 500. STEP was tightened up so that the unemployed from the two priority groups alone would be able to take part in their schemes, with exceptions only for supervisors, managers and skilled manual workers, where no alternatives could be found among the long-term jobless. During 1979–80 only 22 400 unemployed entered STEP, with nearly 70 per cent coming from Scotland, the North, the North West and the Midlands. By March 1980, as a result of the cuts policy, a mere 10 500 people were on STEP schemes. But over three quarters were now from the priority groups. An MSC follow-up survey of STEP participants who entered a scheme in January 1979 found 62 per cent had no formal qualifications and nearly a third had never had a job, while nearly half those who had were previously employed in manual occupations.[12] As many as 45 per cent left STEP for normal, permanent work. Almost half the January 1979 entrants were on schemes sponsored by local authorities and a third sponsored by voluntary or charitable bodies. The rundown of MSC help for the long-term unemployed was the direct result of the government demand for public spending cuts and it had nothing to do with the actual needs of the labour market. On the contrary, the numbers of people on the register for more than six months continue to grow rapidly.

The MSC wrote a letter of protest to Mr Prior on 24 June 1980 in which it argued that the MSC considered its services with present resources were inadequate to meet the needs imposed by mounting unemployment. It went on to point out that under already agreed cuts there would be fewer staff in the employment service by 1983 than at the time of the separation from the unemployment benefit side of the system in 1974, despite the enormous increase in the number of jobless during the intervening period and the calls on it to back training and special employment programmes. 'Needs are growing far faster than we can possibly hope to improve productivity and there is already a great gap between needs and provisions in some cases', claimed the MSC.

> There are now 340 000 people who have been out of work for a year or more and the figure will rise towards half a million over the next two years. The STEP programme, with provision at present for some 12 500 places, is quite plainly inadequate in comparison. Unemployment among certain disadvantaged groups is worsening quickly and we are particularly worried by the situation of ethnic minorities. The community cannot afford to neglect these problems.

But such entreaties failed to persuade Mr Prior that there should not be a further 8 per cent cut in the MSC's staff in the name of government economies, no matter what extra burdens were being imposed on the service by the growing magnitude of the unemployment crisis.

In the autumn of 1980 the MSC was given the go-ahead by the government to expand its places for the long-term unemployed to 25000 by March 1982, far less than the planned growth under the last Labour government. Mr Prior conceived the new community enterprise programme as the successor to STEP. The 1981–5 MSC corporate plan argued:

> The new programme will emphasise work of environmental improvement, encourage greater participation by the private sector in projects arranged by voluntary agencies. It includes funds for partnerships involving the private sector and voluntary and public bodies in the creation of new enterprises, where that can be arranged consistently with the existing government programmes for this purpose.[13]

But the MSC admitted this was 'a very limited response to the problem of the unprecedented levels of long-term unemployment'. The government's view was that nothing much could be done about the long-term unemployed problem until there was a general uplift in the economy.

The failure to tackle the long-term unemployment issue since 1976 indicates a lack of concern among the politicians. Those unskilled and semi-skilled men and women on the fringes of a harsh labour market were seen as expendable. They did not riot and they were not responsible for football hooliganism. Whatever their private bitterness or resignation, few either practised or espoused any mindless philosophy of violence. Nor were they attracted to political extremist groups. In short, the long-term unemployed were conspicuous by their silence, and because they did not make themselves into a public nuisance, they suffered relative neglect.

## YOUNG JOBLESS

Young people are especially vulnerable to unemployment. The PSI study in 1980 found that as many as 36 per cent of the men in their sample of the unemployment flow after six weeks without work were in the 18 to 24-year old age bracket, while 63 per cent were between 18 and 34. Unemployment rose much faster among young people than any other age group during 1980. It shot up by an astonishing 80 per cent for the under nineteens from 106 000 in January 1980 to 191 000 a year later and by 70 per cent for the 19 to 24-year olds (341 000 to 583 000). The only exception was the relatively small rise of 50 per cent among the under 18-year olds who had already had a job since leaving school, though the Manpower Services Commission believed that the main cause for this was 'the fact that school leavers are taking longer to find their first job.'[14] In January 1981 nearly 20 per cent of the registered jobless were under the age of 20, although that age group made up less than one in ten of the working population.

The 19 to 24-year old age group is perhaps the most at risk of experiencing unemployment. In October 1981 as many as a quarter of the total unemployed fell into that category, and they made up 16 per cent of the long-term unemployed. 'In some ways they encounter the same types of problems as their younger contemporaries', observed the Manpower Services Commission. 'They tend to lack the qualifications required for skilled manual and non-manual occupations; they lack sufficient work experience at least in relation to older workers; and they are more likely than older, longer-serving workers to be selected for redundancy. Moreover, they will in some instances find themselves competing for work not only with older, more experienced workers but also with better qualified recent school leavers'.

Indeed unemployment among young people, particularly school-leavers, has aroused considerable 'official' anxiety since the middle seventies. There is no denying that the numbers of jobless in the under 24-year old age bracket rose substantially during the period. Between 1961 and 1972 at each stage in the recovery of the economic cycle, youth unemployment failed to return to the low levels recorded at the start of the sixties. It is now generally accepted that if the male level of unemployment goes up by 1 per cent, the increase amounts to 1.7 per cent for the young.

In 1974 the National Youth Employment Council produced a disturbing report, drawing attention to the problems of youth unemployment. In particular, it pointed out that there had been a net reduction in the number of jobs for young people. Between 1966 and 1971 there was a job loss of 173 000 for boys, 25 per cent over the period, and a 23 per cent fall in the number of employment opportunities for girls. 'Many young people used to work in occupations like delivery-boys, lorry-drivers mates, craftsmen's mates, tea-boys and messenger-boys', argued the study. 'It is occupations like these which suffer most when employers seek to improve productivity'.[15] Evidence was also found that the increase in the youth rates of pay, bringing them more into line with the adult rate was also reducing job chances for young workers. Santosh Mukherjee in a report for the Manpower Services Commission in 1974 pointed out that in the early sixties the proportion of under 20s unemployed was roughly the same as the proportion of

TABLE 1.5 The unemployed: by age

| | Percentage rates | |
|---|---|---|
| | *October 1979* | *October 1980* |
| Under 18 | 11.3 | 19.9 |
| 18–19 | 10.0 | 15.2 |
| 20–24 | 8.0 | 12.7 |
| 25–34 | 5.0 | 7.6 |
| 35–44 | 3.3 | 5.0 |
| 45–54 | 3.4 | 4.8 |
| 55–59 | 4.4 | 5.8 |
| 60 and over | 8.4 | 10.5 |
| All ages | 5.5 | 8.4 |

SOURCE Manpower Services Commission paper to the National Economic Development Council, May 1981, p. 4.

TABLE 1.6 The growth of youth unemployment predictions

| | *Year and quarter* | *School leavers* | *Others* | *Total* | *% of labour force under 18* |
|---|---|---|---|---|---|
| 1980 | Q2 | 132 000 | 92 000 | 224 000 | 24 |
| | Q3 | 316 000 | 115 000 | 431 000 | 32 |
| 1981 | Q2 | 329 000 | 153 000 | 482 000 | 51 |
| | Q3 | 504 000 | 180 000 | 684 000 | 51 |
| 1982 | Q2 | 430 000 | 168 000 | 598 000 | 63 |
| | Q3 | 582 000 | 195 000 | 777 000 | 58 |
| 1983 | Q2 | 464 000 | 172 000 | 636 000 | 68 |
| | Q3 | 603 000 | 197 000 | 800 000 | 60 |
| 1984 | Q2 | 454 000 | 168 000 | 622 000 | 67 |
| | Q3 | 586 000 | 192 000 | 778 000 | 59 |

SOURCE Manpower Services Commission, 'Corporate Plan 1981–85', p. 8.

people of all ages unemployed (1.6 per cent in both cases in 1964), but from 1968 onwards the position of young people grew increasingly worse.[16] By 1972 7.6 per cent of the under 20s were unemployed, compared with 3.6 per cent of people of all ages. Table 1.7 shows the position over ten years.

In May 1977 the Manpower Services Commission published an important report by Geoffrey Holland called 'Young People and Work', which examined the feasibility of launching a programme to help the

TABLE 1.7 The rise of the young jobless, 1971–80

| *January* | *School-leavers under 18* | *Other young people* | *Total number jobless aged 19 and below* | *–of which job-less for more than 6 weeks* |
|---|---|---|---|---|
| 1971 | 6 000 | 76 | 82 000 | 33 000 |
| 1972 | 10 000 | 118 | 128 000 | 69 000 |
| 1973 | 9 000 | 106 | 115 000 | 59 000 |
| 1974 | 5 000 | | | |
| 1975 | 8 000 | | | |
| 1976 | 38 000 | 186 | 224 000 | 148 000 |
| 1977 | 48 000 | 204 | 252 000 | 177 000 |
| 1978 | 57 000 | 217 | 274 000 | 198 000 |
| 1979 | 44 000 | 196 | 240 000 | 180 000 |
| 1980 | 43 000 | 197 | 240 000 | 160 000 |

SOURCE 'Manpower Review', (Manpower Services Commission, 1981) p. 11.

young unemployed. This highlighted some unpleasant facts. Between January 1972 and January 1977 unemployment among 16 to 17-year olds had shot up by 120 per cent, compared with a rise of 45 per cent among the labour force as a whole. Unemployment for the young (16 to 17-year olds) increased as a proportion of total joblessness from 5.4 per cent in January 1971 to 9 per cent in January 1977. Girls were more badly hit than boys. Their proportion of total youth unemployment increased from 35 per cent in January 1970 to 49 per cent by January 1977, while there was a three-fold increase in the number of young unemployed from the ethnic minorities. The median duration of unemployment for the under 18-year olds increased more rapidly over the period than for any other age group. At the same time, the MSC report found disturbing evidence that employers were less than satisfied with the calibre of young people entering the labour market. With every likelihood of a further deterioration in the position of the young worker in the labour market, with the large number of school-leavers looking for work between 1977 and 1982 the MSC proposed a long-term programme with government funding to prepare young people for work through work experience, training workshops and community service. It estimated that it would cost £168.31 million in the first year to launch such a comprehensive programme. Up until that time the official response to youth unemployment had proved rather piecemeal. The job creation programme, launched in October 1975, provided 58 000 employment opportunities for young people in its first 15 months, but the proportion of school-leavers among its beneficiaries had fallen off. A recruitment subsidy for employers to take on school-leavers was introduced in October 1975, but 76 per cent of the firms admitted to the MSC that they would have taken on the youngsters even if they had not been given a subsidy to do so. It was replaced a year later by a youth employment subsidy, which was deliberately designed to aid the long-term young jobless. The work experience scheme was launched in September 1976, open to all 16 to 18-year old young unemployed. In its first seven months it provided 16 500 places for young workers in just over 3000 schemes, with 60 per cent of them in service industries. Community industry had been introduced in 1972 as a 'temporary' measure, By 1977 it had the capacity to take on 4000 young people, a rather modest effort.

The government accepted the main thrust of the Holland report and the resulting Youth Opportunities Programme (YOP) was launched on 1 April 1978, with a target of 187 000 entrants in its first year of operation. The previous schemes to help youngsters were incorporated within the greater MSC effort. By March 1979 162 000 young people had entered the programme. The MSC gave a promise that no young school-leaver from Easter or summer 1978 would be without an offer of a suitable YOP place by Easter 1979, and only 1600 failed to have that undertaking honoured. There was satisfactory evidence in YOP's first year of operation that it did provide a way into more permanent employment. Over 80 per cent of young people leaving the programme were in a job after seven months.

But by 1979 the numbers of young people out of work had risen appreciably, so YOP was expanded to provide 219 000 entrants in its second full year of operation. That figure was pushed up to 230 000 as the employment position worsened for school-leavers in the summer of 1979. By the end of March 1980 only 485 unemployed school-leavers were without an offer of a suitable YOP opportunity and survey evidence continued to show that as many as seven out of ten leaving a YOP scheme went into a full-time job within a few months. There were also encouraging signs that many employers were willing to enable youngsters they employed on work experience on their premises to have off the job further training. 38 per cent of YOP work experience (70 000) entrants enjoyed this facility in the second year of its operation, compared with only 17 per cent (22 000) in 1978–9. Mrs Thatcher's government made severe cutbacks in the manpower programme when it came to power in May 1979, so that an increasingly large proportion of the MSC's expenditure was being devoted to special programmes rather than general manpower policy. In 1976 under 8 per cent had been spent on programmes for the unemployed. By 1981 that figure had risen to 43 per cent and it seems likely to go even higher in the next few years.

However, youth unemployment has continued to take the major share of political concern and this has been provided with far greater resources than government schemes to help other categories of the unemployed.

In November 1980 Mr Prior announced a further expansion in the Youth Opportunities Programme to provide 440 000 opportunities in 1981–2, as many as 180 000 more than had been planned for the previous year and double the number available in 1979–80 (see Table 1.8). The MSC was asked to offer a suitable chance to all unemployed school-leavers by Christmas 1981, rather than Easter 1982, and to provide the same opportunity to any 16 or 17-year old who had been registered as out of work for more than three months. Mr Prior also promised to give more emphasis on courses or schemes within YOP that allowed youngsters who could not find a permanent job after their time on the programme to join another YOP scheme. 'We are trying, as resources permit, to work towards the point where every 16 and 17-year old not in education or a job will be assured of vocational preparation as necessary up to his or her eighteenth birthday', Mr Prior told the Commons (21 November 1980).

TABLE 1.8 How the young dominate the special programmes (£ million at 1980 prices)

| | 1980/1 | 1981/2 | 1982/3 | 1983/4 |
|---|---|---|---|---|
| Youth opportunities | 185.2 | 170.3 | 169.8 | 169.8 |
| Special Temporary Employment Programme | 39.4 | 48.6 | 48.6 | 48.6 |
| Community Industry | 17.4 | 17.4 | 17.4 | 17.4 |

SOURCE Draft of the 'Manpower Services Commission Corporate Plan 1981–85'.

But by the summer of 1981 there were signs of abuse of YOP, as some employers sought to substitute permanent, full-time employees with youngsters paid for by the state for six-month-intervals. An internal MSC survey estimated that nearly one in three of all youngsters on work experience schemes were being substituted for permanent workers, something that began to arouse trade union anxieties.

Moreover by the middle of 1981 only 40 per cent of YOP youngsters were going into permanent jobs after their six-month period on a scheme. Have young unemployed been given a disproportionate amount of public attention? W. W. Daniel and Elizabeth Stilgoe, in their 1977 follow-up study of the unemployed, questioned whether the 18 to 24-year old group, who made up a high proportion of the jobless, were a major cause for concern. 'We found that they had spent very short periods in their last jobs and had generally given them up voluntarily because there was some aspect that they did not like', they wrote. 'They were relatively unconcerned about being out of work because they tended not to have dependants and often lived with their parents where someone else was the main bread-winner. Their chief concern was that limited funds restricted their social activities. They found new jobs relatively very quickly'.[17] The PEP study concluded that the existence of a high number of young adults on the unemployment register was more 'a reflection of relatively short but frequent periods of unemployment rather than the inability of young adults to find any kind of work'. They suggested the government had its priorities wrong on who should benefit from the main thrust of its help for the unemployed.

But the outlook for young people in the labour market is grim. The Warwick University Manpower Research Group estimated in its post-1981 budget forecasts that seasonally adjusted unemployment would stand at 2.8 million by the end of 1983 and school-leaver joblessness would rise from 220 000 to 470 000 over the same period. By 1 January 1984 only 40 per cent of the labour force aged under 18 are expected to have jobs, compared with 70 per cent in 1980. Over 40 per cent of that age category will have had no experience of work at all, a truly frightening statistic with obvious portents for social order. 'Official' concern with the peculiar difficulties of youth unemployment may not seen to have been misplaced after all.

## OTHERS AT RISK

Women workers are also especially vulnerable to unemployment. Between 1975 and 1980 the number of registered jobless female workers rose by as many as 223 per cent – from 141 600 to 457 000, compared with an increase of 59 per cent among unemployed men. While in 1975 women made up 17.9 per cent of the registered jobless, by 1980 they constituted 30.7 per cent of the national total. At the same time, women have become more active in the labour market. Between 1975 and 1980 the number of them in employment rose from 9 094 000 to 9 340 000, an increase of 2.7 per cent, whereas there was an actual drop of 3.3 per cent in the number of men at work. But many women with working husbands fail to register as unemployed, because they are likely to be ineligible for state benefits and they expect to find a new job without using the state manpower services. The Department of Employment reckons there are about 250 000 women seeking work in Britain who do not show up in the unemployment statistics. The Equal Opportunities Commission believes that the real figure for female unemployment is over 700 000, more than 40 per cent greater than the monthly totals suggest. Nearly a third of the PSI cohort unemployment survey sample after six weeks on the register were found to be women in 1980. The heavy impact of the recession on women workers has added to the strain within households. Between 1970 and 1979 the number of employed women in the labour market rose by a million, with a dramatic 25 per cent increase in the number of women working in the service sector. There is a real danger that discrimination against female employment will intensify because of the high level of male joblessness.

Disabled workers also find it very difficult to get a job in a time of deep recession. In November 1981 around 180 000 registered disabled people were unemployed. This represents a jobless rate of 13 per cent for the disabled. On top of this there are known to be almost 90 000 unregistered disabled workers seeking work through the employment services. The Manpower Services Commission has estimated that while it takes about 19 weeks to place a general unemployed worker on average into a new job, the average length of duration for a disabled worker is as much as 62 weeks. During the first eight months of 1981 the number of disabled people placed into jobs by the state service was 50 per cent less than in 1979, compared with a drop of 30 per cent in total placings.

Unemployment among the ethnic minority groups in the labour market rose much faster than total unemployment during 1980. By November 1981 it reached the highest figure ever recorded at 120 000 (4.2 per cent of all unemployed). As the Manpower Services Commission argued: 'Ethnic minority unemployment shows sharper fluctuations than total unemployment and is concentrated in certain areas.'[18] The ethnic workers tend to be younger, unskilled and concentrated in vulnerable industries like metal manufacture, vehicles, textiles and metal goods production. 'In part this disadvantaged position is due to discrimination', conceded the Manpower Services Commission. 'In part it is due to factors such as educational disadvantage, language problems and short or broken duration of British residence.'

David Smith in his 1981 PSI study of the ethnic unemployment crisis agreed that the existing inequalities between different races in the labour market were accentuated during a slump. 'The rate of unemployment has always, or almost always, been higher among the minorities than among whites', he wrote, 'and at times of rising unemployment the minorities are particularly vulnerable. In that way, minorities are another group which, being already at a disadvantage within the labour market, also have a higher than average risk of suffering the more severe deprivations of unemployment.'[19] The ethnic workers are more likely to lose their jobs through dismissal. They tend to have larger families to maintain and they are more ready to take jobs which they find less satisfactory than their old ones. But Smith's detailed analysis makes two important points that must qualify the picture. His sample (taken in mid-1979) among jobless Asians and West Indians did not 'ascribe their difficulties to racial discrimination or prejudice and tended not to react to their misfortune in an extreme or violent manner'. After the riots in the St Pauls district of Bristol in July 1980, Brixton in April and July 1981 and at Toxteth in Liverpool in July 1981, such an observation may well reflect attitudes of an earlier, less desperate time before the recession deepened, though it has been argued that the breakdown of order on those occasions was due almost entirely to a deterioration in the relations between the police and the ethnic communities or racism than to the experience of high unemployment.

More importantly, Smith also stressed that it remains a serious mistake to differentiate too starkly between the position of the black unemployed worker and the white unemployed worker. 'Too much attention to these differences creates a false perspective' he argues.

> 'The extra risk of being unemployed that arises from being an Asian or West Indian is small compared with the extra risk from being an unskilled manual worker rather than a senior manager or a university professor. Once unemployed, the extra deprivation through lack of money that is associated with belonging to a minority group is small compared with the gross deprivation suffered by the great majority of those who are unemployed for a lengthy period regardless of their ethnic group.'

## REGIONAL DIVISIONS

There is another divisive dimension in today's unemployment – its regional variations (see Table 1.9). The older industrialised areas of

TABLE 1.9 Regional unemployment, 1976–81 (annual average)

| | *1976* | *1977* | *1978* | *1979* | *1980* | *1981* |
|---|---|---|---|---|---|---|
| South East | 4.2 | 4.5 | 4.2 | 3.7 | 4.8 | 8.0 |
| Greater London | 4.0 | 4.3 | 4.1 | 3.7 | 4.7 | 7.7 |
| East Anglia | 4.8 | 5.3 | 5.0 | 4.5 | 5.7 | 9.1 |
| South West | 6.4 | 6.8 | 6.5 | 5.7 | 6.8 | 8.7 |
| West Midlands | 5.8 | 5.8 | 5.6 | 5.5 | 7.8 | 13.5 |
| East Midlands | 4.7 | 5.0 | 5.0 | 4.7 | 6.5 | 10.1 |
| Yorkshire and Humberside | 5.5 | 5.8 | 6.0 | 5.7 | 7.8 | 12.1 |
| North West | 6.9 | 7.4 | 7.6 | 7.1 | 9.3 | 13.7 |
| North | 7.5 | 8.3 | 8.8 | 8.6 | 10.7 | 15.0 |
| Wales | 7.3 | 8.0 | 8.4 | 8.0 | 10.3 | 14.5 |
| Scotland | 7.0 | 8.1 | 8.2 | 8.0 | 10.0 | 13.6 |
| Northern Ireland | 10.0 | 11.0 | 11.5 | 11.3 | 13.7 | 18.3 |
| Great Britain | 5.6 | 6.0 | 6.0 | 5.6 | 7.3 | 11.1 |

SOURCE *Employment Gazette*, December 1980 and March 1982.

Britain suffered real decline for much of the seventies, but the scourge of unemployment spread out from the assisted parts of the country to hit former boom areas, particularly the West Midlands, that used to symbolise post-war worker affluence. Regional differences widened during 1980 and 1981. During 1980 the national unemployment rate went up by 3.7 percentage points to 9.1 per cent, but in that same period the rate in the South East of England rose by 2.8 points to 6.3 per cent, while in the West Midlands the increase was as large as 5.3 points, pushing up registered unemployment in Britain's industrial heartland to 10.6 per cent by January 1981.

The startling jump in the dole queues of Britain's most crucial manufacturing region can be seen in Table 1.10 below.

It was not until 1975–6 that the rate of unemployment in the West Midlands exceeded that of the country as a whole for the first time since the Second World War. Between October 1979 and October 1980 there was a 70 per cent jump in the numbers out of work in that region. There has been further sharp deterioration since then. As an MSC study of prospects for the West Midlands up to 1983 concluded: 'Even if recovery does occur, this is unlikely to be reflected in any increase in employment levels in manufacturing industry above those reached at the depth of the recession'.[20] The following table shows the rise in unemployment between 1955 and 1968.

The regional differences mask wide disparities between employment

TABLE 1.10 The arrival of unemployment in the West Midlands

| % | June 1975 | November 1980 | February 1982 |
|---|---|---|---|
| Birmingham | 4.4 | 10.7 | 16.5 |
| Burton on Trent | 2.7 | 6.3 | 10.4 |
| Coventry | 4.4 | 11.6 | 15.5 |
| Oakengates | 5.0 | 14.5 | 20.2 |
| Redditch | 3.0 | 10.6 | 16.2 |
| Rugby | 2.3 | 8.4 | 12.2 |
| Stoke on Trent | 2.3 | 8.8 | 13.7 |
| Walsall | 3.3 | 11.4 | 17.3 |
| Wolverhampton | 3.9 | 11.6 | 16.3 |

SOURCE *Employment Gazette*, July 1975, December 1980 and March 1982

TABLE 1.11 The West Midlands: the rise of unemployment (average annual rate)

| | | | |
|---|---|---|---|
| 1955 | 0.5 | 1969 | 1.8 |
| 1956 | 0.7 | 1970 | 2.0 |
| 1957 | 1.1 | 1971 | 3.0 |
| 1958 | 1.4 | 1972 | 3.6 |
| 1959 | 1.3 | 1973 | 2.2 |
| 1960 | 0.8 | 1974 | — |
| 1961 | 0.9 | 1975 | — |
| 1962 | 1.5 | 1976 | 5.8 |
| 1963 | 1.7 | 1977 | 5.8 |
| 1965 | 0.7 | 1978 | 5.6 |
| 1966 | 0.8 | 1979 | 5.5 |
| 1967 | 1.8 | 1980 | 7.8 |
| 1968 | 2.0 | 1981 | 13.5 |

SOURCE *Employment Gazette*.

areas. In November 1981 Consett in county Durham had the largest proportion of workers jobless (18.4 per cent) in England, because of the closure of the steel plant in the town that autumn. Hartlepool (16.2 per cent), Wearside 15.5 per cent) and Liverpool (15.2 per cent) were not far behind. Every part of the northern region, except for Carlisle and Furness had more than one in ten of its workers unemployed. In Wales there were no exceptions. The highest unemployment blackspot was Ebbw Vale (17.1 per cent) and the lowest was Cardiff with 10.7 per cent. In Scotland Irvine was suffering the most from unemployment with 18.2 per cent jobless, followed by North Lanarkshire (16.9 per cent) and

Dumbarton (15.9 per cent), but the east coast was still enjoying the relative benefits of the North Sea oil industry with only 4.8 per cent unemployed in Aberdeen.

Northern Ireland, an unemployment problem even in the sixties, was in a crisis condition. Strabane had an unemployment rate of 31.2 per cent, the highest in the country, followed by Cookstown (29.7 per cent); Dungannon (28.8 per cent); Newry (26.4 per cent) and Londonderry (22.5 per cent).

But there were also growing signs of the spread of the depression to parts of southern England. The seaside towns of Ramsgate and Southend topped the 10 per cent jobless figure. So did Torbay, Plymouth and Great Yarmouth. Corby new town with 19.8 per cent jobless was a casualty of the contraction in the steel industry. Yet some places continued to register very low levels of unemployment. In November 1980 Hertford and St Albans had 3.6 per cent unemployment, the smallest proportion in Britain, while Watford, Slough, High Wycombe and Crawley remained comparatively unscathed by the deepening recession. There were some parts of London (Hackney, Brixton and Tower Hamlets) with unemployment rates as high as the assisted areas, but much of the capital continued to enjoy buoyant levels of employment. Britain remains a highly centralised country, with most of the important economic and political decision-making power concentrated in the South East of England and it is still possible to live and work there without coming into any direct contact with the unemployment problem. The regional variations, with their unequal impact, underline the intractable nature of the depression and perhaps provide a part of the general explanation for the widespread apathy and indifference about the unemployed.

The inner cities of England are also areas of particularly high unemployment as Table 1.12 shows. The Department of Employment found that between 1971 and 1976 the number of manufacturing jobs in metropolitan areas fell by 20 to 30 per cent in most cases, although 15 per cent of all jobs in the country are based in Newcastle-upon-Tyne, Manchester, Liverpool, Birmingham and London. In October 1978 unemployment in those five cities amounted to 13 per cent of the total jobless figure in the country. Again, the figures reveal that manual workers suffer the most.

In a speech at Swansea in July 1980 Mrs Thatcher suggested that the unemployed should be prepared to look for work outside the area where they lived, but a slump is hardly the best moment to stimulate worker mobility. In July 1979 the rules covering the Employment Transfer

TABLE 1.12 Inner city deprivation: unemployment by occupation group; September 1978 (%)

| | *Managerial* | *Clerical and related* | *Other non-manual* | *Craft and similar* | *General labourers* | *Other manual* |
|---|---|---|---|---|---|---|
| Newcastle | | | | | | |
| inner city | 9 | 12 | 3 | 12 | 45 | 19 |
| TTWA | 7 | 12 | 5 | 16 | 40 | 20 |
| Manchester | | | | | | |
| Salford | | | | | | |
| inner city | 10 | 7 | 5 | 9 | 47 | 22 |
| TTWA | 10 | 13 | 5 | 9 | 42 | 21 |
| Liverpool | | | | | | |
| inner city | 6 | 10 | 5 | 11 | 46 | 21 |
| TTWA | 5 | 11 | 6 | 11 | 44 | 23 |
| Birmingham | | | | | | |
| inner city | 9 | 8 | 5 | 12 | 31 | 36 |
| TTWA | 8 | 11 | 5 | 11 | 32 | 32 |
| London | | | | | | |
| inner city | 12 | 16 | 5 | 12 | 28 | 28 |
| TTWA | 13 | 19 | 5 | 12 | 24 | 27 |
| Great Britain | 9 | 15 | 6 | 10 | 36 | 23 |

(TTWA equals travel to work area)

SOURCE *Department of Employment Gazette*, August 1979, p. 747.

scheme were changed as a move to save taxpayers' money. The most important alteration was to insist in future that workers could only take advantage of its provisions if there was no suitable job in the applicant's home area and no suitable unemployed workers available in the applicant's proposed work area. By removing any obvious incentive for the unemployed in assisted areas to move elsewhere in search of work, the government actually succeeded in reducing the number of successful applicants under the transfer scheme from 22 897 in 1978/9 to a mere 9785 in 1979/80.

The pay limit above which applicants were not eligible for assistance was raised from £100 to £120 a week (£6240 a year) on 1 March 1980 and the grants and allowances were increased by 19 per cent that April. Yet despite the Prime Minister's suggestion that the unemployed should move around for work, this looked an increasingly hopeless option to take as the unemployment crisis grew into one of national, not just regional magnitude. The shortage of unskilled and semi-skilled manual jobs (to judge by the vacancy rates) became acute even in affluent areas like the South East of England and large parts of the diverse London labour market from 1980.

The obstacles to geographical mobility grew increasingly formidable for the unemployed.

As the 1979 MSC report on the inner London labour market argued;

> Although it is theoretically possible for people to travel long distances to work in and around London, and many do, the high and increasing cost of travel and housing tends to reduce mobility, particularly for the low paid and to restrict local labour markets within London. Thus the unemployed and low paid become concentrated in the areas of low cost public housing, while skilled workers and professionals compete for high cost housing which may still be some distance from their work.[21]

Nor did the prospect for moves by workers into a relatively affluent, booming area like Reading look much brighter. A 1979 MSC study of the Reading local labour market suggested: 'without a further upward adjustment in the earnings differential inward mobility of labour is likely to remain rather limited unless low cost rented housing is offered to 'key' skilled workers by local authorities.'[22] A handful of unemployed lathe turners were attracted down from Scotland to work in Bracknell with the help of financial aid from the employment transfer scheme, but the report admitted that 'local MSC officials and employers alike maintain that housing costs and lack of many key worker local authority housing schemes are the main economic block to migration'.

The obstacles to mobility caused by past government intervention in the housing market are real enough. Only in the new towns is population migration directly linked to the provision of housing. Most local councils give priority to their own waiting lists and the rehousing of people covered by their slum clearance programmes. It is very difficult for workers – whether unemployed or not – to move with their families from one part of the country to another as a result. Moreover, the 1974 Housing Act accentuated the collapse of the private rented furnished sector of the market by giving security to tenants for the first time. As Johnson and Salt argue:

> The result has been to reduce the availability of such accommodation, repeating what has happened in the private-rented unfurnished sector and creating a further housing barrier to labour migration. Thus it is in those sectors of the housing market where government has taken

> most control, and which provide relatively cheap accommodation, that there is most restriction on entry for migrants. Yet at the same time these are the sectors most likely to comprise those workers – the lower paid and the unemployed – at whom the government's migration policies are aimed.[23]

Half of Britain's skilled manual workers are now owner occupiers, but it is difficult for them to move from areas of high unemployment to more prosperous parts of Britain like East Anglia and the South East because of the difference in the level of house prices. They find it hard to sell in the depressed region they want to move away from, so they lack the financial base to buy a house in the more buoyant area, where houses often cost twice as much. Mrs Thatcher's government tried to encourage local councils to set aside a certain percentage of their total housing stock as lets for people moving into their area for work, but this has made a limited impact, amounting to only 1 per cent, 2500 lets a year. Unless there is a major stimulus to the private rented property market through the relaxation on the restrictions over tenure and the growth of private shared-ownership (partly mortgage; partly rent) it remains hard to see how many workers can hope to become more mobile when the labour market improves. A deep depression is not the best of times to encourage geographical movement by workers. As the Manpower Services Commission 1981 review argued: 'As unemployment rises and the number of vacancies fall there is considerably less scope for reducing geographical mismatch between unemployed people and unfilled jobs'.[24]

## INDUSTRY IN PERIL

The unequal impact of unemployment on the labour market can also be seen in its wide disparity between different sectors of the economy.

As Table 1.13 shows, private manufacturing industry has taken the brunt of the rundown in jobs. John Hughes estimates that there was a catastrophic fall of over two million jobs in manufacturing during the seventies, a decline of a quarter to around six million by the winter of 1981–2.[25] Manual workers have inevitably suffered the most as a consequence. Again, Hughes has calculated that the total 'input' of manual working hours in British manufacturing by late 1980 was only 60 per cent of its level in the middle of the sixties. This amounts to a 40 per cent fall in total manual working hours in manufacturing in a decade

TABLE 1.13 Where the unemployed came from (%)

| | *Male* | *Pro-fessional* | *Non-manual* | *Skilled* | *Semi-skilled* | *un-skilled* |
|---|---|---|---|---|---|---|
| Manufacturing | 34.7 | 22.8 | 16.8 | 35.2 | 50.3 | 28.2 |
| Construction | 23.2 | 9.3 | 3.7 | 28.7 | 14.7 | 40.6 |
| Gas–electric | 1.0 | 0.5 | 1.1 | 0.8 | 1.0 | 1.7 |
| Transport–communication | 6.6 | 4.1 | 7.0 | 9.1 | 4.4 | 3.8 |
| Distribution | 11.7 | 29.8 | 24.8 | 9.9 | 9.5 | 5.3 |
| Financial services | 1.3 | 4.6 | 8.2 | 0.3 | 0.1 | – |
| Personal services | 8.5 | 18.1 | 14.2 | 5.6 | 9.8 | 7.8 |
| Public administration | 4.6 | 4.1 | 8.5 | 3.1 | 2.5 | 6.1 |
| Agriculture–forestry | 0.7 | – | – | 0.4 | 2.3 | – |
| Mining–quarrying | 1.4 | 2.1 | 0.3 | 2.2 | 0.4 | 1.3 |

SOURCE 'Analysis of the Unemployed Flow: A preliminary report', Policy Studies Institute and Manpower Services Commission, February 1981. Results of interviewing six weeks after registration.

and a half. During the seventies the Warwick Manpower research group calculated that there was a net drop of just over a million jobs in manufacturing. In engineering the fall was 425 200; in textiles and clothing 285 800 (just over 20 per cent of the workforce); in food, drink and tobacco a decline of 85 500 (around 10 per cent).

Redundancy, once the way governments wanted to shake out surplus labour in the name of efficiency, has become common place. During 1980 as many as 390 000 workers lost their jobs, due to redundancies of 10 or more workers. This was two and a half times greater than the number in 1979. Figure 1.2 indicates the growth of redundancy since the late sixties.

Small firms rather than big companies in manufacturing account for a large slice of the unemployment. A quarter of the men who became jobless in the PSI cohort study had worked in establishments employing less than ten people, while 41 per cent had been in work in establishments with no more than 25 workers on their pay-rolls. The median establishment size for working men generally amounts to around 125 workers.

Contrary to popular belief, neither the 1965 Redundancy Payments Act nor the 1975 Employment Protection Act have taken the pain out of the experience of redundancy in a harsh labour market. For many

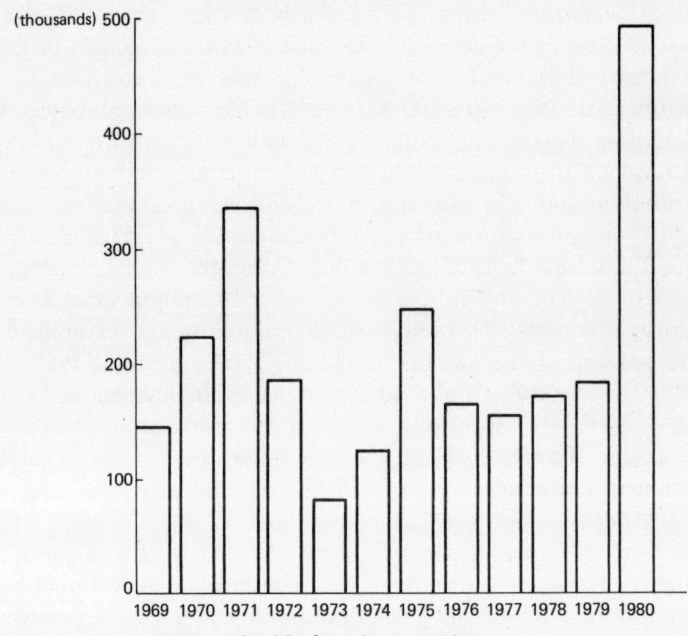


FIGURE 1.2 Redundancies notified to the MSC's Employment Service Division, 1969–80: Great Britain

SOURCE Manpower Services Commision paper to the National Economic Development Council, June 1981.

workers who lose their jobs, new work opportunities are still found quickly without them experiencing unemployment, but the PSI survey discovered that two thirds of those who did register had received no notice at all or no more than a week. Older people in professional occupations were far more likely to have longer notice of their impending redundancy than manual workers.

## THE COST OF UNEMPLOYMENT

Mass unemployment is not just a human tragedy, but a huge financial burden on our society.

The crippling cost of unemployment to the economy is now recognised even by the Treasury. The state loses income tax receipts and national insurance contributions when a worker loses his or her job and it must meet the cost of unemployment and other social security benefits. In February 1981 the Treasury estimated that the direct cost to the Exchequer for every extra 100 000 added to the registered jobless was £340 million. This was made up of £205 million loss in current receipts (£115 million from income tax; £75 million from national insurance contributions; and £15 million from the national insurance surcharge) and £135 million addition to current public spending (£65 million from national insurance benefits; £55 million from other social benefits; £5 million from rent and rate rebates; and £10 million in additional administrative costs). This suggests that every extra person on the dole queue costs the Exchequer as much as £3500 a year (at 1980/1981 prices). The inexorable and dramatic rise in unemployment in 1980–1 made a disastrous impact on the size of the public sector borrowing requirement (PSBR), one of the key indicators in the Thatcher government's economic strategy to defeat inflation.

The Manpower Services Commission in 1980 made detailed calculations on the burden of unemployment. It estimated that a cut in the number of registered jobless from 1.8 million to 700 000 would raise national output by around £6500 million a year (at 1979 prices), as much as 4 per cent of the gross domestic product. Every 100 000 increase in the size of the registered jobless meant a further loss of £590 million in output. The MSC revealed that 2.5 million unemployed represented £10 700 million in lost national production.

The estimated net financial cost in 1979–80 of unemployment rose to as much as £4000 million (40 per cent of the 1979–80 public sector borrowing requirement). The MSC estimated that if the dole queues were halved, costs would fall to £2075 million. Every 100 000 extra unemployed would cost £300 million a year at 1979–80 prices in transfer payments and lost revenue. Two and a half million registered jobless meant a total charge on the Exchequer of £7405 million. Such horrific figures did nothing to deflect the Thatcher government's concentration on limiting the money supply in the battle against inflation. Apparently the added burden of high unemployment on the PSBR was seen by Treasury ministers as a painful but necessary price to be paid in order to restore the country to financial health. Critics of monetarism argued that this was a vicious cycle of decline that pushed Britain further and further into slump conditions. The more ferocious the attempt to cut public expenditure and squeeze the money supply, the greater the size of the numbers out of work and therefore the heavier was the burden of the unemployed on the PSBR, but the larger the PSBR grew the more necessary Treasury ministers argued for the need to deflate the economy. It was this single-minded dogmatic adherence to the money supply targets and the size of the PSBR that made the recession much worse in Britain than elsewhere in the western industrialised world.

The TUC put the waste of unemployment into individual financial terms. The annual bill to the state of one family on the dole on average pay of £6000 a year came out as follows:

| | £ |
|---|---|
| Lost income tax | 1060 |
| Lost indirect tax | 247 |
| Lost national insurance contributions | 1043 |
| Cost of unemployment benefit | 2258 |
| Cost of family income supplement | 231 |
| Rent and rate rebates | 441 |
| Free school meals | 156 |
| Administration | 156 |
| Redundancy pay | 615 |
| **Total** | **6207** |

The personal condition of today's unemployed is not really comparable to the inter-war years. The soup kitchen, the pawn shop and the means test are no longer familiar social landmarks in our society. But on the other hand, there remains little doubt that the vast majority of the unemployed suffer real financial hardship. A study in 1972 of the jobless in Coventry, Newcastle-upon-Tyne and Hammersmith found that in each area around two thirds had incomes of less than £15 a week, while only a sixth had over £20 a week. Average manual worker earnings in each area were found to be substantially above those levels. Two years later a national survey of the unemployed by PEP concluded: 'The costs of unemployment remained substantial for all groups and the idea that the current level of social benefits for the unemployed makes unemployment tolerable was not borne out by our findings'.[26] Nearly three quarters of the PEP sample said it was 'bad' or 'very bad' for them being without a job. As many as 72 per cent mentioned 'lack of money' as their primary cause for concern, while over half the respondents had been unable to meet some of their household financial commitments. 'The greatest difficulty was caused by loans taken on while in work, followed by motor tax and insurance, rent and mortgage payments, and gas, electricity and telephone bills', argued the survey.

A study carried out by the North Tyneside community development project in the middle seventies underlined the desperate condition of most unemployed workers. It discovered that 'more than four out of five unemployed were below 120 per cent of Supplementary Benefit requirements [that is, borderline cases not entitled to benefit], compared to one in twenty of the employed men. None of the unemployed men had an income of more than twice [that is, 200 per cent of] the SB level'.[27] Moreover, 'both single men and men with a wife but no dependent children in the unemployed sample had an average income of about two thirds of their working counterparts, but this figure was considerably higher than the average income of the single working men'. The community development project also found that 'as unemployment continues, potential earnings decrease while the perceived minimum income needed does not'. Apparently, 'those men who had earned wages at or above the regional average were always substantially better off than when they were unemployed, unless they had four or more dependent children'.

The North Tyneside study also highlighted graphically the unsatisfactory character of the social benefits system as it applies to the unemployed. It pointed out that eligibility for the flat rate benefits depends on contributions paid while in work over a relatively short period. The contribution conditions debar important groups of people from entitlement to unemployment benefit such as school-leavers, women or those whose spell in work had not been long enough to enable them to qualify for benefit. Claimants among the unemployed can be refused benefit for up to six weeks after signing on the register if they caused their own loss of work by leaving employment without 'just cause' or had been fired through their own fault. Again, if somebody who is unemployed refuses to 'avail themselves of suitable employment' when it is offered to them or declines to go for an interview for a job, they can be disqualified from benefit for up to six weeks.

Earnings-related benefit is payable to an unemployed person after the second week out of work and it continues for six months bringing the weekly amount up to 85 per cent of previous earnings, but as the North Tyneside study emphasised: 'The payment of both flat rate benefit and earnings-related for the maximum period is dependent on a stable employment pattern before the spell of unemployment begins', and this is not usually the case for many of the jobless.[28] From 1982 the Government abolished the earnings-related supplement and unemployment benefit was taxed after April 1982, further official attacks on the living standards of the jobless.

Evidence to the Royal Commission on the Distribution of Income and Wealth in 1978 from the Centre for Labour Economics argued that the unemployed suffered a sizeable fall in their net weekly income, compared with when they were in work. 'While 30 per cent of those unemployed for under a month are living below 120 per cent of the Supplementary Benefit level, this is the lot of 80 per cent of those who have been out of work for over a year', it argued.[29] 'By contrast less than 10 per cent of those in work are living at this level'. The Centre also pointed out that nearly half the unemployed, when they had worked, had been in the bottom 20 per cent of weekly earnings, while 70 per cent of them had fallen within the bottom 40 per cent of weekly earnings. The unemployed were found to lose on average 25 per cent of their net weekly income as a consequence of being without a job. Estimates produced by the Manpower Services Commission in 1980 demonstrate how most of the unemployed experience a real drop in their living standards as a result of being without a job.

TABLE 1.14 Deprivation on the dole

| *Marital status* | *Sex* | *Dependants* | *Gross weekly earnings* | *Net weekly income in work* | *Disposable weekly income out of work* | *Income out of work as % of income in work* |
|---|---|---|---|---|---|---|
| Single | Female | None | £56.00 | £44.78 | £28.34 | 63 |
| Single | Male | None | £90.50 | £65.17 | £28.34 | 43 |
| Married | Male | Wife | £90.50 | £69.61 | £39.95 | 57 |
| Married | Male | Wife plus two children | £90.50 | £77.79 | £57.26 | 74 |
| Married | Male | Wife plus four children | £90.50 | £94.71 | £82.51 | 87 |

NOTE The gross weekly earnings relate to three quarters of national earnings levels; table relates to persons becoming unemployed in April 1980; out of work income is for those unemployed between 29–52 weeks; calculations assume full claims made for child benefit, rent/rate rebates; free school meals and welfare milk.

SOURCE 'Review of the Services for The Unemployed', Manpower Services Commission, March 1981.

A major study of the unemployed, carried out by the Department of Health and Social Security in 1978, provides further convincing evidence of the financial difficulties of being without a job.[30] It established that most of the unemployed were previously in low paid work. Of the 2300 male sample taken from the register, as many as 40 per cent earned between £40 and £70 a week in their previous full-time job, with a third reporting earnings of under £50 a week. The average pre-tax weekly earnings of the unemployed in their last job was £70, compared with a national average at that time of £86 a week. Only 10 per cent of the labour force as a whole earned under £50 a week. Half the DHSS sample fell into the bottom 20 per cent of the earnings table. The 1978 survey also revealed that less than one in ten of the unemployed received either redundancy pay or pay in lieu of notice from their former employer. It is true that 47 per cent of the men received some form of special payment, when they left their former job, but 32 per cent of them enjoyed only holiday money entitlement and 17 per cent a week's wages in hand. As many as 60 per cent actually received less than £100, while a fifth got between £100 and £300 and the remaining fifth more than £300.

Most could not rest in comfort as they started to cope with the traumas of being unemployed. Forty three per cent said that they (and their wives if they were married) had no savings to draw upon at all, while half again (21 per cent of the sample) said they had less than £250 in savings. Only 9 per cent of the sample claimed to have savings that totalled more than £1250.

It is often argued that nowadays (unlike in the inter-war period) unemployed men can rely on the earnings of their working wives and dependants to see them through a bad spell on the dole. But the 1978 DHSS survey provides precious little comfort that this assumption is true. In the week prior to their husband's registration, only 39 per cent of the wives were either in jobs or seeking work, compared with 58 per cent of all wives. Apparently the wives of the male unemployed are less likely than others to have any part-time work. Moreover, there does appear to be a much higher unemployment rate – both registered and unregistered – among the economically active wives of the male unemployed (17 per cent compared to 4 per cent of all wives). While 2 per cent of the wives also became economically inactive when their husbands became unemployed, 3 per cent sought work.

The DHSS survey reveals a further distressing point – today's unemployed are likely to have experienced previous bouts of worklessness during the recent past. In a period of five years as many as 78 per cent of the sample suffered at least one spell of registered unemployment. More than 40 per cent had actually suffered at least two periods without work and a quarter three or more.

Further evidence of the financial hardship facing the unemployed was published by the Policy Studies Institute in February 1981. The study found that the jobless had previously been in low paid work. For white unemployed men the mean take-home pay from their last job averaged £60.60, only 80 per cent of the mean for manual workers generally. But only three per cent of white men and five per cent of the minority races were actually receiving more in benefits than they had been earning previously. Nearly half of them had previously earned up to £30 a week more than they were getting in benefits. Smith estimated that the incomes of both white and minority men dropped by as much as 46 per cent of its previous level on average as a consequence of unemployment. About half the men said that to be without a job was a very bad experience or the worst thing that had ever happened to them. More than half found it was 'very difficult to manage as far as money is concerned', while the rest found it 'fairly difficult'.[31] About half the men failed to meet one or more of a number of payments. The most important defaulting occurred with rent, mortgage, rates and fuel bills. As many as a third said they suffered some kind of financial hardship because of debt and a substantial minority said they had suffered severely.

A review of the Supplementary Benefits scheme by the Department of Health and Social Security in July 1978 pointed out that 'less than a sixth of the unemployed are currently in receipt of the earnings-related supplement (ERS) of unemployment benefit, which is generally payable from the third to the twenty-eighth week of unemployment and a growing proportion (11 per cent at that time) have their ERS affected because of the rule that total unemployment benefit must not exceed 85 per cent of previous earnings'. 'Flat rate unemployment benefit has been increased regularly in line with prices to maintain its real value', argued the report. 'But ERS has decreased in value, because the figure of earnings up to which it is calculated at the more generous rate of a third of earnings had remained at £30 since 1966'.[32] From April 1982 the government scrapped earnings-related benefit altogether, another harsh attempt to save public money. The 1980 PSI study of the unemployment flow confirmed the difficult financial circumstances facing the jobless. As many as 27 per cent of the sample neither expected nor received any money when they lost their most recent job, while only 17 per cent had any redundancy payment. Only those aged between 55 and 64 received a substantial sum on leaving their previous job, but a mere 4 per cent went away with more than £2000, though 24 per cent of the older age bracket did so.

But the study also found that the unemployed tended to come from low paid jobs in the small firm sector. The manual jobless were paid only around three quarters to 80 per cent of the average paid to their counterparts in the labour force. It is therefore unsurprising that most wanted to avoid any further drop in their earnings in their next job. The higher a worker's previous earnings, the more willing he is to tolerate a much lower wage in the future. As the PSI study argued: 'If people were earning £95 or more in their previous job then they were prepared to entertain the possibility of accepting a job that paid £58 a week less. If however they earned less than £45 in their previous job than their minimum requirement was £18 more than their previous pay.'[33]

Do social benefits provide a disincentive for the unemployed to find work? In 1977 the Supplementary Benefits Commission carried out a small survey of 140 claimants from 55 randomly selected local offices to try and answer that vital question. It concluded: 'on the assumption that these unemployed men would claim all the appropriate means-tested benefits available if they resumed work, 17 of them appeared to be receiving more while on supplementary benefit than the very low wages (plus means-tested benefits) which were all that it was thought they could reasonably expect to obtain on returning to work'.[34] Apparently as many as 88 per cent 'were or appeared likely to be, better off when working, assuming they claimed all appropriate means-tested benefits, than they were when receiving supplementary benefits.' The SBC survey was concerned with unemployed family men only, but if all the unemployed were taken into account it was calculated that as many as 95 per cent of all unemployed claimants in December 1976 would have been better off had they been in full-time employment.

But the family circumstances of the unemployed are crucial to understand the complexities of the incentive-to-work issue. In a study published in October 1977 by PEP, W. W. Daniel and Elizabeth Stilgoe found that the system of 'income maintenance for the unemployed does have an effect on the labour market behaviour and choices of low paid, low skilled men with dependent wives and children'.[35] Through an examination as follow-up to their 1974 national unemployed survey, Daniel and Stilgoe discovered a startling fact: 'Men with working wives had spent nearly two and a half of the three years in work, while men whose wives did no paid work had been employed for only one year and about four months. Men with only one dependent child had spent just over two of the three years in work while those with four or more dependent children had been employed for just under a year'. They argued that the number of children was a 'major influence on unskilled and semi-skilled men's occupational status'. The PEP study found that 'the median weekly benefit income for a married man was £24, less than half the median net earnings for manual workers generally. Even for a married man with four or more children the median benefit was only £35, but the more children a man has the higher wage he needs for working and the more difficulty he finds in getting such a job.

The survey carried out for the Manpower Services Commission in 1979 by Cragg Ross and Associates discovered that a quarter of the long-term unemployed interviewed regarded pay as the dominant constraint on their job flexibility. As it argued: 'Many of these people compared their benefits with the likely pay from jobs which were available and felt the extra was inadequate compensation for the rigours of a job and the expenses incurred by travel and extra food. However, pay levels were rarely the sole unfavourable influence on employability; and a small minority expressed readiness to take almost any job paying more than social security'.[36] But the CRA survey went on to add 'in fairness the pay levels expected from a job rarely seemed unrealistically high', and there was no evidence of the unemployed turning down jobs offered because the pay was too low.

What evidence is there that fraud and scrounging are serious problems among today's unemployed? The Rayner report, published in March 1981, suggested that perhaps as many as 8 per cent or more of the registered jobless were 'unlawfully working and claiming benefits, an estimate that was doubted by the Department of Employment. The study admitted there were 'few hard facts on the extent of fraud', but went on to suggest that those facts that were known were 'disturbing'.[37] In 1979 only 0.24 per cent of the 4.5 million claims from the unemployed led to prosecutions (of which 98 per cent were not successful), but Rayner argued that only the most blatant cases reached that stage and perhaps three times as many were prosecutable fraud. The investigation team looked at the evidence from fraud drives in the North West of England and the West Midlands. It found on average 'positive indications of fraud' in as many as 55 out of 100 cases. Rayner also cited other evidence to suggest that the fraudulent were a sizeable minority among the registered unemployed. In 1977, of every 100 claimants invited in to Unemployment Review Officer interviews about 42 left the register, 13 at once and 29 after the interview. Estimates of moonlighting have varied between 3 and 8 per cent of gross domestic product. 'If only 10 per cent of those working in the black economy are claiming unemployment benefit (probably a large underestimate) the percentage of fraudulent claims for benefit would be in the range of 5 per cent to 13 per cent when the rate of unemployment is 6 per cent', argued Rayner. The study's calculation of 8 per cent fraud would mean that as much as £108 million in benefits was being paid out each year to people who were not genuinely unemployed, with no more than one in ten of the claimants being found out.

In its annual report for 1978 the Supplementary Benefit Commission revealed that the Unemployment Review Officers who seek to find out the reasons why somebody cannot find another job had called in 218 598 of the jobless for an interview and as many as 41 per cent (89 754) stopped drawing benefit as a result.[38] The Thatcher government has been keen to stamp out abuse of the benefit system and the number of review officers has been expanded (from 300 in 1978 to 940 by 1981). In 1979 the officers carried out around 310 000 interviews and about 125 000 people stopped drawing benefit as a consequence. Benefit was withdrawn or refused in 4000 cases. No area is more open to rumour and ill-informed prejudice. 'It is important that the issue of abuse should not be allowed to get out of perspective', argued the Supplementary Benefits Commission in its last annual report in 1979.

> An excessive emphasis on this is likely to discourage genuine claimants from seeking their rights and failure to take up benefits is a much bigger problem than fraudulent take-up, both in terms of the amounts of money involved, and in less obvious ways because of the hardship it can cause. We must not forget that most claimants are honest and most of the unemployed are without work through no fault of theirs.[39]

If politicians devoted as much of their energy and time to publicising the rights of the unemployed as they do the campaign against the fraudulent and the work-shy, they might be to argue with conviction that they want to administer the system in both a firm and humane manner within the law. But the take-up of benefits fails to arouse much concern in 'official' circles. No doubt, the Treasury would lament the extra cost if all claimed their full entitlement.

The introduction of voluntary registration for the unemployed in 1982 puts a big question mark over the entire future of the state placement service. In part, this mistaken move follows the controversial Rayner report, which recommended breaking the link between payment of benefit to the unemployed and their job-seeking through the abolition of compulsory registration. The main safeguard against an abuse of such a radical change by the work-shy was an expansion in the number of Unemployment Review Officers to police the jobless. Rayner suggested that voluntary registration would enable the Jobcentres to cut 2000 more staff and save as much as £13.7 million, while only a further 300 UROs would be required, a figure that the MSC regards as a severe underestimate. It had already been decided to cut the general placing staff from 8167 in April 1980 to 7406 by April 1984. The MSC gave its main objections to a move to voluntary registration in the 1981–5 Corporate plan. Officials feared it would undermine the confidence of employers if it became clear that many recently jobless people were no longer registering with the state service. Even more seriously, there was a worry that while the more active job-seekers continued to sign on the register, the employment service would lose touch with those least able to help themselves in the harsh labour market. An administrative concern was the dangers of the benefit side with the UROs creating a kind of parallel employment service.

Yet it was also admitted that the move from compulsory to voluntary registration carried advantages, especially that in future the placement service would deal only with those who really wanted help.

## CONCLUSION

The United Kingdom remains the only industrial society in the western world that has actually reduced its public spending in real terms on its manpower services in the depths of a recession. Inevitably, much of the idealism and hope of the early years of the MSC has been lost as a result. Government response to unemployment has been half-hearted, grudging, insensitive and harsh. Those without work have far too often been treated as scapegoats, deserving of their fate. The rejection of Keynesian demand management since the middle-seventies was accompanied by a persistent under-playing of the magnitude of the growing unemployment crisis. The rhetoric of most ministers in the Thatcher government was divisive, uncaring and unforgiving. The Conservative cabinet 'Wets' like James Prior, the Employment Secretary (1979–81) and Peter Walker, the Minister for Agriculture, found it hard to convince Mrs Thatcher and her monetarist Treasury team of the mistake of their single-minded economic strategy to defeat inflation through the creation of unemployment.

The jobless remain perhaps too diverse, separate and changeable to constitute a serious threat to the established order. But apathy, stoicism and inertia were no longer the only human responses to unemployment by the summer of 1981. Rioting in the streets did much to sober the overlying complacency of the 'official' mind. Crime and suicide statistics began to climb, with a steep jump in petty theft, muggings and vandalism in the inner city areas. The mindless nihilism of some young unemployed will terrify the old and middle-aged, but this seems unlikely to bring down our society, though it may increase repression. There is an obvious danger of racial strife as extremists seek to exploit social deprivation for their own wicked ends. The future looks bleak.

## NOTES AND REFERENCES

1 *The Workless State*, ed. B. Showler and A. Sinfield (Martin Robertson, 1981). See particularly Alan Deacon's essay, 'Unemployment and politics in Britain since 1945', p. 67. Two other topical and readable books on contemporary unemployment are A. Sinfield, *What Unemployment Means* (Martin Robertson, 1981) and K. Hawkins, *Unemployment* (Penguin, 1979). *See also The Political Quarterly*, Vol. 52, No. 1, January–March 1981.

2 W. W. Daniel, 'Why is High Unemployment Still Somehow Acceptable?', *New Society*, 19 March 1981, pp. 495–7.

3 'Analysis of the Unemployed Flow: A preliminary report', Policy Studies Institute and Manpower Services Commission, February 1981, 11.21.

4 D. J. Smith, 'Unemployment and Racial Minorities', Policy Studies Institute, February 1981, p. 41.

5 'Services for the Unemployed', TUC consultative document, November 1980, pp. 7–8.

6 'A review of unemployment and vacancy statistics', *Employment Gazette*, May 1980. p. 505.

7 S. Moylan and R. Davies, 'The disadvantages of the unemployed', *Employment Gazette*, August 1980, pp. 830–2.

8 'Manpower Services Commission Corporate Plan 1981–1985', December 1980, 2.16.

9 'A Study of the Long-term Unemployed', Manpower Services Commission summaries, January 1980; *see also* M. Colledge and R. Bartholomew 'The long-term unemployed', *Employment Gazette*, January 1980, pp. 9–12.

10 'The Long-term Unemployed', a discussion document, Manpower Services Commission, September 1978, Annex II, 29.

11 'Review of the first year of Special Programmes', Manpower Services Commission, July 1979, p. 28.

12 'Review of the second year of Special Programmes', Manpower Services Commission, July 1980, p. 16.

13 'Manpower Services Commission Corporate plan 1981–1985' pp. 4.28.

14 'Review of the Services for the Unemployed', Manpower Services Commission, March 1981, p. 12.

15 'Unqualified, Untrained, Unemployed', HMSO, 1974, p. 16.

16 S. Mukherjee, 'There's Work To Be Done', Manpower Services Commission, 1974, p. 23.

17 W. W. Daniel and E. Stilgoe, 'Where Are They Now?', PEP, October 1977, pp. 90–1.

18 Review of the Services for the Unemployed, Manpower Services Commission, p. 13.

19 D. J. Smith, pp. 148–9.

20 'Labour Market Trends: Midlands Region 1981–1983', Manpower Services Commission, 1980, p. 51.
21 'MSC Strategy for London', Manpower Services Commission, November 1979, 4.3.
22 'Engineering Skill Shortages in the Reading Area' Manpower Services Commission, 1979, 5.22.
23 J. Johnson and J. Salt, 'Employment Transfer Schemes in Great Britain', *Three Banks Review*, June 1980, p. 37.
24 '*Manpower Review* 1981', Manpower Services Commission, April 1981, p. 23.
25 J. Hughes, *Britain in Crisis*, (Spokesman Books, May 1981) pp. 13–15.
26 'A National Survey of the Unemployed', PEP, October 1974, p. 149.
27 'In and Out of Work', North Tyneside Community Development Project, 1978, pp. 201–2.
28 ibid., p. 130.
29 'The Causes of Poverty', *Royal Commission on the Distribution of Income and Wealth*, No. 5, HMSO, 1978, p. 85.
30 *Employment Gazette*, August 1980, pp. 830–2.
31 D. J. Smith, pp. 153–4.
32 'Review of Supplementary Benefits Scheme', Department of Health and Social Security, July 1978.
33 PSI survey, 1980, iv, 7 and 8.
34 Supplementary Benefits Commission annual report, 1977 p. 16.
35 Daniel and Stilgoe, pp. 92–4.
36 'A Study of the Long-term Unemployed', Manpower Services Commission, January, 1980, 5.26.
37 'Payment of Benefits to Unemployed People', Rayner report, Departments of Employment and Health and Social Security, March 1981, p. 56.
38 Supplementary Benefits Commission annual report, 1978, p. 116.
39 Supplementary Benefits Commission annual report, 1979, p. 40.

# 2 The Wages Jungle

## NEVER HAD IT SO GOOD

Britain's complex pay bargaining system has come in for considerable criticism during the past twenty-five years. It is now widely regarded as a major cause of home-grown inflation, which has helped to ensure the country is increasingly uncompetitive on international markets because of our high unit labour costs. 'We have been pricing ourselves out of markets', warned Sir Geoffrey Howe, the Chancellor of the Exchequer in July 1980. 'Around two thirds of our loss of competitiveness over the past two years has been due to the increase in UK unit labour costs in comparison with competitor countries. Not only have pay levels increased much faster here than overseas, but we have not earned them by faster increases in productivity'.[1] Table 2.1 shows the rise in income over the period 1970–9.

Certainly the figures are alarming. Between 1977 and 1980 the real after-tax incomes of individual workers rose by as much as one sixth, while the real disposable income of industrial and commercial undertakings fell by as much as a quarter and industrial output rose by a derisory 2 per cent. For those in work the slump did not produce a drastic cut in living standards, although profit margins were hit badly, investment was at a virtual standstill, and manufacturing industry suffered its most catastrophic setback since the early thirties. There was a sense of unreality between this stark contrast – of a desperate struggle for survival in the private manufacturing sector and considerable success for many workers (at least until the winter of 1980–1) in keeping ahead of the annual rate of inflation in the value of their pay packets. Unit labour costs rose by a massive 40 per cent between May 1979 and May 1981, compared with an average 12 per cent for Britain's main competitors.

Of course, it would be wrong to overlook the non-wage push factors that at times have contributed to Britain's relatively high inflation rate during the seventies and early eighties. The escalation in energy prices

TABLE 2.1 Britain's pay bonanza in the seventies

| | *Weekly wage rates* | *Weekly earnings* | *Income from employment per head* | *Prices* |
|---|---|---|---|---|
| 1970 | 44.1 | 47.1 | 45.1 | 55.0 |
| 1971 | 49.8 | 52.4 | 50.2 | 59.6 |
| 1972 | 56.7 | 58.9 | 56.7 | 63.5 |
| 1973 | 64.5 | 67.1 | 64.1 | 69.0 |
| 1974 | 77.2 | 79.1 | 77.5 | 80.9 |
| 1975 | 100.0 | 100.0 | 100.0 | 100.0 |
| 1976 | 119.3 | 115.6 | 114.5 | 115.6 |
| 1977 | 127.2 | 127.3 | 126.0 | 133.1 |
| 1978 | 145.4 | 145.7 | 143.6 | 144.5 |
| 1979 | 167.2 | 168.5 | 166.7 | 162.1 |

SOURCE *National Institute Economic Review*, February 1981, pp. 100–1.

that began with the quadrupling of oil prices by the oil exporting countries in 1973–4 made a severe impact on the battle to ensure economic stability. Successive shocks sustained by the international monetary system did not help either. Nor did high interest rates, the fluctuating ups and downs in the value of sterling on foreign exchange markets, the tightening controls on money supply and government austerity measures as well as the explosion in world commodity prices. Yet none of these explanations is adequate to explain why Britain's inflation was so much more virulent than that suffered by the country's major western industrial competitors.

The former chairman of the National Board for Prices and Incomes (1965–71) Aubrey Jones has sketched out the dismal process which makes wage bargaining a major cause of Britain's inflation.[2] 'A leading sector grants wage increases which set the pace for other sectors to follow', he argued.

> Let us suppose that this leading sector is the one in which the growth in productivity is the fastest; then, if similar wage increases follow in the sectors in which productivity is growing more slowly, wages in those will be rising faster than productivity, and prices will accordingly need to be raised if the rate of profit is to remain unchanged. Thus the leading sector would be an important force in the inflationary process, particularly if it is a fast-growing sector.

No doubt, life would be far easier if workers employed in companies that were efficient and productive and profitable could earn big wages, while workers in loss-making enterprises agreed to receive much less, but the wages system does not reflect such differences in the performance of the market economy. In a survey of pay bargaining in 1976 W.W. Daniel concluded that 'the major influences over the level of pay settlements were social and administrative considerations represented essentially by the notions of compensation for increases in the cost of living and of comparability with levels of increase received by other groups of workers doing similar kinds of work'. Apparently 'if wage and salary earners in favourable market or economic circumstances receive the full benefit of their good fortune while those in less favourable circumstances are insulated from their ill fortune by notions of equity strongly backed by union bargaining power, then the result must be wage-push inflation'.[3]

In Jones's opinion, post-war full employment and inflation both arose from the same basic cause: 'the assertion in the economic field of rights enjoyed in the political arena'.[4]

The sociological causes of our present malady of wage inflation should be emphasised. There are few signs that most people in Britain envy the rich or believe in fighting the class war. Indeed, the opinion poll evidence suggests that the majority of workers are surprisingly ready to support a national incomes policy for all in the wider interests of society. Periodic shopfloor revolts against a central government's increasingly plaintive efforts to ensure wage stability have been in no sense worker offensives that challenged the political system in any revolutionary sense. But Goldthorpe has pointed out that what he calls the 'decay of the status order', 'the emergence of a mature working class and an increasing self-realisation by many workers of their rights as citizens in the workplace have all helped to undermine the cohesion and harmony of the wages system.'[5] We have seen in the post-war years in Britain (and elsewhere) a belief in an annual improvement in living standards, no matter what the condition of the economy. The pessimistic rhetoric of Chancellors of the Exchequer from Sir Stafford Cripps to Sir Geoffrey Howe called for self-sacrifice and personal restraint, but in practice most workers have sought to defend and then improve their wages with considerable success. Indeed, you could argue (with some conviction) that workers in Britain enjoyed an unprecedented affluence in the fifties and sixties, in spite of the interventions of government. Full employment was a necessary prerequisite for the maximisation of labour power and in the post-war period we can see a loosening of former rigidities and austerities. Workers began to think and act like capitalists and the values of acquisitiveness became almost universal. It was the impact of those social changes on pay bargaining structures that helped to fuel inflation.

'What the mass of wage and salary earners have learnt from capitalism is not acquisitiveness *per se* – which they have probably never lacked', but of far greater consequence, the practice of exploiting one's market position to the full', maintains Goldthorpe. 'This includes, of course, maximising the gains to be had from any 'strategic' advantage that may present itself; and, more importantly still, using the power of the organisation to improve a weak position or to reinforce and maintain a strong one'. The decline in the 'traditional fatalism' of workers, due in part to a more bouyant labour market in the fifties and early sixties, compulsory universal secondary education and greater expectancy of better times ahead – all these factors helped to enflame the wages scramble, the never-ending struggle which drew 'its energy from an endless stock of hope and envy'. Such developments cracked the centralised character of much of the pay bargaining arrangements in the private manufacturing sector.

'Full employment and cultural changes together have given the workers more independence, hence a shift of power to the shopfloor', wrote Sir Henry Phelps Brown.[6]

> A centrifugal and fissiparous tendency which has been seen to threaten the dissolution of central control whether it be by trade unions or employers' associations or by the accepted organisation of bargaining areas. There is more local bargaining; there is more informal bargaining; there is more individual bargaining. With this has gone a demand by the worker for greater individual control of his working life. He is no longer prepared to accept his traditional place at the place of work in relation to at least the lower echelons of management.

## PRIVATE SECTOR BARGAINING

The most important feature of our wage bargaining system in the private sector is its devolved and fragmented character. Up until the post-war period multi-employer industry-wide wage agreements were prevalent but under changed economic conditions of full employment they began to break up with a strong move to a more decentralised approach. 'The present pay arrangements – massively decentralised and fragmented by comparison with other countries – encourage the pursuit of comparisons and breed competitive bargaining', argues Sisson.

> They are the major sources of disputes – especially as the economy declines. They help to produce the dissatisfaction which fuels inflationary wage claims and contribute to inflation because competitive bargaining adds to the upward movement of pay settlements. For this to happen it is enough that groups of workers seek to keep up with settlements negotiated elsewhere. There does not have to be a clear cut wage round; there does not have to be a recognisable key bargain.[7]

The fragmented bargaining system in the private sector encourages sectionalism among the work groups. There is no closed season on wage negotiations. The multiplicity of bargaining dates and bargaining units invite leap-frogging wage demands, where some workers bid up as high as they can go, while others seek to aspire to reach the same figure irrespective of the strength of their labour power or the financial capacity of their employer to meet what they want.

The 1968 Donovan Royal Commission argued that the 'central defect' of the industrial relations system was 'disorder in factory and workshop relations and pay structures promoted by the conflict between the formal and the informal'. Donovan sought the remedy, not in the reassertion of centralised trade union authority or a return to substantive industry-wide agreements, but through what it called 'effective and orderly collective bargaining over such issues as the control of incentive schemes, the regulation of hours actually worked, the use of job evaluation, work practices and the linking of changes in pay to changes in performance, facilities for shop stewards and disciplinary rules and appeals'.[8] The commission declared its faith in the encouragement of factory agreements through joint union-management regulation, but without any sanctions under the law, to bring them about. Unfortunately Donovan devoted little attention to how such a reform would be reconciled with national incomes policies. Indeed, the commission acknowledged the strength of the CBI's contention that any national planning on incomes was impossible because of fragmented plant bargaining. Donovan agreed that this led to instability in the labour force (through the 'bidding up' for labour to which it gives rise), the increase in the scope for unofficial strikes and other firms of industrial action and a weakening of trade union and employer organisations. But Donovan argued (perhaps more in hope than logic) that 'properly negotiated factory and company agreements' would 'if widely resorted to permit all these tendencies to be brought under control.' Apparently such formalised deals would 'remove many of the causes of unofficial strikes', bring the bidding up for labour into the open and assist the planning of incomes. As Donovan argued: 'Incomes policy must continue a lame and halting exercise so long as it consists in the planning of industry-wide agreements most of which exercise an inadequate control over pay. So long as workplace bargaining remains informal, autonomous and fragmented the drift of earnings away from rates of pay cannot be brought under control. 'Apparently well-regulated company and factory agreements would enable companies to exercise effective control over their own wage – and salary – bills and that in turn would make the control of drift a possibility'. But it was unclear from the Donovan report why workgroups or unions should see advantages in a more regulated bargaining system on the shopfloor, if this entailed greater centralised controls and disciplines.

In the years since Donovan there have been further important developments, which were recently highlighted by a major survey of shopfloor industrial relations by the Warwick University industrial relations research unit in 1981.[9] Firstly, the old multi-employer agreement which used to, at least, provide a 'floor' and raised the wages of everybody, has become more like a 'safety net', aiding only the low paid.

The nationally negotiated rate in industries like engineering and chemicals fails to reflect the actual earnings levels negotiated down at the plant and employer level. As Brown and Terry observed: 'We have met many managements who, though their companies are attached formally to national joint industrial council agreements, never even bother to find out what the NJIC negotiated pay rates are. They find the NJIC agreements useful in setting out the 40-hour week and in advising on the appropriate percentage premium rate for particular shift or overtime conditions, but otherwise they look after themselves'.[10]

Secondly, the Warwick Unit discovered that multi-employer wage agreements were being replaced by single-employer bargaining. They found that only 27 per cent of manual workers in 36 per cent of establishments of 50 or more workers had their earnings principally determined by multi-employer arrangements, compared with the 68 per cent of manual workers in 53 per cent of establishments who had their wages mainly negotiated with their own employer alone. As many as 46 per cent of those manual workers had their wages bargained at about establishment level and the remaining 21 per cent at corporate level covering more than one establishment. By comparison, all but 15 per cent of white-collar workers (in a quarter of establishments of 50 or more employees) were found to be covered by some kind of collective agreement and these were mainly single-employer agreements. Establishment arrangements covered 45 per cent of non-manuals and corporate bargaining covered a further 29 per cent of them.

The Warwick unit argue that during the seventies private sector employers began to exercise a greater control and cohesion over wage bargaining and this helped to stem the extent of wage drift. Industrial relations strategies were becoming much more professional, mainly due to increasing governmental involvement through incomes policies and changes in the labour law. The widespread use of job evaluation by firms has also helped to bring a semblance of order to bargaining at company level. It is worth bearing in mind the high degree of concentration of ownership in the private manufacturing sector of the economy. In 1971 the hundred biggest manufacturing companies accounted for as much as 40 per cent of the country's entire output and that proportion is believed to have risen further during the seventies. Moreover, in those firms with over 2000 employees on their pay-rolls more than 70 per cent belong to trade unions.

## PRIVATE SECTOR SOLUTIONS

The Confederation of British Industry has given careful thought to the problems of the wage bargaining system. In July 1977 it set out its views in a discussion document. In the view of the CBI the crux of the pay problem lies in the 'importance of comparability claims between one group and another'. As the paper argued:

> The pressure for comparability in pay or in pay increases, irrespective of company fortunes, has increased in recent years for a variety of reasons and is now a key problem in our pay determination process. It imposes rigidity on a system that should be fluid. It means that pay increases that reward greater efficiency or which can be justified on commercial or market grounds nevertheless set a 'going rate' for others to follow. The imbalance of bargaining power ensures that for the powerful groups at least this target rate is usually achieved in settlements which are inflationary.[11]

The CBI said that the very instability of the bargaining arrangements fueled the upward push for inflationary wage deals. 'The existence of numerous bargaining groups, each possessing a separate settlement date, means that while one bargaining group will set a 'going rate' another group can exceed this in a subsequent settlement. This process is likely not only to increase the initial level of the 'going rate' but create leap-frogging claims and settlements, producing dissatisfaction and a determination to restore relative positions in future negotiations. This can occur throughout industry and can quickly lead to a lack of control over the general level of pay increases, particularly when the rate of inflation is not constant and the bargaining strength of specific groups fluctuates'.

The CBI laid down guidelines for employers on how to reform their wage bargaining systems through the creation of far fewer and larger bargaining units within plants, companies and industries with a smaller number of settlement dates as a way of trying to eradicate the inflationary implications of a so-called 'going rate' to which workers aspire. The CBI put its faith in longer-term agreements, a greater control over pay structures by employers, above all the need for much more cohesion between companies in standing firm in the face of exorbitant wage demands. An unfavourable comparison was made with West Germany where employers are ready to resort to the use of the lock-out when necessary as a clear sign of their collective strength to act in unity. In Britain employers are far more ready to take advantage of the troubles of their competitors than recognise the need for mutual support in a common cause. As the CBI explained:

> It must be recognised that the individual employer can actually weaken the resistance of others in excessive wage demands. The reactions of major suppliers, of major industrial customers, and of major British competitors at a time of industrial dispute can significantly increase the pressures on a company to settle as quickly as possible, regardless of cost. This has too often enabled trade unions to seek out vulnerable employers to establish high 'going rates' to be sought later through the rest of industry.

In 1977 the CBI drew the conclusion that the future success of pay bargaining required a greater degree of employer solidarity.

The main proposal for change from the CBI was a much shorter bargaining season, with a close link to the annual budget of the government. Two years later it came out in favour of the creation of a 'national economic forum', 'a focal point around which expectations, and so bargaining' could be influenced. CBI did not envisage that the forum would lay down any norm or sit in judgement over the bargaining system. Its main purpose was to be educative, producing regular economic analyses, 'scenarios for the year ahead', publicity, and the provision of information. The forum would take its place alongside better structures, a compressed bargaining round and effective company communications to let their workers know the economic facts of life, as part of the wider CBI solution to the pay problem. The CBI's 1979 proposals were also clear on the need for effective comparability machinery to regulate pay in the public sector, particularly the public services where market disciplines fail to function. 'Having set realistic financial targets, government should not then alter these to accommodate excessive pay awards', it argued. 'Nor should it subsidise the prices of nationalised industries and so cushion the effects of pay settlements. Employees must be allowed to see the price or employment impact of irresponsible bargaining.'

The CBI bargaining season would look like this:

| | |
|---|---|
| May/June | Economic forum takes evidence following the budget and experience of the previous pay round. |
| July/August | Publication of a national economic review. Possible Green paper and parliamentary debate. |
| September/October | The CBI, TUC and party conferences consider the review. |
| November/December | Main bargaining period starts with first settlement operating from 1 November. Government decides cash limits for public sector, and outlines link between pay developments and the next budget. |
| February | Budget presentations by CBI, TUC and others, as at present. |
| March | Tax-dependent public services bargain. April settlement date to coincide with start of financial year. |
| April | Budget taking full account of pay developments. |
| May | Work on next annual review starts. |

Another proposal for a market-style incomes policy was put forward in 1981 by Professor James Meade of Cambridge University. In his opinion, some form of 'financial-monetary restraint' needs to be imposed on society in order to rid workers of the idea that whatever happens they will be provided with confetti money to cover the resulting costs of production no matter how severe the level of inflation.[12] Within that framework of restraint, there would be decentralised pay bargaining with wage rates set to promote full employment. But Meade goes on to argue that there must be a 'more centralised mechanism for determining the absolute level of money pay' through an impartial and independent Pay Commission with powers of compulsory arbitration, which would replace the present anarchic system of monopolistic unions maximising their strength at the expense of other workers. Meade does not duck the sensitive issue of sanctions against either employers or workers who refuse to accept an award laid down by the commission. He suggests that any supplementary benefit paid to support the families of strikers should be treated as a loan to the worker concerned and repaid by deductions through PAYE from future earnings, while any PAYE tax rebates would be withheld by the employer until the dispute was settled. Meade even went so far as to suggest legal immunities from actions taken 'in furtherance or contemplation of a trades dispute' should be removed from those involved in stoppages that defied a commission wage award.

Meade's plan has won some support among the leaders of the new Social Democratic party, but it remains a highly doubtful method for determining wage levels in a free society.

It could risk a dangerous confrontation between the government of the day and the trade union movement, unless the arbitral system was based on the consent of workers, and it remains unclear how such cooperation would be forthcoming. Meade is quite right to point out that the whole aim of his proposal is to ensure workers enjoy real increases in their living standards through a reduction in the rate of inflation in the social market economy rather than merely compensate them with money wage rises for price increases. The all-knowing independent commission would provide the means to call a halt to the senseless, perpetual wage merry-go-round, but this would necessitate a coercive intervention by the agencies of the state into collective bargaining that is unlikely to be based on a shopfloor consensus, and which would probably provoke widespread industrial militancy.

Moreover, the function of the unions in such a system remains unclear. Meade and some Social Democratic party leaders appear to dislike ideas of corporatism, of national bargaining between government, employers and the TUC, on the grounds that this threatens the existence of parliamentary supremacy. Only the Labour party could hope to establish any close understanding with the TUC and it would have to agree on a *quid pro quo* package which would strengthen union power in a way that many people resent. Ties of loyalty and self-interest that exist between Labour and the TUC would be lacking in any kind of union relationship with a Social Democratic–Liberal administration. It would be very difficult, therefore, (some would say impossible) for such a regime to hammer out any 'accord' at the centre which would lead to voluntary self-restraint among union officials and their members in workplace pay bargaining.

An alternative form of incomes policy in the market economy was proposed in the summer of 1981 by Professor Richard Layard of the Centre for Labour Economics and a member of the Social Democratic party. This suggested the introduction of a wage-inflation tax imposed on employers who paid their workers above a government-prescribed norm of what the economy could afford in the growth of hourly earnings. Layard wanted the scheme to be 'revenue-neutral' to prevent any rise in the net tax burden of companies, so at 'appropriate intervals' he suggested that the rate of national insurance surcharge would be set at a lower level than otherwise to balance exactly the previous period's inflation tax receipts. By this method the tax plan would redistribute the tax burden from firms that paid above the norm to those that fell below it. Layard argued that the tax would place a direct downward pressure on pay and it would not bring plant closures because companies that paid the tax would be in the strongest market position.

But the scheme is not entirely problem-free. The tax could well discourage expanding firms from raising wages in order to attract more labour and this must slow down redeployment in the workforce. It would also discourage the spread of productivity deals, but Layard insists that these costs would be worth bearing for the higher employment levels that the tax would ensure by keeping down unit labour costs. There are also dangers that the tax would lead to widespread avoidance by employers, give a boost to the black economy and require widespread government bureaucratic interference to monitor its operation. But the tax plan has some attractive qualities. It avoids corporatist bargaining between government, unions and employers. It does not damage the market economy and it recognises the individualistic, fragmented nature of much (though not all) of our bargaining system. Above all, the tax plan could operate in the teeth of a union veto, giving employers some backbone to resist inflationary wage demands. But Layard admits that the best time to introduce the scheme would be after the imposition of a crude incomes policy that brought down the rate of inflation to an acceptable level. There is no way of avoiding the painful transition to such a system.

## THE PUBLIC SECTOR TROUBLE

It would be wrong to conclude that the dominance of workplace bargaining in manufacturing industry in the private sector encapsulates the entire British pay problem. The country retains a substantial public monopoly sector, where governments possess the ultimate authority over the level of wage settlements. Nearly one in three workers (around seven million) are employed in either the public services or the nationalised industries and their wages account for as much as 70 per cent of the total costs in those still labour intensive areas. Unless there was a sudden and speedy break-up of the entire public monopoly sector and the emergence of a multiplicity of privately owned units of production or services – an unlikely development – it is very hard to see how any government can avoid taking up a position on the appropriate level of pay deals in the sector for which it remains responsible. Yet for the past twenty years successive administrations from Macmillan to Thatcher have found it difficult to resolve the public sector wages conundrum. Douglas Hurd, Heath's political adviser during the early seventies, confessed that the Conservative government of the period wrestled unsuccessfully with the difficulties. 'In a public sector dispute the employee barely suffers', he noted in his diary. 'Any temporary loss of income is usually covered by the union and is in any case quickly recouped out of the eventual settlement. The employer, the actual administrator of the public concern does not suffer at all, for his salary is secure. It is the public, and only the public, which suffers, first as consumer and later, when the bill comes in, as taxpayer. The public picks up the tab for both sides'.[13]

Governments face a genuine dilemma over pay in the public sector. On the one hand, they want to be seen as 'good' employers and they recognise the need for some form of pay comparability between public service workers and those working in the private sector, but at the same time cabinets must struggle with the wider economic problems of the nation that may require some form of government intervention in wage bargaining. The existence of incomes policies of various colours during the sixties and seventies helped to enflame public sector workers, who felt (with some justice) that their levels of pay were being held back in the national interest, whereas everybody else out in the private portion of the labour market was forging ahead. The 1981 conflict between Mrs Thatcher's cabinet and all the civil service unions in impressive unison for once illustrates the trouble. For twenty-five years the pay of civil servants was determined through a system of 'fair comparison', based on the recommendations of a Royal Commission. An independent Pay Research Unit (though staffed by civil servants) built up a sophisticated network of job for job comparisons to discover year on year what the value of each civil servant's worth should be in money terms.[14] Inevitably, by the very nature of the exercise, it necessitated retrospective payments, so that the relationship between civil service and outside wage levels was always a year behind the times. This ensured severe embarrassment to any government. In 1979–80, Britain suffered from an explosive increase in money wages. By the summer of 1980 Mrs Thatcher's cabinet had reached the conclusion that such profligacy could not be allowed to continue in the public sector. There were growing signs of a slowdown in wage increases and shopfloor expectations in private manufacturing industry because of the deepening impact of the recession, but ministers felt that unless they acted decisively the country would have to face yet another wage round of high settlements in the public sector.

Consequently Mrs Thatcher and her cabinet colleagues decided to abolish the whole Pay Research Unit exercise unilaterally and offer civil servants a 7 per cent pay rise and no more within a 6 per cent cash limits incomes policy for the public services. Ministers refused to accept that the civil servants should be allowed arbitration on their pay demand for an increase of 15 per cent in line with what the unions argued was the independent conclusion of the Pay Research Unit's comparability exercise. But there were genuine causes for alarm in the civil service pay system. As Elliott and Fallick have argued: 'In practice comparisons are made with only the better paying employers in the private sector and their rates of pay may be unrepresentative of the sector as a whole. Furthermore, it is difficult to quantify certain key benefits which many public, but only a few private, employees enjoy, such as security of employment and non-contributory index-linked pensions'.[15] Nor did Pay Research take any account of labour market forces of supply and demand or productivity. A committee of inquiry was set up to propose a new system.

Successive governments have failed to bring any coherence or a wide sense of fairness to pay determination in the public services. There has been persistent interference by ministers in the pay awards recommended by *ad hoc* and separate inquiries. This leads inevitably to a deep frustration and anger among many workers, who believe they are being paid far less than they deserve. Purely market forces alone cannot decide the levels of pay in the public services, where the profit motive does not exist.

The need for some form of pay comparability in the public sector was well argued by the short-lived Clegg comparability commission in 1980. 'There is a public interest in scrutinising the justification of pay settlements met largely or entirely from rates and taxes, to give assurance that advantageously-situated groups of public employees are not exploiting their position or, especially in periods of government incomes policy that the government is not using its authority and influence to treat public employees harshly', it asserted.[16] 'There is the special difficulty of determining the appropriate comparisons for the large number of public employees in occupations which are found largely or exclusively in the public sector. Finally, there is a special concern to avoid industrial action in the public services both because strikes in some of them can be particularly disruptive or even dangerous and because of a not uncommon belief that strikes in the public services are morally reprehensible'. But the creation of an 'independent assessment of pay comparisons in the public service' cannot replace the bargaining process between managements and unions. Whether it could become an arbitrator that rewarded or punished is highly debatable. A revived Clegg-style comparability commission might heighten expectations of an inflationary wage bonanza for many aggrieved groups of workers in the public sector. There can be no exact science or a grandiose scheme of national job evaluation that would spirit away conflict and achieve a new consensus on wage determination.

Can labour market forces alone have a major role in deciding the worth of public sector workers? It is hard to see how this can happen unless government dismembered the national wage bargaining machinery in its own sector of the economy. The existence of London weighting allowances in public service wage structures is a clear recognition of the often wide disparity in earnings between people working in the capital and elsewhere, but the deliberate break-up of centralised bargaining would carry serious risks of instability, strife and rough justice. How localised would a labour market have to be in order to establish any precision in matching supply with demand?

## ARE THE UNIONS TO BLAME?

The very existence of trade unions is often blamed for Britain's especially intractable inflation problem. The Confederation of British

Industry have argued that there was 'a major and fundamental shift in the balance of bargaining power' from capital to organised labour during the seventies. 'Instead of being a reasonable compromise between the parties, settlements are too often considered satisfactory only by employees and their trade unions and then only for a short time', it lamented in 1977.[17] The CBI put much of the blame for this on the 'fragmented bargaining structure', the growth of the public sector and the heavy influence on wage settlements of 'factors external to the firm, notably the cost of living and comparability', but the strength of the unions was seen as vital in this process. Research carried out for the Royal Commission on the distribution of income and wealth in 1977 tends to reinforce the view that the unions have proved highly successful bargainers for their members during the past twenty years. While it was found there was no correlation between the level of earnings of white-collar workers and unionisation, women do better in wage negotiations if they belong to a union than if they do not. Male manual workers in unions can expect to enjoy a 'mark-up' of from 20–30 per cent over their comparable colleagues who are outside a union.[18]

'The simple fact is that for years now the unions have increasingly demanded, with effective menaces, excessive wage increases which have inevitably led to excessive cost and price increases', lamented Reginald Maudling, the former Conservative Chancellor of the Exchequer.[19] But this mistakes the trade union as an organisation with the workers it represents. The unions as such have not acquired the negative power to disrupt society in order to win inflationary wage rises. The difficulty rests primarily with workers – whether they belong to a union or not. For example, in 1978–9 it was not the moderate General and Municipal Workers union that stimulated a feeling of militancy among the nation's water workers. Indeed, that union's officials made strenuous attempts to reduce the expectations of the work group, who were threatening to cut off water supplies to the community if they did not get the big wage rise they wanted. Similarly, the national leaders of the Transport and General Workers Union worked through their Christmas holidays in 1978 arguing with oil tanker drivers to settle on a lower wage increase than they had been demanding. To a considerable extent, unions can provide a sense of direction, a cohesion, the necessary collective strength, but they mirror the views of their disparate members in work groups who want large pay rises to keep ahead of the rate of inflation. In the view of Phelps Brown 'our trade unions have become less concerned with the aims of the labour movement and are more like business unions, each concerned with economic gain for its own members'.

## THE PAY STRUCTURE AND EQUITY

There is nothing God-given about our distribution of incomes, but it appears to be very difficult (almost impossible many would say) to make the pay structure more equitable without severe social conflict. Indeed, the paradox persists: despite the apparent fluidity and uncertainties of pay bargaining, there remains an extraordinary stability in the relative position of different groups of wage earners. Routh discovered that 'while differentials between linked occupations have been contracting, dispersion within occupations has been expanding so that overall dispersion has remained fairly stable'.[20] The distribution of incomes between different kinds of worker does fluctuate over time but Routh argues that the disparities regain their former shapes, sometimes after lapses of many years (see Table 2.2). The wage structure of 1971 was startlingly similar to that of 1913. While miners and farmworkers, for example, suffered a relative decline in their earnings position after the First World War, they regained their former positions in the years after 1945. The relative pay of railwaymen and civil servants deteriorated during and immediately after the Second World War, but then those two groups staged a pay recovery during the middle and late fifties. 'There is something elemental in this attachment of a person to his level of income, measured in terms of its purchasing power (the maintenance of

TABLE 2.2 Towards income equality? Changes in shares of total personal income since 1949

| *Quantile group* | *Income shares* | | | *Lower limit of income range 1976–7* |
|---|---|---|---|---|
| | *1949* % | *1959* % | *1976–7* % | £ |
| Before tax | | | | |
| Top one per cent | 11.2 | 8.4 | 5.4 | 11 258 |
| Top 2–10 per cent | 22.0 | 21.0 | 20.4 | 5 686 |
| Top 11–20 per cent | 43.1 | 47.5 | 49.7 | 2 615 |
| Bottom 50 per cent | 23.7 | 23.1 | 24.5 | – |
| After tax | | | | |
| Top one per cent | 6.4 | 5.3 | 3.5 | 7 330 |
| Top 2–10 per cent | 20.7 | 19.9 | 18.9 | 4 418 |
| Top 11–50 per cent | 46.4 | 49.7 | 50.0 | 2 160 |
| Bottom 50 per cent | 26.5 | 25.0 | 27.6 | – |

SOURCE *Royal Commission on the Distribution of Income and Wealth,* Report No. 7, HMSO, 1977, p. 157.

a standard of living) and in terms of the earnings of other occupations, that is not unlike the attachment of an animal to its young', argues Routh. 'It applies to the individual and leads individuals to act in concert with or without trade union organisation; a sense that their work has been devalued can turn a disciplined work force into a surly, disgruntled mob'.

No doubt, life would be far easier if workers who were employed by companies in efficient and productive activity making profits for their employers enjoyed much higher wage increases as a result than workers employed in loss-making enterprises with poor productivity and an inefficient deployment of labour, but our wages system simply does not directly mirror market realities. It is quite mistaken to underplay the persuasive strength of the vague concept of fairness in our unequal and divisive wage bargaining system. Friedrich Engels, Marx's close colleague, confessed that the slogan – 'a fair day's work for a fair day's pay' was an 'old time-honoured watchword' in Britain. Today it is never far from the lips of union bargainers and their members, even if the meaning of equity in the wages jungle remains highly subjective, dependent on time, circumstances, and the balance of strength between the parties at the negotiating table. Yet the Pay Board recognised, in a report it published in January 1974, that 'fairness' was as important as 'labour market' factors in determining the wage relationships between different workers.[21]

As it acknowledged: 'People's views of the fairness of their pay in relation to that of others frequently lead to changes or pressures for changes in wage levels and these may conflict with the operation of market forces'. Indeed, notions of fairness lie at the heart of the intractable problem of wage relativities. 'The main consequence of the pervasive notion of fairness is that no pay increase stands alone', argued the Pay Board. 'Pay increases negotiated for whatever reasons by employers and trade union representatives become part of the grounds for claims by other groups. It is thus difficult for a group to move ahead and stay ahead!

Most democratic Socialists, who believe in an incomes policy for the labour market, do so because they see it as a method of securing more social justice in a deeply unequal society. As we have already seen, the distribution of income in Britain shows just how far this country has to go before it can achieve any substantial measure of egalitarianism, so that the arguments in favour of an incomes policy which involves a real redistributive change is the direction of pay levels remain powerful. And after all, as Sir Frank Figgures, chairman of the defunct Pay Board once remarked: 'The purpose of an incomes policy is to induce people to accept, overall, something less than they feel they could have got by negotiation'.[22] Yet can we really expect the vast majority of workers to cooperate freely with such a strategy if it is clearly designed to achieve greater equality between the earnings of different groups on grounds of equity and fairness?

Barbara Wootton, in her classic *Social Foundations of Wage Policy*, recognised the difficulties as long ago as 1955, when she suggested that the relative neglect of egalitarian ideas in the Labour movement during the thirties and forties, stemmed from 'the conversion of the trade union movement from its role as a defence of manual workers against the depredations of their economic betters into a highly organised machine, professionally operated for the protection of sectionalist interests at all levels'.[23] The growth of unionisation among the white-collar salariat in the sixties and seventies has ensured a more sturdy defence of existing pay and fringe benefit differentials and relativities from erosion by manual workers. Indeed, some white-collar unions (despite their professed adherence to left-wing Socialism) have made an appeal of calculated self-interest and snobbery over status to the frustrated and increasingly militant ranks of staff in both the private and public sectors who used to display either fear or contempt for the very idea of trade unionism in the past. For their part, skilled manual workers have fought a rearguard action to defend and improve their relative wage position *vis-à-vis* the low paid. Unlike the Swedish manual workers movement (the LO) the British TUC has always kept clear of any radical commitment to an egalitarian incomes policy, in part because it would involve a squeeze on the pay of those on or above the average wage to enable the less fortunate to catch up. The wide variety of occupational and industrial interests that must work together within the TUC makes it very hard for that body to champion one section of workers if this means doing so at the expense of other workers. This is not to say that the TUC cannot for a period successfully exercise its influence with a Government in achieving a pay understanding, but severe limits to any long-term arrangement remain.

It is true that most workers share a vague notion of what constitutes 'fairness' in pay bargaining, however imprecise and subjective that may turn out to be in practice. But this falls far short of any egalitarian approach towards the wages system. Indeed, the vast majority hold narrow terms of reference when they compare the size of their pay packets with those of others. As W. G. Runciman explained, 'Dissatisfaction with the system of privileges and rewards in society is never felt in an even proportion to the degree of inequality to which its various members are subject'. In his study, Runciman made the surprising discovery that few workers believed that anybody else was doing better than they were. Such blood-curdling cries of 'make the rich squeal' do not appear to find any sympathetic echo among manual workers, who more than any other occupational group, tended to evaluate their own position in society relative to other people in the same position as themselves. 'Most people's lives are governed more by the resentment of narrow inequalities, the cultivation of modest ambitions and the preservation of small differentials than by attitudes to public policy or the social structure as such', Runciman concluded. His findings provide crucial evidence that workers do not either question or even use the pay rates of others beyond their day to day experience in the workplace to justify their own demands.[24] In 1976 W. W. Daniel of the Policy Studies Institute confirmed those attitudes were still present among workers, despite the existence of incomes policies in the sixties and middle seventies. As he wrote: 'Surprisingly few people in Britain felt that there was anybody else doing better than they were. Moreover the lower people were placed in the social hierarchy, the less they were to feel that anyone else was doing better than them'.[25] This was even found to be true in the case of trade union negotiators, with as many as 70 per cent of them believing nobody was any better off than their own members in the plant. 'It is people's positions relative to others in the

TABLE 2.3 Earnings: regional differences

| | *Full-time manual men* | | *Full-time non-manual men* | |
|---|---|---|---|---|
| | *1974* £ | *1981* £ | *1974* £ | *1981* £ |
| South East | 44.80 | 126.2 | 59.10 | 174.6 |
| East Anglia | 41.50 | 116.7 | 50.70 | 157.6 |
| South West | 40.80 | 114.4 | 51.20 | 153.3 |
| West Midlands | 45.50 | 117.1 | 51.70 | 152.7 |
| East Midlands | 42.40 | 122.5 | 49.70 | 151.5 |
| Yorkshire and Humberside | 42.90 | 121.0 | 50.10 | 153.4 |
| North West | 43.10 | 119.8 | 52.30 | 158.1 |
| North | 43.60 | 122.9 | 52.00 | 155.7 |
| Wales | 43.70 | 120.3 | 51.90 | 152.7 |
| Scotland | 42.90 | 121.5 | 51.80 | 161.8 |
| Greater London | 45.90 | 131.9 | 63.20 | 185.9 |

SOURCE 'New Earnings Survey', 1974 and 1981.

*same* social class that influences their evaluations of their own circumstances rather than their position compared to that of people in other classes', argued Daniel. 'Disputes over pay relativities spring more from the system of collective bargaining of which they are part than from any spontaneous or deep felt sense of injustice on the part of workers they represent in disputes', he concluded.

There appears to have been a narrowing of the regional disparities in the earnings of manual workers since the middle seventies (see Table 2.3). The most noticeable difference lies in the relative deterioration in the earnings power of West Midland manual workers. In 1974 they were a mere 40 pence behind the average earnings in greater London, but six years later they had dropped back to ninth regional position. This reflects the sharp decline in the fortunes of Britain's main manufacturing region during the present recession. From being an area of promise, of high wage packets and affluent life styles, the West Midlands is in serious danger of remaining a region of relatively low wages and high unemployment during the eighties.

## THE FAILURE OF INCOMES POLICY

National incomes policies during the sixties and seventies did not bring about much redistribution between workers. Andrew Dean concluded that there was 'little evidence, apart from the higher income groups that there has been a strong compression of pay brought about directly by incomes policies'.[26] Even the 1975–6 flat rate £6 policy with a cut off point for no rises at all beyond salaries of £8500 a year had 'very little effect at aggregate level'. Certainly (as we have seen) the dispersion of earnings between groups of workers has hardly changed this century, though during the seventies the miners did recover much lost ground as a result of their industrial actions in 1972 and 1974 and the revival of importance in coal as a strategic fuel after the quadrupling of oil prices in 1973–4. The position of the lowest decile of male manual workers in 1980 was broadly the same as it had been in 1886 (69.4 per cent in 1981 compared with 68.6 per cent in 1886). Most of the changes over time have come in a narrowing of incomes in the higher income groups *vis-à-vis* the median. However since 1967 there was a noticeable compression of the relative position of skilled manual workers against production workers in the engineering and motor car industries, whether an incomes policy was in operation or not.

Such empirical evidence should dampen the enthusiasms of those egalitarian Socialists who wish to reform our pay structure in the name of social justice. By contrast with Sweden, our manual and non-manual workers seem uninterested in the pursuit of greater equality in their earnings relative to others and up until now the Labour movement has proved unsuccessful in either stimulating a greater awareness of inequity or generating more solidarity between workgroups about pay determination. It is difficult to see how the low pay problem can really be solved through an incomes policy that contains a national minimum wage because other workers are likely to press at once for a restoration of their hallowed pay differentials. Moreover, any special bid to aid the low paid in the midst of a slump is likely to lead to more workers being priced out of their jobs, something that hardly looks conducive to their future well-being.

Governments that want to pursue more equality between wage earners will have to look to reforms in the tax system and even here we can see genuine limitations on progress as manual workers have revolted (in the late seventies as well as the late sixties) against the burdens of income tax on those earning below as well as above the average wage. The Royal Commission on the Distribution of Income and Wealth suggested that poverty was not simply a problem caused by low wages. In many families with more than one breadwinner there is usually enough money coming in to pull the household above any poverty line, even if the individual level of earnings is low. Government spending of taxpayer's money should also help to ease the low pay problem through better social benefits. The upvaluation of child benefits and the family income settlement look a more sensible method of helping the less well off than any direct government intervention in the pay bargaining system of a redistributive kind. There is depressing enough evidence to suggest that the political parties are only too aware of the pitfalls in the implementation of any overall incomes policy.

According to H. A. Turner, Britain suffers from an electoral cycle that enjoys a direct connection to the wages system. Parties come into office when the rate of pay rises is accelerating and then they seek, after a time, to apply some form of wage restraint, which is then followed by the collapse of such an approach in a welter of inflationary wage rises as the next general election approaches. The pattern of industrial relations also tends to reflect a similar dismal cycle. As Turner explains:

'Each government starts with a heritage of wage claims from its predecessor's last year, which is legitimised by comparability with the recent wage leaders. At some point, the effects drive them to a wage/price restraint, which initially has some measure of TUC and/or

CBI cooperation. But this does not seem enough. So the government also takes back more in taxation and cuts demand and employment – which prejudices worker and employer support.'[27]

Frustrations begin to accumulate in the wage system as some groups of workers feel themselves to be more restrained by government policy than others. Through higher rates of personal taxation and pay restraint there is a real impact on workers' living standards in the middle years of the electoral cycle. As the economy begins to grow (even slowly) and profits are made by more successful employers who want to pay their workers more than the imposed norm to attract labour, the unions come under pressure from their rank and file to ensure that there is a rapid return to 'free' collective bargaining. Attempts are made valiantly to hold the line by devices such as productivity payments 'special' cases and the rest, and governments try to recover what is lost through wage drift by use of the income tax system. Both the TUC and the CBI, hardly strong institutions at the best of times, come under inevitable internal strain, which eventually breaks down in a general wages bonanza.

Any incomes policy has to have a general application across a diverse and competitive labour force. If any major group of workers can establish a bridge head with a huge wage rise, far above an agreed or imposed norm, then it is very difficult to hold the line against others following suit. Nobody wants to feel left behind in the ensuing spree. But again as Turner points out for most workers the pay merry-go-round does not actually mean a boost to their living standards. 'On a broad view of real and relative income distribution, the effect is negligible', he argues. 'Average real living standards in the long run remain tied to productivity growth. From year to year they are determined much more by changing government fiscal and monetary policies than by the relationship between pay and cost increases.'

Over the past twenty years successive attempts have been made by both Labour and Conservative governments to introduce and sustain an incomes policy in order to reduce the rate of inflation in the economy, but in the end they have all suffered ultimate failure. Action from the centre to halt the rise in the level of prices through wage norms (mainly statutory) between 1965 and 1969 ended in a huge wage explosion. Derek Robinson concluded a study of that period with the observation that 'as far as actual earnings of manual workers were concerned the policy had little overall effect but slowed down the rate of increase in the first half',[28] but 'the immense stresses and strains imposed on the labour market and on the relations between the unions and the Labour government were an excessive price to pay for merely postponing wage increases'. Paul Ormerod and S. G. B. Henry at the National Institute of Economic and Social Research argued in a study of wage inflation and incomes policies from 1961 to 1977 that 'wage increases in the period immediately following the ending of the policies were higher than they would otherwise have been and these increases match losses incurred during the operation of the incomes policy'.[29] Since the 1948 wage freeze experiments in incomes policy in Britain have always originated as attempts to restrain the growth of incomes. Invariably they have been crudely devised norms to deal with an economic crisis. But, by the very nature of emergency measures, they were manifestly imperfect, leading to the inevitable distortions in the pay structure that generated rank and file grievances on many a shopfloor. In turn, this provoked growing labour militancy and the eventual collapse of the policy under a flood of inflationary wage deals. Governments have never enjoyed enough time to construct a more permanent and flexible structure to determine wage bargaining through consent.

## WAYS OUT OF THE JUNGLE

The pay issue lies at the heart of our tangled industrial politics, so that every major political party in succession has managed to exploit an electoral advantage out of denouncing the restrictive pay strategy of the government in power. The obvious lack of any bipartisanship on pay between the parties is a problem that other western democratic countries suffer from much less. Yet to some on the Left the system known as 'free' collective bargaining is nothing better than the law of the jungle, an arbitrary and unfair approach that rewards the strong and penalises the weak. The unions, however, tend to see incomes policy as an attempt to shackle the unions and keep down living standards.

In his introduction to the May 1979 Labour party general election manifesto Callaghan reaffirmed his conviction that free collective bargaining was no longer a sensible method of pay determination. 'Each year there will be three-way talks between ministers, management and unions to consider the best way forward for our country's economy', argued Callaghan.[30] 'Germany's Social Democratic government under Willy Brandt and Helmut Schmidt has proved that this is a good way to reach agreement on how to expand output, incomes and living standards. I am realistic enough to know that there are bound to be set-backs, but experience reinforces what all of us know in our hearts – there is no sound alternative to working together. A Conservative free-for-all in pay and prices would mean endless pitched battles that would be fatal to the interests of all of us'. But most union leaders were unsympathetic to any such idea and after Labour's decisive defeat they returned to the reckless enjoyment of the pay jungle, with considerable results for those of their members who were fortunate enough to stay in work over the next two years. Attempts to cobble together a new form of words in a national understanding to provide for wage restraint as part of an economic recovery programme will be very difficult.

The leaders of the Welsh TUC were brave enough to raise the pay issue in an imaginative policy document – The Social Plan – in February 1981. They castigated free collective bargaining as 'fundamentally anti-Socialist', 'taken straight from the capitalist rule book which dictates that only the strongest will survive'.[31] The document continued:

> The argument that the bargaining of powerful union groups sets the tempo and creates breaches in employers' and government resistance, which effectively 'pulls' the weakly organised worker through does not stand up to critical examination. If anything, the lower paid worker (by definition those with weak or constrained bargaining positions) has gained marginally more in real terms during periods of incomes policy, than he or she has during times when free collective bargaining has prevailed. . . . The suggestion that we can all be 'free' to bargain over pay has an increasingly hollow ring to it. The last decade has shown clearly that governments can operate very effective wage restraint policies in the public sector by the crude application of cash limits – without formally declaring an incomes policy and whilst apparently favouring the exercise of market forces to determine pay levels.

The Welsh TUC plan made it clear that the kind of incomes policy it had in mind was not a system of pay restraint. Its fundamental aim would be to 'maintain and advance real living standards.' The document advocated a legal minimum wage; increases in pay to be never less than the increase in the inflation rate; the creation of an Incomes Planning Board to avoid severe distortions in pay; the index-linking of pay of public service workers to retail prices under the principle of comparability. The Welsh TUC also wanted an annual tripartite pay assessment and a maximum wage so that nobody earned more than four times average earnings.

But delegates to the 1981 Welsh Trades Union Congress lost no time in giving the document the thumbs down, mainly because of its section on incomes policy. One militant suggested that the policy contained 'Social Democratic' arguments, the ultimate insult. There is simply no prospect whatsoever of a commitment by the trade union movement to any form of incomes policy. No doubt, Labour politicians might seek a vague commitment over pay in the run-up to the next general election, but they will find it hard to win union cooperation on this sensitive issue. For the time being, the Labour party will push ahead with its plans for a highly controlled economy, combined with a wages free for all, seeing nothing incompatible between Socialism and unfettered pay bargaining.

Nor are the Conservatives in a much better mood to establish a voluntary incomes policy. During the years in opposition from March 1974 to May 1979 they reappraised their views on the question and came to the conclusion that its difficulties were insuperable. In *The Right Approach*, published in October 1976, the Conservatives cast doubt on whether statutory incomes policies were really enforceable. They required an extension of bureaucracy; rigidity; a compression of pay differentials and they acted as a provocation for union militants. Nor were the Conservatives any more enthusiastic about a voluntary understanding on pay between government and the unions. The 'social contract' approach came under withering scorn. 'Unions tend to demand and obtain policies in exchange for restraint which either damage the national interest as a whole (such as tight price controls) or which they hope will further their own interests at the expense of the rest of the community. The basic bargain is likely to mean that the government promises to do things that ought not to be done, in exchange for a promise of wage restraint which is in everybody's interest anyway'.[32] Such national bargaining was also seen by the Conservatives as an usurpation of the role of Parliament. It failed to include other interest groups in society and it eroded the authority of moderate union leaders by exposing them to pressure from their militants. *The Right Approach* enthused about the West German's approach to wage determination through Concerted Action, where 'without any elaborate machinery' they were able to 'establish each year a generally agreed basis for responsible wage bargaining' through widespread consultation with interested parties. But the Conservatives were under no illusions that such an approach could be introduced either easily or quickly into Britain. Apparently 'monetary restraint, including the setting of targets for monetary expansion' was to become 'a key feature' of future Conservative economic policy.

'Excessive wage claims should clearly not be accommodated by an easy expansion in bank lending', the Conservatives argued. Cash limits were to be imposed in the public sector so that every organisation was 'put into a position in which workers and management are obliged to face together the inescapable choice between realistic wage levels and job security, or excessive earnings and a doubtful future'. In *The Right Approach to the Economy*, published in October 1977, the Conservatives were even more emphatic in their rejection of an incomes policy, which they argued led to a distortion of the economy by undermining the system of collective bargaining operated by employers and unions. It was the function of government to provide a climate in which wage negotiations were carried out responsibly. Through a 'strict control of the money supply' and 'firm cash limits on public expenditure', the Conservatives would ensure a new sense of economic realism in wage bargaining. There was to be no recognition of any such device as a 'going' rate. As the Conservatives argued:

> With freedom to bargain there will, and should be, a wide variation in wage increases for different groups. This is another old lesson that needs to be relearned. Employers, public and private, face an infinite variety of market conditions: some face weak demand; some need more of one sort of labour, some need less; some have adequate profits in real terms for survival and even for necessary expansion and investment; some have not. Some skills are scarce; some are not. Some firms can increase productivity more or less sharply, so as to absorb part or all of increased pay; some cannot or will not. Some have strong bargaining positions; some do not.[33]

Mrs Thatcher and her colleagues wanted to make quite clear the 'important and direct links' they saw between unit labour costs, prices and jobs.

There was to be no question of the government stepping in to act as Father Christmas by ensuring excessive wage rises were paid out to workers in the public sector through an increase in the money supply, an expansion in the cash limits, subsidies, or a cut in investment to fund current spending on wages.

The Conservatives in opposition were divided in the value they attached to any idea of a pay norm for bargaining purposes, but the 1977 document conceded that 'in framing its monetary and other policies the Government must come to *some* conclusions' about the likely scope for pay increases if excess public expenditure or large-scale unemployment was to be avoided. It was proposed to use the National Economic Development Council as an economic forum in which efforts could be made to find 'common ground about the economy', with scope for a Commons Select Committee on Expenditure to scrutinise the process.

The 1979 Conservative party election manifesto was much blunter on what it promised. Pay bargaining in the private sector was to be left to companies and workers to carry out, with no interference from the government. In the public sector there was to be a clear difference between 'the great public corporations' and the public services in the way in which pay negotiations were to proceed. In the case of the former it was to be left to each to negotiate what it could afford, though there was to be 'no question of subsidising excessive pay deals'.[34] For the latter cash limits were somehow to be reconciled with the demands of the unions, taking into account what the taxpayer and ratepayer could afford to pay. The Conservatives hoped to reach 'no strike agreements in a few essential services'. Above all, they wanted to 'put bargaining on a sounder economic footing, so that public sector pay deals took more notice of supply and demand, regional differences, manning levels, job security and pension arrangements.

Some Conservatives did point out that the British system of fragmented and multifarious bargaining failed to mirror the simplicities of a pure market economy where economic laws determined the value of a worker's labour power. Nicholas Ridley, a former junior industry minister, sketched out the 'tough postulates' that any such free collective bargaining would need. 'Neither participant in any negotiation about wages must have market power', he wrote in a confidential memorandum to the Conservative Shadow Cabinet.[35] 'Employers and workers alike must negotiate in isolation or in numerous small groups. Neither side must be a large enough element in the market to be able to significantly affect the price offered or demanded for labour. Under these conditions the outcome will be determined by the cost of labour (which determines its supply), its productivity (which determines demand) and the balance between the two.' Ridley added that as well as this 'neither participant in any negotiation must have political power of a kind or strength sufficient to induce the authorities to over-ride or influence the outcome of negotiations in the market place', while 'negotiations must be frequent enough to ensure that supply and demand do not get out of balance to any significant extent and wages must be easily adjustable downwards as well as upwards, in both real and money terms.' In his view, if that last proposition was 'unattainable', then negotiators must 'have fairly accurate information about economic trends and government policy – for example towards the money supply – if they were to bargain realistically and responsibly in their own interests, bargains which did not divert greatly from what the future course of supply and demand would dictate'. But Ridley accepted that 'none of these conditions' were met 'in every part of the economy'.

How did the Conservative approach to pay work in practice? Mrs Thatcher's first year (May 1979–May 1980) was an unmitigated disaster, as the government presided over a huge wage explosion in the public sector. Professor Hugh Clegg's comparability commission was made the scapegoat for such profligacy from a government that was elected to power with the clear mandate to take a tough line on pay in the public sector. It is true that Mrs Thatcher made a rash pledge in the heat of the general election campaign to honour the Clegg awards, but the huge wage rises handed out in the public sector extended far beyond the specific groups of public service workers who had been referred to the comparability commission (see Table 2.4).

For all the rhetoric of gloom and despair, workers who held onto their jobs enjoyed a *real* increase in their living standards during Mrs Thatcher's first two years in office that kept them well above the annual rate of inflation. Between 1978 and 1980 real earnings rose by an astonishing 17 per cent, while in 1980 there was a 15 per cent nose-dive in manufacturing output, the steepest decline in any 12-month period since the inter-war depression, though output per manhours was broadly maintained.

Yet there is little doubt that, from the summer of 1980 onwards, fear of the dole queue began to condition the wage expectations of millions of private manufacturing workers in vulnerable sectors of the economy. In

TABLE 2.4 Mrs Thatcher's wage spree, April 1979–April 1980 – % increases in average gross weekly earnings

| | *Full-time men aged 21 and over* | | | *Full-time women aged 18 and over* | | |
|---|---|---|---|---|---|---|
| | *Manual* | *Non-manual* | *All* | *Manual* | *Non-manual* | *All* |
| Central government | 33.7 | 33.5 | 34.4 | 31.5 | 31.9 | 31.8 |
| Local government | 28.6 | 25.1 | 25.9 | 26.6 | 21.9 | 22.8 |
| Public corporations | 21.0 | 24.2 | 22.1 | 31.2 | 24.1 | 25.4 |
| Public sector | 23.5 | 27.0 | 25.6 | 29.6 | 26.1 | 26.6 |
| Private sector | 18.4 | 22.8 | 20.6 | 20.2 | 23.6 | 22.5 |
| All industries and services | 20.0 | 24.5 | 22.4 | 22.8 | 25.2 | 24.8 |
| (All industries, April 1980, £) | 111.70 | 141.30 | 124.50 | 68.00 | 82.70 | 78.80 |

SOURCE *National Institute Economic Review*, No. 95, February 1981, p. 11.

the 1980–1 wage round key companies like Ford (8.8–9.2 per cent rises); BL (5 per cent); Vauxhall (6.5–8.0 per cent) and Metal Box (8.9–9.2 per cent) settled on wage rises below 10 per cent. One of the most dramatic turn-arounds in worker pay power came in the road haulage industry where lorry drivers (at the forefront of the 1978–9 wages offensive) swallowed wage rises of 3 to 7 per cent to bring their basic weekly rate up to around £80. Overtime opportunities collapsed for most lorry drivers as the recession bit deep and productivity bonuses were also hard to earn. The only fortunate group of drivers who found themselves able to insulate their position in the labour market were those employed by the oil companies, where a proven strength to disrupt supplies to the customer continued to dominate the character of collective bargaining in their sector. They enjoyed wage rises of around 14 per cent, more than twice the figures reached by other lorry drivers.

Even in the depths of the worst slump since the thirties some groups of workers were able to use their collective strength to exact huge wage rises without any regard to productivity improvements. The men of muscle – the miners; the power workers; the water workers; the gas workers – continued to demonstrate that they were almost immune to the harsh realities experienced in the rest of the labour market. As long as we have large public utility monopolies on which society depends for its livelihood, workers in those industries will continue to enjoy an almost unchallenged power.

Sir Geoffrey Howe's spring 1981 budget reinforced the commitment to monetarism and it added to the mounting squeeze on workers' purchasing power. Ministers congratulated themselves on what they saw as the new sense of realism in most pay bargaining. But there is no good reason to believe that this amounts to a genuine and permanent self-restraint among millions of workers in a depressed labour market. The old attitudes are more likely to have frozen over for the moment because of the cold winds blowing through the economy, but in any thaw we must expect a reacceleration of the wages merry-go-round. We can expect reluctant, sullen acquiescence in wage settlements that fall below the Retail Price Index, but enormous frustration, bitterness and a growing sense of injustice are likely to build up among workers. The urge to restore a perceived, lost position will become irresistible and any government in the run-up to a general election is going to find it very hard to resist. Tax cuts and some modicum of economic growth – however modest it may turn out to be – may start to smooth away the wrinkles.

## CONCLUSION

Pay will remain one of the central problems of our industrial politics during the eighties. Hopes of achieving any common purpose, a consensus between employers, union negotiators and government look remote, though no doubt intermittent attempts will be made to achieve such an arrangement. But nobody has devised any practical and workable way of resolving the three major difficulties inherent in our collective bargaining system. The decentralised multi-plant bargaining in private manufacturing ensures it is hard to enforce any national or industry-wide approach to pay. The existence of a strong and highly unionised public sector, where many organised groups of workers know they possess enormous strength to paralyse the country, makes it extremely hard for any government to reconcile its role as manager of the entire economy with that of being a 'good' employer to its own workers. But perhaps the biggest single headache for governments rests on the expectations of the shopfloor in a democratic society. Workers have been used to annual wage rises (in real and money terms) since the immediate post-war years of full employment and labour scarcity. They work and live in a society that places a premium on material acquistiveness, on the satisfaction of wants, on competition and individualism, even if so much of our industry and service sector is dominated by large national and multinational conglomerates.

While it is true that workers are neither upset nor militant about wide disparities of wealth and income in our unequal society, they are aware enough to resent and challenge any concerted effort to diminish their living standards in the 'national' interest. Unlike more successful economies in western Europe, Britain lacks strong, centralised and representative institutions of organised capital and labour that are needed for the achievement of any long-term consensus. We must live with the consequences. These will be often harsh, unjust and morally indefensible. The dominance of the workgroup in pay bargaining, the triumph of sectionalism and the decline in solidarity, are likely to outlive the present recession.

As in so many other areas of our national life, we are not short of blueprints and panaceas to right the wrongs of our wage-bargaining system. But there is a lack of will to change engrained attitudes, a belief that collective self-restraint to achieve a higher standard of living for all is impossible because some groups will always take advantage of their market strength to steal a march on everybody else. Nor can we expect any coherent response from a weakened and divided trade union movement. Free collective bargaining, the doctrine of smash and grab, will continue to find its champions among those who claim to be Socialists, believing in a more planned and collectivised society. Demands for a legal minimum wage and help for the low paid will co-exist with pressure to maintain pay relativities and differentials at all costs. Union negotiators are bound by the very nature of their work to uphold the existing earnings relationship, which is fixed by custom and practice as much as by economic calculation. This is why (whether they like it or not) unions tend to buttress the existing unequal labour market and through their actions ensure that it is not modified so that the strong can help the weak. The most militantly Socialist of trade union negotiators will continue to thrive as aggressive practitioners of a bargaining system that mirrors the inequalities of the market economy. The result will be a continuation of the evils associated with the pay free for all – high unit labour costs; low real wages and desperately poor relative levels of productivity.

No doubt, workers would be much better off if the British economy could achieve a miraculous breakthrough into higher growth and higher productivity, what the Treasury calls the 'virtuous circle'. But how can workers be convinced that it is in their own interests to hold back in the short term to ensure a more prosperous future? At bottom, all those who recognise the inadequacy of our wages jungle and want to see a more rational and ordered approach find themselves moving irresistibly into authoritarian arguments. The price of wages stability through centralised controls and bureaucratic intervention by the state may well be much too high to tolerate. A statutory wage norm laid down by a government, an independent all-knowing commission, backed up by sanctions of a penal kind against workers and unions would fail to carry the consent of our democratic society and threaten individual liberty. Such an approach would necessitate the destruction of free trade unionism and the introduction of a highly planned economy. This system is now in force in eastern Europe, with resulting food shortages, repression and low living standards. A belief in the wisdom of an incomes policy must come from a recognition of a wider political commitment to consensus, community, the sense of duties and obligations that we need to underpin a free society. As one participant argued in a recent OECD conference: 'Attitudes to collective bargaining undoubtedly reflect not only vested interests but also political beliefs. Those who find the free, peaceful, localised solution of social problems a source of value in itself will wish to encourage the further development of collective bargaining within the framework of certain, workable laws with a minimum of government intervention. Others – and recent experience suggests they are a large and growing group – will attach importance to the establishment (or re-establishment) of a stable total economic environment within which free individuals and free social relationships may develop'.[36]

An incomes policy, moving with the grain of market forces, remains central for any remedy to Britain's economic crisis, but it must rest on a consensus that we lack in our divided, *laissez-faire* society. We are thus left with an insoluble dilemma: we cannot live with much hope except through a common approach to wage bargaining and yet we lack the means to achieve any such agreement. In the future, as in the recent past, governments will therefore lurch from one desperate expedient to another as the economy spirals into further decline. Drifting incoherently downhill looks hardly like an heroic pose, but governments are likely to claim some success if they can slow down wage expectations for only short periods of time. In 1980–2 cash limits and supposed control of the money supply were the rough disciplines as an alternative to an industrial consensus, but this brought more and more unemployment. It is not the men of muscle in the core of the labour market who will price themselves out of work as a result of inflationary wage deals, but those less well placed than themselves in a society tempered neither by mercy nor justice.

## NOTES AND REFERENCES


1 Treasury press release, 22 July 1980.
2 A. Jones, *The New Inflation: The Politics of Prices and Incomes* (André Deutsch, 1973) p. 9.
3 W. W. Daniel, 'Wage Determination in Industry', PEP, June 1976, p. 25.
4 Jones, op. cit., p. 26.
5 The Political Economy of Inflation, ed. F. Hirsch and J. H. Goldthorpe (Martin Robertson, 1978) pp. 186–212.
6 'Wage Determination', OECD, 1974, p. 357.
7 F. Blackaby (ed.), *The Future of Pay Bargaining* (Heinemann, 1980) p. 100.
8 *Royal Commission on Trade Unions and Employers' Associations*, HMSO, June 1968, p. 143.
9 *The Changing Contours of Britain's Industrial Relations*, ed. W. Brown (Basil Blackwell, 1981).
10 W. Brown and M. Terry, 'The Changing Nature of National Wage Agreements', *Scottish Journal of Political Economy*, Vol. 25, No. 2, 1978, p. 124.
11 'The Future of Pay Determination', CBI, 1977, p. 34.

12 J. E. Meade, *Stagflation*, vol. 1, *Wage Fixing* (Allen and Unwin, 1982).
13 D. Hurd, *No End of Promise* (Collins, 1979) p. 128.
14 P. B. Beaumont, 'Government as Employer, Setting an Example?', Royal Institute of Public Administration, 1981.
15 R. F. Elliott and J. L. Fallick, *Pay in the Public Sector* (Macmillan, 1981) pp. 58–9.
16 'Standing Commission on Pay Comparability', Final Report, HMSO, 1980, p. 6.
17 CBI, p. 44.
18 Low Incomes', *Royal Commission on the Distribution of Income and Wealth*, Report No. 6, HMSO, 1978, pp. 58–9.
19 R. Maudling, *Memoirs* (Sidgwick & Jackson, 1978) p. 266.
20 G. Routh, *Occupation and Pay in Great Britain 1906–1979* (Macmillan, 1980) p. 214.
21 'Relativities', Pay Board Advisory Report 2, HMSO, 1974, pp. 3–4.
22 Press release, Pay Board, March 1974, p. 7.
23 B. Wootton, *The Social Foundations of Wage Policy* (Allen & Unwin, 1955) p. 175.
24 W. G. Runciman, *Relative Deprivation and Social Justice* (Routledge & Kegan Paul, 1966) p. 66.
25 W. W. Daniel, 'Wage Determination in Industry', PEP, 1976, p. 14.
26 A. Dean, 'Incomes Policies and Differentials', *National Institute Economic Review*, No. 85, August 1978, p. 48.
27 H. A. Turner, 'Wages of Fear' *New Society*, 1 February 1979, pp. 243–4.
28 *The Labour Government's Economic Record 1964–1970*, ed. Wilfred Beckerman (Duckworth, 1972) p. 314.
29 S. G. B. Henry and P. A. Ormerod, 'Incomes Policy and Wage Inflation', *National Institute Economic Review*, No. 85, August 1978, p. 39.
30 Labour party election manifesto, May 1979.
31 The Social Plan, Welsh TUC, 1981, pp. 35–8.
32 'The Right Approach', Conservative party, October 1976, pp. 37–8.
33 'The Right Approach to the Economy', Conservative party, October 1977, pp. 13–15.
34 Conservative party general election manifesto, May 1979.
35 The Ridley memorandum (undated), copy in the hands of the author.
36 C. A. Blyth, 'Collective Bargaining and Government Policies', Organisation for Economic Co-operation and Development, 1979, p. 90.

# 3 The Productivity Problem

Britain's productivity performance, measured by output per worker employed, has proved little short of appalling over the past twenty years, as our relative post-war economic decline has worsened. In the decade up to 1973 the average output per worker in British manufacturing industry rose at an annual rate of 3.5 per cent, but while our manufacturing output per worker rose by just over three quarters between 1955 and 1973 the average level of productivity in the member states of the European Economic Community increased by as much as one and a half times. For the rest of the seventies – with short, exceptional bursts in 1973 and 1979 – the country's output per head spluttered along at a disastrously low rate, in contrast to what was happening on the continent of Western Europe. Lack of competitiveness in the UK (shown in Figure 3.1) has become a major obstacle to the creation of any sustained economic growth, though it recovered by 11 per cent between January 1981 and January 1982.

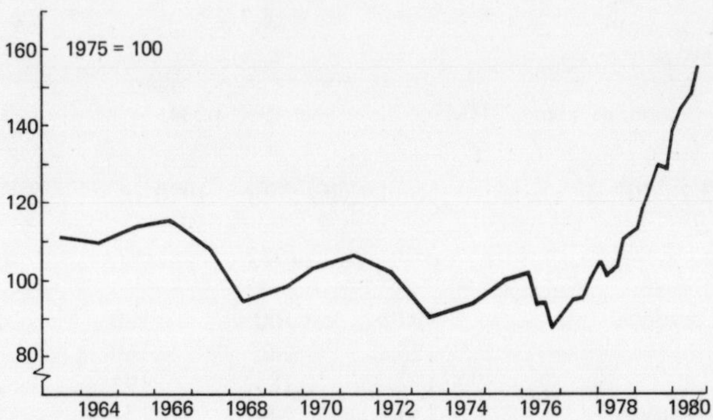


FIGURE 3.1 Loss of UK competitiveness – UK unit labour costs in manufacturing relative to main competitors

Note: A rise indicates a loss of UK competitiveness

SOURCE 'The Will To Win', CBI, March 1981, p. 12.

The statistics in Tables 3.1, 3.2 and 3.3 indicate the magnitude of the problem. The slump may have gone some way to improve productivity performance in parts of private manufacturing, but the laudable aim of bringing British levels of output per head up to continental western European standards looks problematic. Our relative productivity failure is due to a variety of reasons. Lack of investment in new plant and machinery remains central. The low rate of return on capital and the profits squeeze of the seventies were real enough. The inability to apply original research to business practice must also take much of the blame. The marketing efforts of too many companies have been complacent

TABLE 3.1 Britain's output per head, 1969–80

| | *Whole economy* | *Index of production industries* | *Manufacturing industries* |
|---|---|---|---|
| 1969 | 92.5 | 90.6 | 88.0 |
| 1970 | 94.5 | 92.0 | 88.6 |
| 1971 | 97.4 | 94.6 | 90.6 |
| 1972 | 100.1 | 98.7 | 95.8 |
| 1973 | 103.6 | 105.1 | 104.1 |
| 1974 | 101.5 | 101.6 | 102.6 |
| 1975 | 100.0 | 100.0 | 100.0 |
| 1976 | 103.0 | 105.1 | 105.4 |
| 1977 | 105.5 | 109.7 | 107.1 |
| 1978 | 108.6 | 114.1 | 108.3 |
| 1979 | 110.0 | 117.6 | 109.8 |
| 1980 (2nd qtr) | 108.5 | 114.7 | 106.2 |

SOURCE 'Economic Trends', HMSO, November 1980, p. 34.

TABLE 3.2 Britain's relative productivity failure, 1970–7

| | *1970* | *1973* | *1975* | *1977* |
|---|---|---|---|---|
| United Kingdom | 100 | 100 | 100 | 100 |
| Belgium | 156 | 146 | 160 | na |
| France | 177 | 185 | 197 | 205 |
| West Germany | 153 | 146 | 151 | 165 |
| Italy | 138 | 117 | 111 | 120 |
| Japan | 215 | 238 | 233 | 263 |
| United States | 340 | 336 | 338 | 360 |

SOURCE 'Finniston Committee of Inquiry into the Engineering Profession', HMSO, January 1980, p. 14.

TABLE 3.3 Britain's labour costs and output in the seventies

| | *Income per unit of output* | *Output per person of gross domestic product* |
|---|---|---|
| 1970 | 47.8 | 94.5 |
| 1971 | 51.6 | 97.4 |
| 1972 | 66.5 | 100.1 |
| 1973 | 61.9 | 103.6 |
| 1974 | 76.3 | 101.5 |
| 1975 | 100.0 | 100.0 |
| 1976 | 111.3 | 103.0 |
| 1977 | 119.7 | 105.5 |
| 1978 | 132.2 | 108.6 |
| 1979 | 151.0 | 110.0 |

SOURCE *National Institute Economic Review*, No. 95 February 1981, p. 100–1.

and amateurish. British manufacturers have not taken their full share in the international tendency for advanced countries to trade up-market with an increasingly sophisticated range of goods. As the Finniston inquiry argued, while other major industrialised powers have moved into high quality high value products to sell at competitive prices in rising markets, 'Britain has struggled with a product range for which world demand, including that from home customers, has grown relatively slowly.'[1] In 1975 the UK and West Germany both sold about 22 per cent of their total exports of metal-forming machinery to developing nations, but whereas the unit value of the British machines was only $1628, that of the German products was $4951 and the total value of the German sales was over four times greater than that for the UK.

In the view of the Brookings Institution in its 1980 report, the British malaise 'stems largely from its productivity problem, whose origins lie deep in the social system'.[2] The purpose of this chapter is to examine the nature of labour inefficiencies in Britain and to argue that the trouble lies *not* in trade union restrictive power but in the tenacity of the work group.

Trade unions have been blamed especially for this lamentable performance. Sir Keith Joseph, then industry minister, believed they were more anxious to protect existing jobs in dying industries than in the creation of new ones elsewhere in the economy as well as being hostile to the profit motive. He wrote in a memorandum to the National Economic Development Council in October 1979[3].

> Trade union attitudes make good management difficult. Many at shop-floor level seem hostile to the need for industrial efficiency. Many are encouraged to feel that reductions in working hours or increases in real pay are feasible without improvements in productivity or that inter-union disputes which keep major new facilities idle do no lasting damage to employment in their industry. Just as important, negotiated labour agreements are less dependable in the UK and restrictive practices – reflected in a reluctance by labour to agree to the elimination of unnecessary work and rules – are too prevalent. Yet these practices all contribute to overmanning; to the inefficient use of plant and to a loss of competitiveness.

Graham Hutton, in his 1979 Wincott lecture, suggested that 'our union leaders are preoccupied with job security (that is over-manning) to the exclusion of bigger wage increases for fewer, but more productive workers. They have thereby kept real earnings in Britain nearer the 'dole' than have unions in any other western country.[4]

Such criticisms have become over-familiar in the past few years, but they are nothing new. From their origins in the early nineteenth century trade unions were seen as hostile associations by economists and employers, not only because they were forces of potential subversion to the existing order, but also dangerous monopolistic enemies of a free market economy where the laws of supply and demand among self-regarding individuals determined the price of labour's value. It was the classical economist Alfred Marshall who wrote of the 1897 engineering dispute: 'Unless the ASE (the Amalgamated Society of Engineers) concedes to the employers the right to put a single man to work on an easy machine, or even two or more of them, the progress of the English working classes from the position of hewers of wood and drawers of water to masters of nature's forces, will, I believe, receive a lasting check'.[5]

But can unions as reactive, voluntary, collective organisations really be held responsible for the persistence of restrictive labour practices in so much of British industry today? The main argument of this chapter is that the craft mentality remains deeply rooted in the traditional hallowed culture of the workgroup and the trade union reflects and represents (for the most part) the collective expression of an attitude of mind pervasive among workers themselves. As Kahn-Freund has argued: our industrial system is dominated 'by the desire of one group of workers to attain and maintain privileges as against other groups of workers and to map out for itself a reserved area in which other workers are not allowed to trespass'.[6] This view is not just limited to skilled manual workers. It exists everywhere in our society, far beyond the boundaries of the union. The legal profession, for example, is riddled with restrictions over access to jobs, status protectionism, and demarcation lines.

It is no exaggeration to maintain that the resulting sectionalism of the workgroup (whether among barriesters or bricklayers; bus drivers or television producers) remains a formidable characteristic of our work organisation. In the *laissez-faire* economy of mid-Victorian England the trade union was often regarded by the workers who joined it as 'a device for getting more money for the same work; it was a joint stock company for selling labour; and like any other similar undertaking, it hoped to make a handsome profit over and above the costs of supplying its product'.[7] The restrictions on entry into a defined trade through the time-served apprenticeship system were a legacy from the medieval guilds. In the name of job protection this was the method of maximising the bargaining strength of the union against employers.

The 1968 Donovan Royal Commission was careful to draw a distinction between the union as such and the workgroup for the persistence of restrictive labour practices, which it defined as 'an arrangement under which labour is not used efficiently and which is not justifiable on social grounds'.[8] As that report insisted:

> Where practices of this kind exist, insistence on retaining them usually comes from workers themselves, acting as groups which have certain interests in common which they try as best they can to further, rather than from trade unions. Most responsible union leaders deplore the habitual use of overtime. If time-keeping is bad, it is because management has been slack, not because trade unions have encouraged it. It is not trade union policy, that mates should be underemployed.

The 1969 Labour government's ill-fated *In Place of Strife* White Paper made the same important distinction between unions and workers. 'There can be no doubt that equipment and manpower are not always used as efficiently in this country as in other comparable industrial countries'.[9]

> This is partly due to customs and practices which restrict the efficient use of resources including manpower. On the whole such practices are operated, not by unions themselves but by groups of employees, who

see them as a way of protecting their jobs or of maintaining their earnings. Because of this, any attempt to get rid of such practices without adequate compensation is seen as a threat, either to earnings or to security of employment'.

Some trade union leaders recognise that the obstacles to changes in working practices stem from the workgroup. Len Murray, the TUC's general secretary said in his 1980 Granada lecture: 'It is less difficult for unions to win from their members acceptance of temporary wage restraint than it is for them to win agreement to changes in manpower practices. Indeed, Britain's poor economic record since the war is due much more to the ineffective use of our resources than to excessive wage settlements.'[10] Union leaders like Clive Jenkins of the Association of Scientific, Technical and Managerial Staffs and John Lyons of the Engineers' and Managers' Association have welcomed increased efficiency in a positive manner. The Post Office Engineering Union under Lord Delacourt Smith in the sixties seized the initiative in productivity bargaining with the Post Office. Initially this brought promising results, though the 1977 Carter review committee did suggest that Britain's telecommunications remained 'significantly less efficient than the best of its foreign competitors'.[11]

The Electrical, Electronic, Telecommunication and Plumbing Union under Les Cannon, and later Frank Chapple, cooperated fully with the modernisation of the supply industry, a point that was recognised by the 1971 Wilberforce inquiry.

Indeed, the recent performance of the electricity supply industry looks impressive. Between 1965–6 and 1979–80 there was a 75 per cent improvement in output per head, with a 49 per cent increase in the total number of Gigawatts supplied per year and a 20 per cent cutback in the total manpower of the Central Electricity Generating Board. During the seventies the manual workforce was reduced by a quarter, while there was a 10 per cent rise in the size of the numbers employed in scientific and technical work. These impressive changes took place with little fuss after a break through in productivity agreements between 1964 and 1968, mainly through the introduction of shift or staggered work patterns (any five days from seven). In the middle sixties the existing work rate norm was only around 60 per cent of 'standard performance', but by the end of the seventies that figure had reached around 99 per cent. A flexibility of working was introduced into electricity supply after 1967, which enabled management to use craftsmen to carry out associated work within their competence, require higher grade staff to perform lower grade work and the cross-grading and mobility of operators, attendants and managers. There was a clear slowdown in productivity improvements during the late seventies, due to the delay in the commissioning of new power stations. Consequently higher staffing numbers and the curse of overtime began to creep back into the industry. A 1981 Monopolies and Mergers Commission report expressed some concern that during the seventies real total labour costs had risen by 46 per cent in supply (compared with a 38 per cent rise in output per head). It called for more job evaluation and work measurement among clerical and managerial grades to improve performance.

During the sixties the National Union of Mineworkers – despite serious doubts among some of its leaders – did not resist the rundown on the coalfields and went along with the abolition of the divisive piecework payment system and its replacement by a day wage structure for all miners. In the words of the 1972 Wilberforce inquiry: 'This rundown, which was brought about with the cooperation of the miners and their union, is without parallel in British industry in terms of the social and economic costs it has inevitably entailed for the mining community as a whole'.[12] NUM president, Joe Gormley, championed the principle of a pit incentive scheme as a method of improving productivity, and this was eventually introduced in 1978 at area level. It has brought a marked improvement in output per manshift at the coal face and elsewhere underground, so that the British coal industry bears effective comparison in its productivity performance with the rest of Europe during the past few years. In 1981–2 overall output per manshift was 2.4 tonnes, the highest figure ever recorded.

These examples should help to qualify the picture of total trade union hostility or indifference to the cause of higher labour productivity. But it is also true that very few unions take much consistent interest in the question. In his study of productivity C. F. Pratten discovered that 'union officials make little study of what constitutes labour productivity'.[13] 'Only one of the unions consulted had made any comparisons of labour productivity within or between international companies, or any international comparisons of labour productivity,' he wrote. 'The Transport and General Workers had obtained comparisons of productivity for wage claims it submitted to Ford and ICI'. However, contrary to popular belief, trade unions are not formidable bureaucratic organisations with enormous power and influence over their members or the running of industry. As Pratten concluded: 'One of the more surprising features of this part of the study was the loose control shown to apply within unions. In some unions, local branches control a substantial proportion of the unions' finances and have a good deal of autonomy for determining policy for negotiations and in disputes'.

The emergence of the independent power of the work groups since the Second World War, with the resulting elevation of the shop steward and the recent arrival of the combine committee outside the formalised organisation of the unions was shaped by the needs of industry. The devolution of authority down the line to the shop-floor, especially in pay bargaining, but also in the everlasting struggle over 'the frontiers of control' at the workplace between workers and management over work organisation, made it much harder for the trade unions to win the consent of their members to changes in restrictive labour practices in the name of higher productivity.

Of course, where a trade union controls the actual supply of labour entering an industry or occupation, it might be more vulnerable to the charge of holding back productivity improvements. A 1980 study at the London School of Economics found that as many as one in every four trade unionists in this country are covered by a closed shop or 100 per cent union membership agreement. This amounts to around 5 200 000 workers. Around 14 per cent of that figure (837 000) are estimated to belong to pre-entry closed shops, where 'a union seeks to control the supply of labour to employers by restricting entry to the union and by insisting at the same time that job applicants hold an appropriate union card before being considered for appointment'.[14]

Two industries are particularly involved in this arrangement. These are printing, paper and publishing, and shipbuilding and marine engineering. Neither has a good record of productivity performance. The national newspaper industry suffers from some of the worst restrictive labour practices in the country, operating in a jungle of leap-frogging wage claims and high manning levels, which were highlighted in the famous 1966 report by the Economist Intelligence Unit. If anything the situation in Fleet Street has worsened considerably since that time, with crises at the *Observer* and Times Newspapers. But again, it is difficult to pin the blame for the troubles of the industry onto the print unions. Power on national newspapers rests primarily with the chapel (the work group) and not the union branch meeting. Failure to comply with a union directive can incur fines on erring members and, in the last resort, the loss of the union card, which is a meal ticket for life, but although such sanctions exist in the union rule books, they are seldom threatened, let alone used. Time and time again union officials have found their own position *vis-à-vis* their own members undermined by the willingness of weak Fleet Street managements to give way to the demands of the chapels that possess the proven disruptive power to halt newspaper production with the resulting damage for the well-being of the title. As Keith Sisson acknowledged in his study of Fleet Street: 'It must be obvious that the control which the chapels have been able to establish over the payment system and the demand and supply of labour goes some of the way towards explaining the high pay and overmanning'.[15] A survey carried out by the Advisory, Conciliation and Arbitration Service for the McGregor Royal Commission in the newspaper industry in 1977 found that as many as 21.5 per cent of its production workers were more than sixty years of age and 6.5 per cent of them even over 65. With around 55 000 people working in Fleet Street, 12 000 of them as production workers and 4600 as casual part-timers, it is hardly suggestive of great efficiency. National print union leaders like Bill Keys of SOGAT and Joe Wade of the National Graphical Association have recognised the problem, but they appear almost powerless to do anything about it. In 1977 they all drew up an enlightened document – *Programme for Action*. This was a blueprint for the newspaper industry in the new technological age, complete with generous severance payments for older workers who were no longer needed to operate the labour-saving machinery. Both sides of the industry accepted that it was vital to have a gradual, planned rundown on a voluntary basis so that no worker suffered any unnecessary hardship. But only a majority of the journalists agreed to the trade union inspired package, while the rest of the Fleet Street workforce turned down the reform programme in a secret ballot. The skilled compositors and machine men of the National Graphical Association are most vulnerable to the loss of their skills with the move away from mechanical type-setting to photo-composition and press-button, computerised technology because their whole *raison d'être* has been brought into question. They have responded in a militant, uncompromising manner, in many cases (though not all) and their union officials have had to reflect their views whether they agreed with them or not.

The power of the work group is also considerable in Britain's shipyards, despite the existence of pre-entry closed shop agreements. In August 1971 the Commission on Industrial Relations published a hard-hitting report on the organisation of work in the yards. As it argued: 'Because the work lends itself to self-supervision, the traditions of the industry protect the autonomy of the work group. It is a common feature of the industry that this often extends to some control over the times when the work actually starts and finishes. It also affects decisions about manning and about the allocation and distribution of overtime'.[16] The CIR study went on to say that 'the extent and organisation of the craft content of the work has led to the emergence of a large number of distinct craft specialisations, each with its own skill, pride in work and control of much of the work process. Division into craft groups has been reinforced by union organisation which coincides with craft organisation, and by the development of social and work group attitudes within closely-knit communities'. The (until recently) casual hire and fire methods of shipbuilding employers, the ups and downs of the economic cycle in the industry and the life-span of ship construction helped to solidify the independence of the sectionalist work groups, who fought to protect themselves from losing their jobs through a perpetuation of ancient demarcation lines, which were enshrined in custom and practice but no longer made any sense at all. In the words of the CIR report, the result was the continuation of 'the uneconomic use of labour'. It was sectionalism that stood 'in the way of wider job opportunities' and prevented 'differences over pay from being settled with the interests of all employees being taken into account at the same time'.

Since the nationalisation of the shipbuilding industry in 1978, joint management-union initiatives have given a high priority to improving productivity performance. A national industry-wide pay system has replaced the old fragmented, sectionalist yard bargaining and a major drive has removed many – though by no means all – of the demarcation lines between work that used to hamper efficiency. But nobody doubts that British shipbuilders have a long way to go in boosting output per head at a time of world recession in the industry. In March 1979 Britain's yards were disclosed to be only half as efficient as Japan's. An internal study revealed that as much as three hours and five minutes of every working day was lost in production through the misuse of working time.

The difficulties of translating good intentions from the national bargaining table to the workplace remain considerable in shipbuilding, where workers may feel they will work themselves out of a job if they improve their performance. A similar problem exists in the nationalised steel industry. In 1976 all the trade unions in steel signed an agreement with the British Steel Corporation to reduce labour costs and improve productivity. One clause in that document said that there would have to be 'very significant changes in the organisation and structure of work' to make sure that 'working practices match those of the Corporation's competitors'. Another stated 'the need to man jobs flexibly in such matters as working light, broadening of job content and mobility, particularly in regard to the undertaking of alternative work without restrictions imposed by traditional union and branch boundaries'.[17] At that time BSC released productivity statistics to show it needed only 64 000 Japanese steel workers or 87 000 American steel workers to achieve levels of output of liquid steel that it took 182 000 British steel workers to produce. Yet four years later BSC management complained that the 1976 joint agreement had simply failed to be implemented down at the plants, despite the sincere efforts of union officials to win the cooperation of workers to carry through the necessary changes in working practices.

Comparative studies carried out by the iron and steel sector working party for the National Economic Development Office between similar plants in Britain, Holland and Sweden during 1979 revealed substantial differences in performance, although the lower labour costs in Britain did help to ensure a more balanced result than would otherwise have been the case. The report concluded that 'the clearest difference between the United Kingdom and the continental plants was in the relationship and demarcation between production and maintenance employees'.[18] On the continent production workers are trained to be flexible enough to move around the plant to carry out different kinds of work when needed to do so. 'The benefits of such flexibility were in the ability to cover for those not at work without recourse to overtime and in increasing the job interest by job rotation', said the NEDO report. At the British steel plants surveyed a separate group of semi-skilled maintenance hands or labourers are employed to fetch and carry for the craftsmen. These don't exist at the continental plants, where production workers are expected to carry out such work themselves. Moreover, the continental plants have far fewer workers performing separate craft skills'. 'Typically a mechanical craftsman combines the skills of a mechanical fitter, pipe fitter, welder/boilermaker'. In Britain we have many varieties of craftsmen working inflexibly in a given, narrow skill that is not interchangeable. At continental steel plants the lack of demarcation in labour practices between production and maintenance is also reflected in the absence of separate trade unions for both groups. In Britain we suffer from multiplicity of different unions in the steel industry that adds to the complexity of collective bargaining and work organisation at the plants.

Similar common problems as steel were discovered in 1972 by the NEDO office when working practices were contrasted between chemical plants in Britain, West Germany and Holland. The report argued that manning levels for production workers were about the same in all three countries in chemicals, but in the maintenance area the UK plants compared unfavourably, needing 50 per cent more men per unit of output than on the continent. The NEDO study suggested that the main explanations for the differences were less shift working on the continent; all workers on the continental maintenance teams being fully skilled; greater mobility between plants on the same site; more freedom to use outside contract workers on the continent and greater flexibility between their process operators and craftsmen. The craftsman's mate is an unknown figure at continental plants, because all workers are trained 'to as high a level as their abilities allowed'. As the NEDO report argued

> The result of continental companies having such a high proportion of skilled men among maintenance employees was enhanced efficiency. For example, on small repair jobs requiring two men, both would be skilled and both would be allowed to do any part of the job, thus ensuring a quick finish. This increase in flexibility resulted in an overall cost reduction despite the greater use of more expensive skilled labour.[19]

In steel and chemicals, the trade unions tend to mirror the customs and practices laid down by the work groups. The same remains broadly true of the troubled motor car industry, where low productivity is a major headache. In 1975 the Central Policy Review Staff stated bluntly: 'It takes almost twice as many man-hours to assemble similar cars using the same or comparable plant and equipment in Britain as it does on the continent'.[20] The CPRS blamed low productivity on overmanning. Apparently it needed 41 per cent more workers in Britain compared with the continental plants to trim, finally assemble and dress the car engine and as many as 69 per cent to 78 per cent more plant maintenance workers.

> Overmanning in maintenance is also an example of the impact of trade demarcations on efficiency. If a multiweld machine used to weld body panels together breaks down in Britain, six maintenance men would be required to repair it – an electrician, a jig fitter, a pipe fitter, a mechanical fitter, a tool man and a repair man. On the continent only two men, one mechanical and the other electrical would accomplish the same job.

But even when car production lines in plants are manned at competitive levels, output in Britain fails to reach the same volume. The CPRS document highlighted the 'slow work pace' as a major obstacle with 'slower line speeds, late starts, frequent stoppages between and during shifts and delays in correcting mechanical problems'. Other barriers to improved productivity in the car industry were shortage of materials due to disputes affecting suppliers; poor quality control (plants in Britain need twice as much rectification time as continental car plants) and poor maintenance. The management and the work groups must take much of the blame for this, but trade unions cannot entirely escape from criticism. The CPRS report thought that the 'fragmented union structure' in the car plants was a factor 'which affects the continuity of production by provoking disputes over recruitment and demarcation'. Extremism among militant political minorities in the plants was also given as an explanation by the CPRS.

The highly critical CPRS report was a direct challenge to the Ryder study on British Leyland that tended to place the main blame for poor productivity on lack of new plant and machinery. But it is also worth bearing in mind what BL chairman Sir Michael Edwardes told the Commons industry and trade committee in March 1981 when he was asked to contrast Japanese productivity with British in car manufacture. 'The problem about productivity comparisons is that generally speaking they are apples and pears and I have even heard very responsible ministers making very irresponsible comparisons on productivity', explained Edwardes. He pointed out that the Japanese companies import bulk of the car they manufacture into the plant from their suppliers. With 70 per cent of the components brought into the plant from elsewhere it was not surprising that the output per head of the Japanese car worker was higher than elsewhere. The major cause of the collapse in the competitiveness of BL during 1979 to 1980 was not low labour productivity from workers, but the very high value of sterling on overseas exchange markets. Edwardes told the Commons committee that the situation had deteriorated by as much as 57 per cent against the Japanese yen in just two years. 'In some cases the Japanese are selling cars in certain markets at prices based on the present yen which, even with no labour content in ours, are lower,' argued Edwardes. But from 1980 productivity improved dramatically with an average jump in output per man of 30 per cent between 1981 and 1982. From under eight cars per man per year built in 1980, the total rose to nearly 17, within a year. At Longbridge there was more than 100 per cent improvement on the Mini Metro line in 1981 over 1980.

The British construction industry also emerges badly from comparative study. A 1976 joint working report from NEDO concluded that British construction projects in the power, chemical and oil industries took far longer than similar ones either in the United States or in continental Europe, requiring more workers and taking more man-hours on site. The study found the ratio of unskilled to skilled workers was worse here than anywhere else and more supervision was carried out. It also recorded that less than a third of the working day on British sites examined was actually spent on construction work, while a substantial amount of the day in some cases was actually used by the workers 'not on plot'.[21] The NEDO report concluded that British construction workers were less ready to work in the rain, had prolonged tea breaks and their proneness to disruption was greater than their counterparts on the continent. A 1979 joint NEDO study comparing British with American performance in the construction equipment and mobile cranes industry produced a familiarly depressing picture. The report was impressed by the use of the three year labour contract in the United States which ensured job security and earnings stability and the one union plant structure that avoided inter-union rivalry between skills and allowed for labour flexibility.

Nor is the engineering industry very different. A 1979 study by the Engineering Employers Federation concluded that 'the greatest barrier to productivity is inefficient practices within individual firms', although it was also stressed that the level of demand in the economy was the major constraint to improvements.[22] Of the 12 firms that currently reported depressed markets for their products in the EEF study, as many as ten reported 'inefficient levels of labour utilisation described by most as overmanning – which held down current productivity levels'. A 1975 research project at Birmingham University examined the distribution of time during a working day by operatives and machines in forty engineering and metal working firms during the 1968–72 period and a further 45 firms in 1970–4. It discovered that the machines were idle for half the working time and on average operatives spent 16 per cent of their working day simply 'waiting'.[23]

Britain's railway system has some of the lowest labour productivity in western Europe, argued a Commons Select Committee in 1977. Criticism was levelled in particular at the use of the second man in the railway cab of high speed trains (a relic from the steam age); the use of guards on freight trains; the low amount of driving time achieved by drivers (between 3½ and 3¾ hours in an eight-hour shift) and the large number of tickets and station staff employed. An internal British Rail study published in March 1980 concluded that 'the longer hours worked by British railwaymen do not, in general, lead to equivalent higher levels of output per man than those achieved' by other continental railways.[24] This was mainly because the standard working week runs from Monday to Saturday in Britain and not over seven days as on the Continent. While the study found a favourable productivity comparison between passenger services, Britain along with Italy had a poor efficiency level on freight and parcels services, with the need for twice as many train crews to run a freight train as the most efficient, mainly because other railway companies had abolished guards and/or drivers assistants on their freight trains.

The 1980 Monopolies and Mergers Commission report on British Rail's London and South East commuter services highlighted the painful lack of progress during the seventies to greater labour productivity.[25] Whereas between the middle fifties and the late sixties British Rail's overall workforce was cut back by over 57 per cent, while output measured in terms of traffic units (passenger miles/net freight tonne miles) fell by under 16 per cent, thus achieving a 97 per cent rise in productivity (traffic units per worker), during the seventies there was only a manpower reduction of 14 per cent against a fall of 9 per cent in traffic units, ensuring a puny 5 per cent improvement in productivity. Between 1977 and 1980 management and unions negotiated for an incredible 120 000 man-days without any breakthroughs. Once again, it is clear that most of the resistance to more efficient working practices was coming not from the union negotiators but from their members. There was strong localised resistance among many guards during the period to the proposal that they should collect unpaid fares, and issue tickets as part of their duties on rural routes. In March 1980 BR reached agreement with the National Union of Railwaymen for guards to perform commercial duties in return for an extra £2 a week payment, but it had to be paid out to all the guards whether or not they were being asked to carry out these added functions and there was still much opposition to the move in the Eastern Region and in Scotland.

A number of conditions laid down in the national agreements at BR positively impede efficiency. First, there are inflexible shift patterns, for the agreements guarantee an eight-hour day for train crew and permit rostered turns in excess of this only with agreement. Second, national agreements entitle rail drivers to what are known as 'physical needs breaks' of half an hour between the third and fifth hours of their turn, although in numerous cases the break falls during commuter peak times. Third, much time is spent on local joint management-union departmental committees making sure that the work programmes of single manned drivers are in compliance with national agreements. The Monopolies and Mergers Commission found that almost all day every Thursday was spent by those committees on southern region examining this problem for the following week.

Fourth, there are debilitating obstacles to job opportunity on BR under national agreements. Any new arrival in the footplate grades has to be under the age of 23 and no-one can qualify to be a driver before he reaches 21. Drivers are not promoted by ability but through seniority based on service. Railway workers who enter the footplate line of promotion from other grades retain no seniority in respect of service outside the footplate. These restrictions both restrict the available supply of labour to BR and hamper efficiency.

The Monopolies and Mergers Commission report also highlighted the considerable absenteeism among railway workers. It commented:

> The frequency of absence is highest for train crews, there is substantial variation between different locations, the performance of supervision in containing absenteeism also appears to vary and there is a shortage of data regarding uncertificated sickness absence which could assist monitoring and control. There is in our view a risk that the abuse of uncertificated sick leave arrangements is becoming a commonly accepted feature of BR employment in London and the South East. The staff have adopted their own terminology to describe it; in Southern Region they refer to 'Awaydays' and in Eastern Region to 'blow outs'.

The rail unions have taken a strong public stand against the excessive use of overtime, rest day and Sunday working by their members, but such official disapproval seems to make little impact down on the ground. On Southern Region, local management does not recruit to establishment level in order to provide plenty of opportunities for their employees to ensure adequate earnings through working longer hours than the basic week. In the words of the Monopolies and Mergers Commission:

> It is the official policy of all three rail unions to oppose this practice, which they believe undermines their objective of improving relative basic pay and contributes to the decline in their membership. At local levels in London and south east however, members cooperate in keeping actual employment levels below establishment and we have

> been told of cases where they have used their influence to ensure that recruitment does not rise even to the budgeted levels.

Strong local depot resistance was also found to exist to any changes in work allocations, because workers saw the need to hold on to existing work to ensure their established earnings levels were maintained. 'This has seriously inhibited management's ability to reallocate work between depots in order to maximise operating efficiency', commented the report.

A similar conflict between a union and its members over efficiency can be found in the Post Office. A 1980 report from the Monopolies and Mergers Commission on the state of the postal services in inner London revealed that the Post Office is unable to provide a continuous monitoring of the volume of flow in postal traffic through each sorting office, because it alleged there was opposition from the Communication Workers union. Resistance from the union was also blamed for the slow progress towards a mechanisation of the sorting offices during the 1970s. But a closer reading of the evidence in the report suggests that the problem – painfully familiar – lay not with the union as such but the workers themselves in the sorting offices. In their submission to the Commission the union asserted that it was in the interests of their members to achieve a highly mechanised and more productive business with a reduced but better paid labour force. However, the report from the Commission noted that 'this view appears to us not always to have been reflected in local branches, whose members in the absence of a work-related pay system are principally concerned to protect their existing privileges in relation to seniority, concessions or access to overtime to the almost complete exclusion of consideration of the long-term prospects of the postal service and of their future employment'.[26]

In the last resort, as a democratic union, the Communication Workers must respect the views of their members, so on thorny issues like the employment of part-time and seasonal workers, the function of postmen in the higher grade and the organisation of work, union officials often have to act against their own opinion by defending the indefensible.

It is usual to heap the blame for poor productivity on the shoulders of the trade unions, but the power of the work group remains crucial for an understanding of the problem. However, this does not mean that trade unions are entirely immune from criticism over low productivity. Demarcation disputes between groups of workers have become less frequent in the past decade, but the existence of separate unions in a plant to represent divergent occupational interests can make it very difficult to make any progress on productivity bargaining. Marathon disputes like those at Hunterston terminal in Scotland and the Isle of Grain power station in 1979–80 did reflect divisions between workers of a genuine kind, but there is little doubt that personal union rivalries and antagonisms made those troubles much worse than they should have been.

Union bargainers are not always ready to see the value of greater labour efficiency as a way of boosting the living standards of workers in the long run, even if it does mean some sacrifice in the here and now. It remains a depressing British habit of mind, and by no means confined to union officials or their members, that restrictive practices can only be bought out with immediate monetary rewards. Moreover, the incessant competition between trade unions for members makes it difficult for union leaders to trade jobs for money or cooperate with a firm to boost output per head if it means fewer opportunities and not more. Dislike of the profit motive also exists among too many union officials, who often blind themselves to the value of technological change in bettering the living standards of their members and their families.

The removal of bad labour practices will only come through the action of employers. Yet, unlike their foreign rivals, companies pay little attention to the issue in a humane manner. The resistance of so many work groups to change is not surprising. As an economist argued recently:

> Since the managers tend to place much greater emphasis on productivity than job security, a real and important conflict of priorities may easily arise. It seems that managers in western Europe and Japan have been more successful than the UK's managers in reconciling these two priorities by coupling relatively faster labour-saving innovation with faster product innovation and greater marketing effort, so that, in parallel to a high growth in labour productivity and (therefore real wages) also a high output (and therefore job security) have been achieved.[27]

In the words of Len Murray in his 1980 Granada lecture:

> Workers can only be got to accept changes in manning and working practices if they are convinced of the need for and benefits of change and if they are protected against its adversities. They ask – fairly in my book – why they should accept the adverse consequences of decisions made for their own purposes by faceless boards of directors or by managements, or indeed by governments.[28]

The present slump is a difficult time to press major reforms in working practices. Workers fear they could make themselves unemployed, if they cooperate too eagerly with change.

But despite such understandable anxieties, many companies have been able to take advantage of the change in the balance of economic power resulting from the slump to reassert the right to manage. In BL, for example, there was the unilateral imposition of a radical change in working practices by the company in 1980. Down at plant level that meant the abolition of many shop-floor gains achieved over the past twenty years.

Similarly, the British Steel Corporation by-passed intransigent union officials nationally to reach productivity deals down at plant level that broke through the old restrictions on the mobility of labour. Impressive improvements were recorded in labour efficiency at the Port Talbot and Llanwern plants as a result. During 1981–2 there was some evidence that the very severity of the slump had forced companies to streamline their operations and remove many practices that hampered output in the past. Whether such gains in productivity will grow in any upturn in the economy must remain questionable. The trouble with unilateral management change is that it can invite shop-floor counter-attack when the crude economic balance of power moves away from the employer. A 1981 survey from the Confederation of British Industry suggests that few companies bother to keep their employees fully informed on performance, so they can hardly expect unquestioning support for any reform of manpower practices. The use of fear to motivate necessary change can prove to be a mistaken psychological weapon that breaks to pieces in better times.

But workers and their unions will respond to the challenge of change if they are treated as necessary partners in a strategy of national survival and not as enemies or outsiders. During the Second World War, especially after August 1941, this country achieved levels of industrial output that became the envy of the Nazi war machine through the suspension of demarcation lines, the dilution and mobility of skilled labour and the establishment of joint production committees and works councils, with the full cooperation of the unions with management. The mobilisation of the British economy for total war produced impressive results that helped to ensure eventual victory. Tragically, in the deceptively easier years of peace, custom and practice, over-manning and all the other familiar restrictive habits of British society once more became predominant in industry. The central problem remains with no obvious solution in the eighties: how to achieve a breakthrough in productivity performance when we lack the obvious external stimulus of a nation under threat of occupation by a foreign power to motivate necessary change. The burdens of history, of our voluntarist traditions and the power of the work group, remain formidable obstacles and the present slump looks unlikely to change those fundamental attitudes of mind.

## NOTES AND REFERENCES


1 'Engineering Our Future', report of the Committee of Inquiry into the engineering profession, January 1980, p. 16.

2 *Britain's Economic Performance*, ed. R. E. Caves and L. B. Krause (Washington DC: Brookings Institution, 1980) p. 19. See in particular R. E. Caves, 'Productivity Differences among Industries' pp. 135–98.

3 Memorandum from the Secretary of State for Industry to the National Economic Development Council, October 1979, p. 1.

4 G. Hutton, 'Whatever Happened to Productivity?' Institute of Economic Affairs, 1980, p. 19.

5 *Memorials of Alfred Marshall*, ed. A. C. Pigou (Macmillan, 1925) p. 398, quoted in *Trade Unions, Public Goods or Public Bads?* (IEA, 1978) p. 9.

6 O. Kahn-Freund, *Labour Relations: Heritage and Adjustment* (Oxford University Press, 1979) p. 43.

7 R. Currie, *Industrial Politics* (Oxford University Press, 1979) p. 31.

8 *Royal Commission on Trade Unions and Employers' Associations*, HMSO, June 1968, p. 77.

9 'In Place of Strife' White Paper, HMSO, January 1969, p. 3.

10 'The Role of the Trade Unions', Granada Guildhall lectures, 1980 (Granada, 1980) p. 75.

11 'Report of the Post Office Review Committee', HMSO, July 1977, pp. 18–19.

12 'Court of Inquiry into the Coal Mining Industry', HMSO, 1972, p. 5.

13 C. F. Pratten, 'Labour Productivity Differentials within International Companies' (Cambridge, 1976) p. 67.

14 'The extent of closed shop arrangements in British industry', *Employment Gazette*, January 1980, pp. 16–22.

15 K. Sisson, *Industrial Relations in Fleet Street* (Blackwell, 1974) p. 37.

16 'Shipbuilding and Shiprepairing' Commission on Industrial Relations Report, No. 22, HMSO, 1971, pp. 109–18.

17 Joint agreement between BSC and the Steel Unions, February 1976.

18 'A Hard Look At Steel', National Economic Development Office, 1980.

19 'Chemicals Manpower in Europe', National Economic Development Office, 1973, p. 19.

20 'The Future of the British Car Industry', report from the Central Policy Review Staff, HMSO, 1975, pp. 79–83.

21 'Engineering Construction Performance', National Economic Development Office, 1976, pp. 19–20.

22 'A Pilot Study of Performance and Productivity in the UK Engineering Industry', Engineering Employers Federation, July 1979, pp. 43–4.
23 'Midlands Tomorrow', West Midland Economic Planning Council, No. 8, 1975, pp. 3–5.
24 'European Railways Performance Comparisons', British Rail, March 1980, p. 18.
25 'BR south east region', Monopolies and Mergers Commission, HMSO, 1980.
26 'The Inner London Letter Post', Monopolies and Mergers Commission, HMSO, March 1980, p. 86.
27 *Slow Growth in Britain: Causes and Consequences* (Oxford University Press, 1979). Essay by Stanislaw Gomulka, p. 190.
28 Granada lecture, op. cit. (see note 10).

# 4 The Training Scandal

The shortage of skilled labour has been almost a persistent complaint by many employers in manufacturing industry during much of the past thirty five years. Even during the depths of the recession some companies still found it hard to recruit and retain the qualified workers that they wanted for their production needs. "The value of training is not generally recognised or accepted in Britain',[1] complained Sir Richard O'Brien, the chairman of the Manpower Services Commission, to a meeting of the National Economic Development Council in November 1980. 'It is costly, the pay-off may take a long time and employers' perspectives are often short. Not enough training is done: much that is done is misdirected or wasted. As a result many people are less productive at work and derive less reward from their work than they might. Although there are many examples of excellent training our performance overall is patchy and our arrangements inflexible'. Likely developments over the next few years do not suggest our training system is going to improve radically. Indeed, there are signs that it could worsen, ensuring a chronic shortage of skilled workers during an economic upturn. The low priority given to training by our society until recently is nothing short of scandalous because there can be no doubt that lack of appropriately skilled manpower remains a serious obstacle to Britain's future economic growth.

Indeed, Britain's system of industrial training for its workers remains one of the worst in the western industrialised world. Apart from Ireland, this country has the highest proportion of school-leavers receiving neither an apprenticeship training in a recognised skill nor any form of full-time vocational education as the preparation for a job. According to a survey of training facilities in the countries of the European Economic Community, as many as 44 per cent of Britain's boys and girls who enter the labour market every year go into a job with no training at all, while only 14 per cent acquire a time-served apprenticeship, 10 per cent enjoy full-time vocational training and 32 per cent enter some form of higher education.[2] Compare this with West Germany, where only six per cent of school-leavers start work without any training at all, compared with 50 per cent who have an apprenticeship, 19 per cent going into full-time vocational education and 21 per cent into higher education. Even France now provides far more than it used to do in vocational education opportunities for youngsters who fail to benefit from that country's highly competitive education system. While 19 per cent of French boys and girls in 1978 went straight from school into a job, 40 per cent were enjoying some full-time vocational education through the *lycées d'enseignement* and *lycées techniques* and 27 per cent began higher education.

Professor S J Prais of the National Institute of Economic and Social Research has estimated that as many as two thirds of Britain's workers have no kind of vocational educational qualification, compared with a third of the workers in West Germany. As a Manpower Services Commission report on training explained in July 1980, 'In practice only about 14 per cent of young people in Great Britain who leave school at 16 and do not obtain a craft apprenticeship receive any part-time further education and vocational preparation as part of their first employment. Thirty seven per cent of 16-year old boys and 8 per cent of 16-year old girl school-leavers enter a craft apprenticeship.[3] This means that over 300 000 youngsters entered the world of work each summer, acquiring dead-end jobs without prospects, interspersed with periods on the dole. No other modern democratic industrial state wasted its own human resources in such a scandalous manner.

There is nothing new about Britain's indifference towards the training needs of its labour force . Until recently training was left almost entirely to the personal whims of employers in a *laissez-faire* system, where the state played only a marginal role. In many sectors of manufacturing and some areas of the service industries employment training was based firmly on the concept of the time-served apprentice, the 16-year old school-leaver who learns a specified trade over a fixed period of usually up to four years. No doubt, some merit can be found in this method. It does foster a pride in the acquired skill and ensures high standards of workmanship. But the drawbacks to the system far outweigh its virtues.

The 1968 Donovan Royal Commission gave a cogent description of the serious obstacles to job opportunities imposed by the time-served apprenticeship system. As it argued: 'The knowledge that they have virtually committed themselves to a craft for life makes men alert to guard what they consider to be their own preserve, and to oppose relaxations in practices, which, however desirable and even essential to efficiency, may seem to constitute a threat to their whole way of life.[4]

Donovan went on: 'If the only normal method of entry into the craft is via the apprenticeship, supply will respond slowly and inadequately to demand. Where expansion is required it will be delayed. Where technological innovation reduces the demand for a given craft then there will be waste and suffering among the men whose livelihoods and expectations for the future are bound up with its continuing existence'.

Indeed, the whole apprenticeship system is tragically rigid and inflexible in practice. It prevents workers in a plant from acquiring new skills or a wider knowledge of the work process and thereby penalises them for the whole of their working lives by setting a limit on their own capacities for self-advancement. Again, the Donovan report's wise and sadly forgotten words preserve their relevance. 'As industries decline and others expand, workers have to change jobs. They must be free to acquire new skills. There would be neither social justice nor economic sense in denying them training simply because the jobs for which they had originally trained had disappeared, and they are now past the age of apprenticeship. For the future it will be less and less reasonable to regard an apprenticeship as equipping a worker with a skill for life. It must be accepted as normal for men and women to undergo retraining and further training at intervals during their working lives so as to adapt their capabilities to new techniques'.

Next to nothing was really done to further Donovan's practical and sensible training objectives. Our system of apprenticeship training displays remarkable tenacity in the face of technological progress. The Central Policy Review Staff published a report in May 1980 with some trenchant criticisms of Britain's industrial training. Like so many reports before, it highlighted the serious drawbacks of the system. In particular, the study mentioned two problems.

> First, a number of key skilled trades – notably in the engineering industry – are effectively reserved to workers who have undergone apprenticeship or similar training at the outset of their careers: these trades are not therefore generally accessible to those who seek to acquire skill by any other route or at any other time in their career. A corollary of this is that adult training and retraining is relatively neglected: much of industry's training effort is concentrated on young new entrants to the labour force and systematic provision for updating and upgrading skills is given relatively little encouragement or support from the education and training institutions that establish the framework for training in industry. Second, a large proportion of formal training in industry is concentrated on a relatively narrow

> range of occupations: the majority of workers in the less skilled occupations receive hardly any training.[5]

In sum, the CPRS report condemned the training system as 'rigid, conservative and slow to respond to new industrial requirements', and it added: 'The failings will become increasingly apparent as the shift in the industrial structure of Britain accelerates'. Enlightened people on both sides of industry now recognise the folly of the present training system. The Confederation of British Industry made some outspoken comments on the apprenticeship methods in a discussion paper, published in January 1980. 'It seems clear that the traditional system of "time-served" apprenticeships will become increasingly inadequate;' it asserted. 'Qualifications and therefore training will need to be based on the attainment of standards and not the passage of time. There should be no bars to training and retraining at any age, and the attitude of some unions to so-called dilutees need to change'.[6] In evidence to the MSC's review body on training in 1980, the TUC took a surprisingly progressive view of the problems as well. It argued:

> In craft and technician training, the length of training should be based on what has to be taught and on the rate of learning of the individual, subject to sufficient time being allowed to acquire maturity. There should be incentives for trainees to become qualified as quickly as possible. The need for flexibility on age of entry and in opportunities for the later acquisition and updating of skills would be for the consideration and agreements by employers and trade unions.[7]

The TUC document does not suggest craft and sectionalist attitudes have been allowed to dominate trade union thought about training, at least at the national level. The TUC accepts that all training should lead to acquired, recognised standards in appropriate skills and be of a high enough quality to assist worker mobility.

In an enlightened policy document passed by the 1979 Congress, the TUC spurned any Luddite view of the revolution in microtechnology and came out in favour of new technology agreements that would ensure labour flexibility in return for job and income security.

But as with so many facets of British life, good intentions differ from the reality on the ground. Resistance to change in the training system by employers and workers alike remains frighteningly strong, and the forces for reform are still too weak to make any radical impact. The fundamental trouble lies in the basic philosophy that employers should provide for their own training needs, just as they provide for their own investment in capital equipment. As a result, the size of the apprenticeship intake moves up and down sharply with the business cycle. As an MSC discussion paper explained in 1975: 'In times of economic downturn employers tend to reduce their intake, influenced by considerations of cash flow and current judgement of their longer-term needs for craftsmen and technicians; but then later on they often face a shortage of skill when industry is booming'.[8] It means that young people who suffer the misfortune of entering the labour market in a slump cannot acquire an apprenticeship, although if they had by chance left school in a boom they would have found little difficulty in acquiring a training place with an employer.

In the words of the MSC paper:

> Since it is in principle open to employers to let others go to the expense and trouble of providing training in long-term transferable skills and then to recruit ready trained workers when needed, the present system carries the risk of a chronic shortfall in quantity. The position is made worse by the effect of the cyclical swings in the economy. For various reasons – poor short-term business prospects, cash shortage, lack of work for existing skilled employees – this form of training is heavily pruned at times of recession. One consequence of this is that fewer newly trained craftsmen are becoming available just when an upswing in the economy means they are most needed. There are also unfortunate social consequences in that chance plays a big part in deciding how many long-term training opportunities will be open to young people each year.

During the seventies there was a noticeable downward trend in recruitment for long-term training occupations.

The collapse in the number of youngsters who are being apprenticed in British industry (shown in Table 4.1) has been horrifying in its speed. In 1980, 239 500 (202 000 males and 37 500 females) were experiencing some form of training in manufacturing, with 149 500 as apprentices and 90 000 undergoing some other form of training. Compare this with the 445 800 in 1968 (359 100 males and 86 700 females) of whom 236 200 were being apprenticed and the rest receiving other kinds of training. In 1968 5.6 per cent of the workforce in manufacturing were involved in training; by 1980 that proportion had shrunk to 3.6 per cent. The major decline took place during the early seventies and there are no signs that this is likely to be reversed in the present decade, with obvious grave

TABLE 4.1 Britain's decline in training, 1968–80 (in thousands, male and female)

| | *1968* | *1969* | *1970* | *1971* | *1972* | *1973* | *1974* | *1975* | *1976* | *1977* | *1978* | *1979* | *1980* |
|---|---|---|---|---|---|---|---|---|---|---|---|---|---|
| Apprentices | 236.2 | 232.1 | 218.6 | 208.1 | 186.9 | 155.5 | 139.6 | 155.3 | 148.6 | 153.1 | 156.2 | 155.0 | 149.5 |
| Other trainees | 209.6 | 295.3 | 202.1 | 173.8 | 159.7 | 157.0 | 156.6 | 135.2 | 116.3 | 125.1 | 116.3 | 111.3 | 90.0 |
| As proportion of all workers in manufacturing | 5.6 | 5.4 | 5.2 | 4.9 | 4.6 | 4.4 | 4.2 | 3.9 | 3.8 | 3.9 | 3.9 | 3.9 | 3.6 |

SOURCE *Employment Gazette*, September 1980, p. 947.

long-term consequences for the future of our manufacturing and technological based industries. In part, the net fall is due to the overall contraction in the number of workers employed in the manufacturing sector, but this does not provide a complete explanation for what has been happening. There has been a real drop in the proportion of workers who are receiving formal training at work.

In the words of an MSC–Department of Employment consultative document in June 1976:

> There is good reason to believe that, taking all employers together, industry has never provided as much training in vital skills as the economy requires. Since recruitment is cut back most heavily in periods of recession and training in transferable skills takes some years to complete, the effects of the cutback tend to become apparent just as demand is increasing with economic upturn. By definition the gap between supply and demand cannot be plugged rapidly by long-term training.[9]

What is good enough for one employer may be of little use for the needs of the whole industry, let alone the national interest in acquiring a versatile, mobile and skilled workforce, but the main thrust of the training system remains obstinately concerned with the requirements of the individual company. It will not be easy to even modify the present system. In 1978 the Engineering Industry Training Board made an attempt to introduce some sensible reforms in the way the engineering industry trained its skilled workers. It pointed out the severe contraction in the actual number of craftsmen in companies covered by the EITB – from 700 000 in 1967 to 550 000 ten years later. The 1980 intake of craft apprentices was only around 21 000 (made up of 18 000 first year off-the-job and 3000 first year on-the-job with day release). Around a quarter of the annual intake never last out the full four-year training period, while a further 4000 learn a craft without making use of the recommended EITB module approach, which has become a standard method used in other industries as well as in engineering.

In 1981–2 the training position deteriorated further in the engineering industry. In September 1981 there was a total recruitment of only 14 731 new first-year craft and technician apprentices, as many as 5000 less than the training board estimated was necessary to meet the long-term needs of engineering. That overall figure was reached only through extra financial aid from the Manpower Services Commission which aided around 4000 of the apprentices. Industry itself was in such deep recession that it could fund only 10 500 youngsters, the lowest figure on record. In 1982 the numbers fell even lower.

Only about 40 per cent a year actually pass through the system and acquire the skills provided by the EITB's two-module training programme. In a consultative document, which was circulated widely throughout the industry, the EITB spelt out the grave drawbacks of the system. 'There is a good deal of anecdotal evidence to suggest that the four-year apprenticeship required of a 16-year old school-leaver acts as a deterrent to recruitment, and that is one of the reasons why so many apprentices leave before completing their training',[10] it argued. 'There is no doubt that the engineering industry faces severe competition from what are seen as more attractive occupations, attractive in terms of security and status as well as pay. Additionally, there is an increasing tendency to stay on at school beyond the statutory school-leaving age'. The EITB paper was highly critical of the schools. 'The inability of many school-leavers to cope with craft training without remedial education because of their lack of facility in mathematical skills gives widespread cause for concern', it alleged.

A number of changes were proposed to improve the training system. The EITB suggested that there ought to be a closer link between the schools and the world of work during the last two years of formal education, with the development of more practical courses in mathematics, applied science, technology and craft practice, where the EITB could play a direct role. An incentive to this approach for the youngster would be to ensure that if he or she achieved a statisfactory grade at the CSE level in a practical subject this would count as the equivalent of reaching a standard of six month's training in a first year engineering training centre.

On leaving school with those required standards, apprentices would spend a first year in off-the-job full-time training and associated further education in the two EITB modules, followed by a second year on-the-job training in industry, practising what they had learned. A certificate of craftsmanship would be awarded to every successful apprentice who passed through the necessary tests to reach the acquired standards. The EITB saw this approach as a necessary and belated escape from the time-served apprenticeship method, so that abler youngsters could reach the maturity of interchangeable craft skills on an adult rate of pay more quickly.

Unfortunately the EITB proposals, a logical development rather than a root and branch reform, failed to win much support. The educationalists were outraged at any suggestion that industry should intervene directly in the classroom in a practical way, even though very few teachers have any direct knowledge of shop-floor life. The craft unions gave the proposals the thumbs down and reaffirmed their historic faith in the virtues of the time-served apprenticeship, while most employers displayed indifference, with the smaller and medium-sized companies grumbling that they could not possibly afford to pay adult rates to their young workers before they reached the age of 20.

But technological change is not going to wait patiently for long overdue modifications in the training system. Indeed, the whole concept of craft skills will be brought into serious question during the eighties, whatever employers and unions might say. Already the precise and rigid boundaries of what constitutes a skilled job are settled on an often arbitrary basis through workplace bargaining. The characteristics of a particular skill differ not only from industry to industry as a result, but also from plant to plant in the same company. A survey of industry's needs, carried out by the PA management consultants in 1977 for the MSC suggested that the whole apprenticeship system had become irrelevant to modern requirements. The emphasis will move from the need to train workers in single skills to a more flexible approach. 'Skilled workers will need a broader understanding of the overall technology or process rather than a physical dexterity. They will need to know how a machine works and be capable of diagnostic and even problem-solving skills, in particular areas of maintenance', said the PA survey. 'The new skills will not be learnt by on the job "sitting by nelly".'[11] The need is for broad-based trainees, with the flexibility of interchanging between one task and another. 'We must give young people a broad base of skill which will give them adaptability to the changing requirements of the future', MSC chief executive, John Cassels once argued.

Kahn-Freund observed that the British industrial system is imbued with the craft spirit, for 'the demarcation policy has come to dominate large areas of industry in which there is no apprenticeship system at all'.[12] The apprenticeship method of training upholds this form of job control that has its origins in the pre-industrial guilds. Unless we recognise that hallowed custom and practice block the road to reform in our industrial training, there is no possibility of any change for the better. Employers, trade unions and the existing skilled workers have a vested interest in propping up and maintaining the present archaisms, which prevent change that would bring greater job opportunities and prosperity to millions of workers.

State intervention in industrial training is at the moment peripheral to the total effort, but it will have to be expanded over the next few years, if this country intends to have an educated, flexible labour force to take advantage of the new technology. The 1980 MSC review of training recognised the need for more public involvement. As it noted, 'Both theory and experience suggest that, left to themselves, individual firms will not undertake enough training fully to meet the needs of the economy for transferable skills'.[13] The present mainly voluntarist employer-based system simply cannot train enough people to meet the needs of the economy. A report on computer skill shortages produced by NEDO in 1980 found a serious shortfall of nearly 25 000 in the number of people with computer-related skills (275 000 of them at present). 'Not enough training is being done', it argued. 'These key skill shortfalls, by fuelling mobility and thus high training costs, are inhibiting employers from recruiting and training sufficient new entrants, and are discouraging new applications. These feedback effects will worsen, in our view'.[14] The forces of the market economy are incapable of providing the skills that we need in high technology. The state will have to take a more direct role if Britain is to have the necessary provision of training places in computer-related skills. The MSC training review argued

> Public authorities are better placed than any other institution to act as 'honest broker' in bringing together employers and trade unions to overcome industrial relations obstacles to reform of training practice. The state cannot simply stand aside where differences in perspective and interest between employers, trade unions and others lead to conflicts or the taking up of rigid positions which threaten the public interest and inhibit the flexibility of training response needed to match the economic achievement of our major competitors.[15]

In fact, government involvement really only dates from the 1964 Industrial Training Act and the creation of industrial training boards

(ITBs). This was the belated response to the worries about skill labour shortages in the fifties. About 55 per cent of the workforce was covered by the existing 23 training boards in 1981. Their original purpose was to prepare recommendations for training in occupations in their specified industries and to impose a levy on employers, paying out grants to employers who trained satisfactorily. After a review of the ITBs in the early seventies the Heath government passed the Employment and Training Act in 1973, which modified the financial arrangements. It changed the levy/grant system, with the provision of exemptions for firms that were found to train adequately for their own purposes. As a result the levy income of the ITBs has declined, while the amount of government financial support has gone up rapidly since the middle sixties. The MSC's review body concluded that the ITBs had 'achieved some success in regard to the quantity of training' but highlighted defects, notably the limited impact of levy exemption, the difficulties of dealing with the training needs of small firms and the failure to ensure training arrangements were able to meet cross-sector skill problems in the labour market.[16] There has been considerable criticism, particularly from the unions, about the way in which the exemption procedures work in practice. The current arrangements have meant a substantial fall in the financial resource of many of the ITBs. The larger the number of companies opting out of the system, the more difficult it becomes for the training boards to enjoy an independent life of their own. As a result of the dependence on state resources for administrative costs, many of the ITBs are viewed with suspicion by industry, who fear they may become too concerned with training for its own sake and less preoccupied with the particular requirements of employers. The MSC review body recommended that the ITB's administrative costs should be met by the employers and not the state. In November 1981 the government decided to abolish 16 of the boards and pass operating costs for the others on to industry alone.

But it would be a mistake to leave reform as purely a change in administrative and financial procedures. As long as the *laissez-faire* system continues to operate this country will suffer from persistent skill labour shortages. A 1975 MSC discussion paper said quite bluntly: 'it is doubtful whether financial incentives at the margin can be sufficiently influential to secure the amount of training which is needed, and there is a strong case for moving towards a system in which the cost of off-the-job training during at any rate the first year of employment would no longer fall on individual employers but be borne collectively in some way'.[17] It suggested this would involve a cost of around £150 million a year. A year later a consultative document went over the same ground and floated the idea of collective funding, a scheme whereby employers were repaid the whole or a proportion of the cost of initial training. In this way, companies would be discouraged from deciding on the number of young people they recruited by the ups and downs of the economic cycle. Under the existing system no formal mechanism exists for fixed targets in the volume of training to be funded from grants. The collective fund would be a method that could ensure 'a high and stable intake into training for vital skills which at the same time' was 'flexible in operation, so as to meet the widely differing patterns of need in different industries, and yet had the same fundamental impact on training levels'. Unfortunately no action followed this proposal. It was lost in a bureaucratic fog as all sides sought to question its wisdom. Perhaps lack of political will by the Labour government, backed up by the Civil Service, consigned collective funding to the wastepaper basket in 1977. Certainly the emergency cash injections provided on a *ad hoc* basis by the Manpower Services Commission to meet apprecenticeship shortfalls were an unsatisfactory response to a problem that had been diagnosed long enough without any sign of determined reforming zeal from government.

The MSC's corporate plan for 1980–4 recognised the constrained role of the state in training. In 1978–9 just over £90 million was provided by the MSC to boost the ITBs to finance 12 897 workers in training programmes, while around £15 million was allocated to key training grants and £41 million to special measures for the provision of 42 000 training places. Apparently industry is unable to train enough people as computer programmers, North Sea oil-riggers and those who want jobs in high technology, so the MSC acts as an ambulance wagon in these vital areas with puny resources. But in the words of the MSC plan 'the primary responsibility for training must rest with industry'.[18] Despite the multiplicity of recent studies that emphasise the inadequacy of the present system to provide the training needed in the wider interests of the economy, the MSC goes on to say: 'These problems (skill shortages) will only be overcome if suitably qualified men and women are attracted to and retained in key occupations; if their skills are fully utilised and if rigidities in recruitment and deployment of manpower are removed. These matters are in the main regulated through collective agreements between employers and unions and by custom and practice, and the MSC's powers of intervention or persuasion are necessarily limited.'

It was only in August 1972 that the state launched a massive effort to provide training facilities for adult workers under the training opportunities scheme (TOPS). Before that time government efforts had been extremely modest. After the war disabled and ex-servicemen were trained at rehabilitation centres. From 1963 onwards there was a limited growth in the numbers of adults passing through government training centres, but by 1971–2 only 17 000 did so. The Heath government recognised the inadequacy of the state provision for industrial training, with long waiting lists for many courses. In a discussion document – 'Training for the Future' – the aim was to develop facilities so that 100 000 people a year could have some training. By 1979–80 there were 74 489 completions, with as many as 41 555 of them through centres of further education, 21 879 at 'skillcentres' and 10 434 on employers' premises. In 1979–80 the Thatcher government cut back training places as part of its plan to reduce public expenditure, with the closure of some skillcentres and reduction in course opportunities in less popular subjects.

TOPS training lasts usually up to six months, so it remains a highly intensive form of education. A review of the first six years of the scheme declared in 1978 that 'It is not yet genuinely accepted that it may be necessary or beneficial for a worker to refurbish or change his skills twice or thrice in a lifetime; and there is widespread ignorance of the TOPS scheme among potential employers'.[19] A number of surveys of the TOPS trainees found that nearly half were not making use of their acquired skills in the jobs they were doing afterwards, with the worst results in those areas with the longest dole queues. Richard Berthoud found 69 per cent of his sample in Dundee and Stoke-on-Trent who had been on TOPS had found a job 'in trade' and just over two fifths of them were working 'in trade' at the time of the survey. Nearly a third of the men in his study did not succeed even in getting a start 'in trade', while no less than 60 per cent of the men whose first jobs were 'in trade' had left those jobs by the time of the survey.[20] A 1978 survey for the MSC, by Industrial Facts and Forecasting Ltd, discovered that as many as a quarter of trainees who left their first employer did so because they were judged to be insufficiently skilled.[21] There is some evidence to suggest that many trainees try to hide their skillcentre credentials when they take a skilled job and move on quickly in their employment, but the signs of union or employer resistance are not always so obvious as common mythology might suppose.

But the TOPS survey warned, 'there is a long-standing prejudice on the shop-floor against the dilutee. He may be seen as a threat to standards, to the job chances of existing union members, or to the maintenance of restrictive conditions favourable to pay'. Most employers prefer time-served apprentices any time to skillcentre trainees and in a recession they can become particularly choosy about the person they hire. As a result, it can be more difficult when demand is low to encourage adult workers to train or retrain in a skill, with little obvious prospect of an immediate job in their neighbourhood.

Many employers seem indifferent to the government training effort, even when they are complaining about their alleged skill shortages, and surprisingly few bother to take advantage of sponsored training for their own employees through the MSC's services. In 1979–80 only 41 441 workers benefited from direct training services at a cost of £5.6 million, with nearly half being firms' supervisors. A mere 8870 workers were on sponsored TOPS courses with their companies who paid out £1.3 million in fees, though the whole programme cost £3.2 million. It is to be hoped the sponsored training services can expand through a much closer partnership between TOPS and employers during the next few years. Less than 10 per cent of places in skillcentres are occupied by workers on direct sponsored courses. Nor is much use being made of government mobile instructors in industry. In the 1979–80 year only 7196 firms' workers were trained in this way on their premises at a cost of £714 000. This suggests that the government training effort is a neglected and under-used resource for private employers, but it was hoped that by 1981–2 50 000 employed people would be undergoing sponsored training.

There is an imbalance in the TOPS provisions, so that long waiting lists exist of over a year for courses such as carpentry and joinery, motor vehicle repair and radio and television servicing, while vacancies are widespread for engineering skills at government skillcentres. In 1977, 61 per cent of TOPS trainees were trained in occupations accounting for only 12 per cent of all employment. Clerical and secretarial skills were mostly catered for, with nearly 40 per cent in the late seventies in this occupational category. The present government has cut back the opportunities for this particular category of worker, while the numbers trained to technician level has been expanded. None of this suggests that adult workers who will learn a skill will become more numerous during the next few years.

Yet the biggest scandal in Britain's hit and miss training system continues to lie in the neglect of the needs of those who enter the labour market without any chance of learning a skill at all, however it may be defined. Again, the trouble was highlighted some years ago. In 1974 a working party established by the National Youth Employment Council published a hard-hitting report which spoke about the 'great deficiency and inequality' of treatment for young people looking for work below the craft level. 'If the provision of training was improved and made more universally available, the opportunity would be provided (in many cases) for young people to protect themselves as individuals against the forces of cyclical change and regional imbalance', it argued.[22] 'At present the state is prepared to spend a great deal of money in educating those who have academic ability. Industry is prepared, in its own interests, to provide excellent training for those who have other kinds of ability; yet no one seems prepared to do very much about those abilities which have not been identified or developed'. Two years later an MSC discussion paper drew public attention to the same problem. It estimated 300 000 boys and girls received little or no training from their employers. The report argued, 'it seems certain that properly conceived vocational training preparation would raise substantially the ability of many of these young workers. More important still, the experience of 'learning to learn' things relevant to work would help them to adapt to change more readily and therefore work more effectively throughout their lives. Proper training for young people would raise the whole potential of the workforce'.[23] That document made the bold recommendation that: 'all employees should be given the right to a certain period of release for training or education to be taken at a time and in form of their choice with the cost of the training or education borne by the state, but with the employer required to continue to pay wages and to offer continued employment if the employee so wished'. But it was not until the spring of 1979, just before leaving office, that the Labour government made the tentative proposal for a 'universal scheme of education and training opportunities' for the 16 to 18-year old age group.

The unified vocational preparation programme launched in 1976 is still only a modest experiment. As the MSC corporate plan for 1980–4 argued: 'Vocational preparation is a combination of education and training based directly on experience at work. The broad aim is to help young people to acquire the skills needed to carry out specific tasks at work and develop attitudes and knowledge which will enable them to play their part in the working community'.[24] But in 1980/1981 only around 340 schemes were under way and only 3400 youngsters were involved. In 1981–2 the MSC hoped to increase the numbers to 6500 at a cost of £7 million.

The 1980 MSC review body report provided some hope that a more considered training response could be established to remedy the present inadequate system. There is little point in wishing the admirable West German training approach onto our society, because we start from different cultural and organisational positions. The abolition of time-served apprenticeships must be as ultimate objective, over the years more thorough and less wasteful methods are needed to train the whole labour force in a multiplicity of different skills. We need to give a high priority to training adult workers and to giving young unqualified people a basic grounding in the tools for survival in the harsh labour market of the eighties.

Alan Brown, head of the MSC's training services division saw the causes of the present inadequacies in the 'take it or leave it mentality' that exists in Britain. 'There is a lack of incentive in our society', he told me. 'People do not believe thay have a field marshal's baton in their knapsack. We fail to view so many jobs as an opening to a career'. The MSC would like to relax many of the internal restrictions that handicap workers of all ages from making an advance in their job prospects and well-being. Barriers exist everywhere – in the age limits on jobs; in shop-floor resistance to adult training; in the status distinctions between blue and white collar; in the lack of security and poor wage prospects of skilled manual workers; in the tenacity of demarcation lines between jobs when they have so often lost all meaning through technological change.

It is very easy to blame workers for all this and especially the unions, many of whom depend for their existence on the persistence of craft and non-craft differences. But the main initiative for belated change in training (as in so many other areas) must rest with the employers. As the MSC hard hard to fill vacancy report in September 1979 admitted:

> There is no doubt that in the past employers tended to cut back their apprentice intake during recessions, and that the subsequent lower output of trained men was one factor in skilled labour shortages which choked off expansion. In the last few years the level of apprentice intakes has been made more stable by the special measures operated by the MSC and the ITBs which should, other things remaining the same, result in a higher flow of skilled men into industry over the next few years'.[25]

But, understandably, firms take a short-term view and they always will do. 'Most pay inadequate attention to future skilled labour requirements, rarely forecasting sufficiently far ahead to adjust apprentice intakes in the light of future expectations', added the MSC report. The immediate rewards of an apprenticeship may not be attractive enough to young people who want to make money quickly, but in the present recession this has not brought any shortage of applicants for a training. The main thrust of future training should come from the state itself, which has already been compelled to underpin the inadequacy of the present system during a time of recession. It is all very well for organisations like the Engineering Employers Association to be hostile to the idea of social priorities in training, but we need to provide a national sense of urgency to our training efforts. The curious and fatal combination of *laissez-faire* in manpower planning and inflexibility in the organisation of work in industry has become a formidable barrier to the open, flexible adaptable workforce which is needed at all levels. By ridding industry of preconceived notions about apprenticeship training, skills could be placed into a more up-to-date perspective. Only in this way can Britain hope to acquire, not just the kind of workers needed to take advantage of the age of microtechnology, but also those required for the future development of industry in a changing world.

The sad, sorry tale of delay and prevarication continued. In May 1981 the MSC produced a 'new training initiative'. Its central argument was the same as that produced in the Donovan Royal Commission thirteen years earlier.

> For too long we have treated training and education as a once for all experience at the start of life – as if circumstances and requirements would remain unchanged. In consequence, there have been few chances for adults to start afresh or add to what they have. Employers have too often taken or been forced by financial problems to take a short term view and relied heavily on being able to buy in the skills they need from the market place. Training has been seen as a dispensable overhead rather than an investment for the future. In some parts of the country trade unionists have taken an equally short-sighted view in the restrictions that have been placed on the acquisition of skills and their subsequent use or updating.[26]

The MSC discussion document proposed three major initiatives to improve training. It wanted to see more training in a number of basic skills for young workers, which would ensure adaptability throughout their working lives. It favoured achieving a position where every youngester under the age of 18 was assured of staying on in full-time education or entering training or a period of planned work experience which combined education with training. Finally it suggested a widening of opportunities for adult workers to take advantage of technological change.

Norman Tebbit, the Employment Secretary, gave his response in a White Paper published in December 1981, which aroused widespread criticism among the unions, careers offices and the educational world. The main proposal was for a new £1000-million-a-year Youth Training Scheme to be launched from September 1983 with the aim of guaranteeing a place for every 16-year-old unemployed school-leaver on a year-long 'foundation' course. This was seen as a replacement for the Youth Opportunities Programme and built on the limited Unified Vocational Preparation arrangements. In the words of the document, 'The new scheme will aim to equip unemployed young people to adapt successfully to the demands of employment; to have a fuller appreciation of the world of industry, business and technology in which they will be working; and to develop basic and recognised skills which employers will require in the future'.[27] The appropriate skills would be acquired by youngsters in 'planned and supervised work experience and properly designed opportunities for off-the-job training or further education'. Youngsters who were not 16-year-old unemployed school-leavers would not rate so high a priority and there would be no guarantee of a training place for them. The trainees would receive around £15 a week and they would not be entitled to supplementary benefit if they turned down a place, though their families could claim child benefit for them. The lowness of the proposed allowance (it compared with £25 a week under YOP from 1 January 1982) and the element of compulsion brought protests that the government was going to introduce 'slave labour'. The Manpower Services Commission expressed its dissatisfaction with the Tebbit plan because it did not extend the training scheme to all young people in the under-18 category, whether they found jobs or not. The piecemeal approach might have been dictated by financial stringencies but it gave a third-rate quality to the look of the Youth Training Scheme as a super-YOP on a miserly allowance.

Union opposition to such an idea will make it much more difficult for the government to move to a system of apprenticeship training based on reaching required standards of proficiency rather than the time-served element by 1985 at the latest, as it wants to do. The threat that the government would reduce or eliminate its financial support for skill training in industry if there were no acceptance of the new yardstick of proficiency seems unlikely to make employers fall into line.

In early 1982 there was a growing feeling that the government had failed to take a radical enough view of the national training scandal. A political desire to remove over 300 000 youngsters from the registered unemployment figures appeared to take a higher priority than a sober recognition of the long-term needs of industry. Around 2.5 per cent of Britain's gross domestic product has gone into vocational education and training in recent years, but this is hardly enough to meet the challenge and it is diffused through a bewildering multiplicity of organisations. In November 1981 the government appeared to show some belated recognition of the crisis, but far too much was left open for more endless debate and delay. In May 1982 both the TUC and CBI backed an MSC scheme to cover all 16-year old school-leavers with a £25 a week allowance on work experience and off the job training for a year from September 1983.

But is any fundamental change in our inadequate training system really possible without state intervention in a much more dynamic way in the labour market? The MSC 'New Training Initiative' suggested that 'the main instrument for change must be collective agreement at the level of the sector and the company. Progress depends on positive steps being taken by individual employers and trade unions. They are best placed to work out the kind of arrangements which fit their own circumstances'. Yet it is precisely because of this *laissez-faire* approach that we have skill shortage problems.

Two of our major continental competitors are less hamstrung by vested interests and lack of 'official' willpower. Under laws passed in 1971 and 1978 every French worker has the right to paid leave for education and training purposes. It is the state's responsibility in France to ensure that every 16 to 18-year old school leaver has some form of vocational training if they cannot get a job. From 1 January 1982 the system was extended to cover all young French people up to the age of 23 and for workers employed for less than two years in the last five. In West Germany the 1969 Vocational Training Act makes three-year long apprenticeships available to all young people seeking them. In 1980 half the school-leavers in West Germany entered apprenticeships on finishing school. The West German authorities hope by 1982 to ensure that no more than 3 per cent of school-leavers who cannot find a job are unable to receive post-compulsory school training or education. Neither France nor West Germany has any ideological hang-ups about the crucial need for state intervention to assist those workers in their societies who cannot help themselves, by providing the money and the facilities for training any modern technological based society needs if it means to prosper and survive.

## NOTES AND REFERENCES

1 'Training: Questions for the 1980s', Sir Richard O'Brien, memorandum to the National Economic Development Council, November 1980, p. 1.
2 'International Comparisons of vocational training provision', Chris Hayes Associates, April 1980, p. 5. *See also* 'Outlook on Training: Review of the Employment and Training Act 1973', Manpower Services Commission, April 1980, and 'Youth Unemployment and the Bridge from School to Work', Anglo-German Foundation, 1980.
3 'Outlook on Training', p. 1.
4 *Royal Commission on Trade Unions and Employers' Associations*, HMSO, June 1968, pp. 87–8.
5 'Education, Training and Industrial Performance', report from the Central Policy Review Staff, 1980, p. 17.
6 Training Review, Confederation of British Industry, March 1980, p. 6.
7 'TUC review of the Employment and Training Act 1973', March 1980, p. 7.
8 'Vocational Preparation for Young People', Manpower Services Commission discussion paper, May 1975, p. 19.
9 'Training for Vital Skills: a consultative document', Department of Employment and Manpower Services Commission, June 1976, p. 8.
10 'Review of craft apprenticeship in engineering', Engineering Industry Training Board, March 1978, p. 2; *see also* 'The Craftsman in Engineering' from the Training Board, 1980.
11 'Training for Skills: A Programme for Action', Manpower Services Commission, 1977, p. 37.
12 *Labour Relations: Heritage and Adjustment* (Oxford University Press, 1979) p. 42.
13 'Outlook on Training', op cit., p. 33.
14 'Computer Manpower in the Eighties', National Economic Development Office, May 1980, pp. 202–3.
15 'Outlook on Training', op. cit., p. 25.
16 'Outlook on Training', op. cit., p. 4.
17 'Vocational Preparation for Young People', Manpower Services Commission, July 1975, p. 19.
18 'Manpower Services Commission Corporate Plan 1980–1984', p. 12.
19 *TOPS Review*, Manpower Services Commission, 1978, p. 23.
20 R. Berthoud, 'Training Adults for Skilled Jobs', PSI, April 1978, pp. 83–5.
21 *TOPS Review*, p. 14.
22 'Unqualified, Untrained, Unemployed', HMSO, 1974, p. 47.
23 'Vocational Preparation for Young People', op. cit., p. 24(?)
24 'Manpower Services Commission Corporate Plan 1980–1984', p. 52.
25 'Hard to Fill Vacancies', Manpower Services Commission, 1979, p. 3.20.
26 'A New Training Initiative', Manpower Services Commission, May 1981, p. 3.
27 'A New Training Initiative: A Programme for Action', Department of Employment, November 1981, p. 7.

# 5 Inequalities at the Workplace

Inequality of status and treatment between manual and non-manual workers remains an indefensible relic of Britain's industrial system. The stigma of being a worker by hand is far more tenacious in this country than perhaps almost anywhere else in the western industrialised world. Moves towards a harmonisation of conditions of service, bringing the shop-floor into line with the office, have begun only recently in any systematic way. A number of manual trade unions, notably the Amalgamated Union of Engineering Workers, have started to make the issue a major bargaining priority after a long period of neglect and shop-floor indifference. The present depression is hardly the best of times to achieve any lasting breakthrough towards work-place equality, but a growing number of employers recognise the justice of the demand and they are making belated efforts to remedy the injustice. White-collar staff – in many cases well-organised in unions – can be expected to press for new privileges to differentiate themselves from manual workers. Some white-collar unions are even quite ready to appeal openly to snobbery and status in their recruitment drives, while they continue to claim they stand on the left of the Labour movement. Until now, not enough manual workers have been either upset or angry at the discrimination they have suffered at work and neither their unions nor the Labour party have made any conscious effort to highlight the issue or launch a radical policy to eradicate its worst abuses.

## WAGE INEQUALITY

The most obvious and painful inequality between manual and non-manual lies both in the size and make-up of the weekly wage packet. In April 1980 male full-time manual workers aged 21 and over averaged a pre-tax weekly wage of £111.70, compared with £141.30 for male white-collar workers.

The disparity in earning power is more startling when you examine the difference between occupations. In April 1980 university academic staff enjoyed a median wage before tax of £203.10 a week, medical practitioners £220.00, finance, tax and insurance specialists £187.10, marketing, sales managers and executives £156.30 and company secretaries £165.40. There are some low paid non-manual occupations. Records and library clerks had a median weekly wage of only £84.90, while salesmen and shop assistants earned a median £78.40 a week. The lowest median weekly wage among manual workers was earned by kitchen hands (£74.70 a week) followed by general farm workers (£74.90); butchers and meat cutters (£77.30) and barmen (£79.20). The highest paid male manual workers are faced-trained miners (median wage of £147.00 a week) followed by stevedores and dockers (£127.30 a week); steel erectors and scaffolders (£126.30 a week); gas fitters (£124.80) and electricians (£124.10). The overall figures in Table 5.1, taken from the 1980 New Earnings Survey, illustrate the wide gap that exists between the level of earnings between the manual and non-manual occupations.

TABLE 5.1 Median incomes, April 1980 (£)

| | *Gross weekly earnings* | | | | |
|---|---|---|---|---|---|
| | *Lowest decile* | *Lower quartile* | *Median* | *Upper quartile* | *Highest decile* |
| All non-manual male occupations | 80.30 | 100.40 | 127.70 | 163.80 | 215.00 |
| All male manual occupations | 71.80 | 86.30 | 105.00 | 129.00 | 156.70 |
| All occupations | 74.70 | 90.70 | 113.30 | 143.40 | 183.10 |

SOURCE 'New Earnings Survey', 1980, Part D, HMSO, January 1981, D 27.

As much as 26 per cent of the male manual worker's weekly pay packet is derived from supplements on top of his basic rate. Overtime pay accounted for 14.1 per cent (£15.80), payment by results, bonuses and commissions a further 8.7 per cent (£9.80) and shift premia etc. 3.3 per cent (£3.70). Without these additions to their basic pay, most male manual workers would simply be unable to enjoy a tolerable standard of living, particularly after the crushing extra burden of direct taxation imposed on lower paid workers over the past decade, in the name of the 'social wage'.

Here, the contrast with white-collar staff is stark enough. On average a mere 6.7 per cent of the non-manuals' gross weekly earnings arose from additions to their basic pay (£9.50 a week), with only 3.5 per cent derived from overtime working (£4.90), 2.6 per cent from payment by results, bonuses and commissions (£3.70) and 0.6 per cent from shift premia (90 pence a week). While as many as 54.3 per cent of male manuals received overtime pay (£29.10 on average a week), as few as 19.6 per cent of male white-collars did so (£25.20 a week). Only 12.0 per cent of male white-collars earned an average payment of £30.80 in April 1980 through payment by results, bonuses and commissions, compared with 42.3 per cent of male manuals who made an average £23.10 a week by doing so. There was a similar disparity in the payment of shift premia, with only 5.7 per cent of male white-collars receiving such money (£15.50 a week on average), contrasting with the 23.0 per cent of male manuals who did so (£16.00 a week on average).

Most full-time male manuals reach the height of their earning capacity at a relatively young age – between 30 and 39 (an average of £118.10 a week in April 1980). This follows a pre-tax pay packet average of £111.80 for the 25 to 29-year olds and £116.80 for the 40 to 49-year old age bracket. Male manuals in their thirties are usually bringing up a family, with mortgage and hire purchase commitments to meet and the probability is that their previously working wives are at home looking after the children, meaning a fall in household income. The longer hours worked (6.4 hours on top of a basic 40-hour week on average) provide the extra cash which is needed.

This is also the age when male manual workers are at their most agile physically to work longer hours without undue hazards to their health. By the time they reach their fifties, the gross weekly wage packet of a male manual worker has begun to fall quite sharply (£108.80 a week on average – down £8 a week from a forties age bracket) and it drops even more to £102.40 a week for the 60 to 64-year olds.

The contrast with the male non-manuals is quite startling. They reach the prime of their earnings power during their forties (£158.60 a week on average, compared with £120.00 in the 25 to 29-year old age bracket and £147.60 for the 30 to 39-year olds) with only a slight dip to £151.30 for the 50 to 59-year olds. Indeed, up to the age of 25 the average male manual worker is earning more each week than the white-collar male in the same age bracket.

A major difference arises from the lack of any career structure or progression in most manual male worker jobs. Regular annual increments and promotional opportunities remain rare in manual jobs but they are commonplace in office work, enabling non-manual workers to plan their careers. In a survey for the Office of Manpower Economics in 1973 it was discovered that only 3 per cent of all manual workers were paid any increments at all, compared with a massive 90 per cent among white-collar staff. Richard Layard and his LSE colleagues emphasised in their evidence to the Royal Commission on the Distribution of Wealth and Income: 'No manual jobs offer much prospect of real wage increases (other than from economic growth) after the first ten years. So in a sense more than half the labour force are in jobs without prospects.'[1]

There is no reason to believe that this particular inequality between manual and non-manual workers has improved very much since the middle seventies. Indeed, prospects for individual advancement are much more restricted now for workers in the depression than they were a decade ago. Jobs like first-line supervisors and foremen are now being increasingly taken up by young graduates or highly qualified recruits with formal educational qualifications. Movement off the shop-floor for manual males has become more difficult as a result.

Far more manual workers have their wages determined by a payment by results system such as piecework. In April 1980 as many as 42.3 per cent of male manuals received an average £23.10 a week through payment by results such as bonuses, productivity payments, profit-sharing or commissions. This contrasted with 12.0 per cent of male non-manuals who benefited from a payment by results system to the tune of an average £30.80 a week. An industrial breakdown of payment by results shows that the main beneficiaries are the miners (£28.30 a week out of the average gross earnings of £154.80 come from the incentive scheme for underground workers); pottery workers; furniture workers; rubber workers; gas workers; water workers; and workers in ordnance and small arms manufacture. During the seventies there was a spread of work study techniques on which payments by results were based. This development helped to reduce the amount of wage drift from agreed pay rates for manual workers. But there has been a substantial reduction in the extent of payments by results in a number of industries in recent years, most notably vehicle assembly, and shipbuilding and the docks, where measured daywork replaced piece work systems, and there was a move to fewer and wider bargaining units.

Another inequality suffered by male manual workers arises from the fluctuations in their weekly pay packets, particularly during a slump. Most white-collar staff receive the same net earnings week by week, or month by month between wage settlements, but pay on the shop-floor can move up and down quite drastically, mainly because it is determined by hourly rates and these can vary depending on the level of activity in the plant. Lay-offs, whatever their cause, are widespread in much of manufacturing industry. We can see evidence of this in the rapid growth of short-time working in recent years (see Table 5.2). This hits the manual workers far more harshly than the office staff.

TABLE 5.2 The rise of short-time working

| *1980 week ended* | *Stood off for whole week* | | *Working part of the week* | | *% of operatives working part of week* |
|---|---|---|---|---|---|
| | *Operative* | *Hours* | *Operatives* | *Hours lost* | |
| January 12 | 5 000 | 181 000 | 80 000 | 992 000 | 12.4 |
| April 19 | 13 000 | 524 000 | 143 000 | 1 579 000 | 11.0 |
| June 14 | 14 000 | 546 000 | 192 000 | 2 218 000 | 11.6 |
| September 13 | 33 000 | 1 304 000 | 336 000 | 4 081 000 | 12.1 |
| November 15 | 26 000 | 1 053 000 | 503 000 | 6 373 000 | 12.7 |
| *1981* | | | | | |
| January 17 | 41 000 | 1 626 000 | 553 000 | 6 830 000 | 12.4 |
| April 11 | 18 000 | 741 000 | 416 000 | 4 928 000 | 11.9 |
| June 13 | 10 000 | 386 000 | 291 000 | 3 251 000 | 11.2 |
| September 12 | 8 600 | 317 000 | 181 000 | 1 943 000 | 10.7 |
| November 14 | 6 000 | 259 000 | 174 000 | 1 782 000 | 10.2 |

SOURCE *Employment Gazette.*

A temporary short-time working compensation scheme was introduced by the government in April 1979 as a way of encouraging employers not to carry through redundancies by providing financial support to enable them to keep on their manual workers. It was decided to pay 75 per cent of normal pay of workers for each day they were without work, with a maximum period of support restricted to six months in order to give hard-pressed companies some breathing space before they felt compelled to cut their labour forces. Fairly strict conditions were laid down about eligibility for such cash aid. An employer had to show that he genuinely intended to make 10 or more workers redundant if he did not receive assistance and consultations about those threatened redundancies had to have already begun with the unions and notified to the Department of Employment. Union agreement was also necessary in the application to take advantage of the short-time working scheme and the employer had to demonstrate that his company was not about to become insolvent. In November 1980 Jim

Prior, the employment secretary, made various changes in the scheme, extending the maximum period of support to nine months and at the same time reducing the level of reimbursement to 50 per cent of the worker's normal pay.

The experience of short-time is invariably suffered most by manual workers and they can expect a considerable fall in the level of their take-home pay as a consequence.

The persistent insecurity of wage expectations for male manual workers makes it more difficult for them to plan a family budget without genuine worries about making ends meet. In some cases, it can encourage a 'live for today' mentality and confirm the cynical view that life is just a lottery in an economic and social system that thrives on greed and the pursuit of money and scorns social justice and collective solidarity.

In Britain the actual method of payment of wages differs noticeably between manual and non-manual. Most white-collar workers are paid usually either with a cheque or by credit transfer that goes straight into their bank accounts. But a survey carried out in 1979 by the Interbank Research Organisation discovered that as many as 78 per cent of manual workers were paid by the employers each week with cash in the hand. Only around 57 per cent of workers had a bank account in 1979. A Price Commission report published in 1978 revealed that as many as 94 per cent of all payments over 50 pence were made by individuals paying in cash. This extraordinary British habit must be compared with the United States where 99 per cent of the working population is paid through the banking system and France where the figure is a high 95 per cent. It is an often overlooked but vital distinction that persists between manual and non-manual workers in this country. Some employers have made a big effort in the late seventies to move to non-cash methods of wage payment, but no more than 1 per cent of the workforce a year has switched. Up until 1960 the law of the land required that all manual workers had to be paid in cash. It was seen as a necessary safeguard to avoid their exploitation by their employers through such devices as the 'truck' system (whereby workers were paid in goods rather than cash) or the 'tommy shop' arrangement (this required employees to exchange vouchers or credits at the employer's own shop for goods). The 1831 Truck Act required employers to pay certain kinds of workmen in the coin of the realm and it prohibited employers from imposing any restrictions on how or where a worker should spend his pay. By 1887 the measure's provisions covered all workmen in manual employment except domestic servants. Under the 1960 Payment of Wages Act a worker can make out a written request to be paid in a non-cash form, and if the employer agrees within two weeks the payment can be made through credit transfer, postal order or money order and from 1963 by cheque.

During the seventies there is some evidence that a growing number of non-manual workers moved away from payment by cash to other forms of payment. The Interbank Research Organisation in 1979 found that 91 per cent of manual workers but only 44 per cent of non-manual were paid either weekly or fortnightly, compared with only 9 per cent of manuals paid once a month or every four weeks and 56 per cent of non-manuals.[2] It will not be easy to break the weekly cash in the hand habit among manual workers. Traditionally there is a love of the rustle of pound notes on a Friday afternoon, the desire among male manual workers to keep the size of their wage packets secret from their families and a suspicion about the middle-class image of the clearing banks with their difficult opening hours and lack of obvious interest in attracting the lower paid manual workers into the bank account system. During the seventies, under the influence of the French government, there was a successful move to mensualisation among manual workers in France. Here, apathy, inertia and indifference combine to perpetuate the manual–non manual distinction.

## WORKING TIME

Another severe inequality between manual and non-manual workers lies in the number and pattern of hours they work. In April 1980 manual male workers worked an average of 45.4 hours a week, 5.7 of which was overtime. As many as 54.3 per cent of male manuals actually worked overtime, averaging 10.3 hours a week. A total of 26.7 per cent of male manuals clocked on for more than 48 hours of work a week. Unskilled railway staff put in a massive average of 54.1 hours a week in April 1980, of which 14.1 hours was overtime for a gross wage of £104.10, with £32.70 coming from overtime payments. Bakery workers averaged 14.2 hours of overtime in a 54.5 hour week, while males in civil engineering construction and mechanical engineering construction worked 11.0 and 10.9 hours of overtime respectively in just over 51 hours a week of working time. By contrast, the white-collar male worked only a 38.7 hour week of which no more than 1.6 hours was worked in overtime. In April 1980 as many as 23.3 per cent of non-manual males worked less than 36 hours a week, compared with only 1.8 per cent of male manuals who did so. While 57.8 per cent of white-collar males worked 36 to 40 hours, 41.2 per cent of male manuals fell into the same period of working time, but 30.3 per cent of male manuals worked between 40 and 48 hours, compared with only 13.2 per cent of the non-manuals. The working hours of our white-collar workers are broadly in line with their colleagues in continental western Europe, but Britain's manual workers work much longer hours than most others in the industrialised west (see Table 5.3). What limited experiments there have been in so-called flexible working hours in Britain have tended to involve white-collar staff mainly in the public services and not manual workers.

TABLE 5.3 Britain's long hours of work

| | | | |
|---|---|---|---|
| United Kingdom | 1902 | Italy | 1678 |
| West Germany | 1762 | Holland | 1622 |
| Denmark | 1725 | Belgium | 1611 |
| France | 1706 | Sweden | 1513 |
| Austria | 1703 | | |

Actual hours of work of manual workers in engineering on annual basis 1979.

SOURCE From Swedish Engineering Employers Federation in 'Unemployment and Working Time', TUC, February 1981, p. 7.

However, there were clear moves towards a reduction in the basic working week during the 1979/80 wage round, particularly in the aftermath of the damaging national engineering workers' dispute that broke through the employer resistance to moves away from the 40-hour week. In early 1981 the TUC estimated that as many as four million manual workers in employment had achieved agreements which provided for a basic working week of under 40 hours, almost half all full-time manual workers. Both the deepening recession and the planned cut in working time helped to cut back the levels of overtime being worked by manual workers. The average weekly overtime hours per male manual worker dropped from 6.3 to 5.7 between April 1979 and April 1980. The actual total weekly overtime hours per operative in manufacturing industry fell from 15 million in 1979 to below 10 million by November 1980 and this trend has continued since then, though the main cause of this cut back has been the fall in the number of workers working overtime. The average weekly hours per worker (male and female) working ovetime in manufacturing dropped by only a few percentage points – from 8.7 to 8.1. Yet the TUC found that the statistics on overtime since 1974 suggested the rise in unemployment over the period made little impact on the amount of overtime worked per overtime worker (see Table 5.4). A cut in overtime working would help to provide more job opportunities for unemployed manual workers. The TUC reckons that if all hours worked above 40 could be parcelled out and converted into full-time jobs, some 200 000 jobs might be saved in manufacturing industry and 600 000 in the economy as a whole.

TABLE 5.4 The overtime scandal, 1974–80

| | *1974* | *1979* | *1980* | *1981* |
|---|---|---|---|---|
| Overtime workers as % of all male manual workers | 60.7 | 58.5 | 54.3 | 46.8 |
| Average weekly overtime of all male workers (hrs) | 6.5 | 6.3 | 5.7 | 3.8 |
| Average weekly overtime of male manual workers (hrs) working overtime | 10.6 | 10.6 | 10.3 | 9.5 |
| Total male manual unemployment | 647 000 | 1 340 000 | 1 520 000 | 2 734 000 |

SOURCE 'New Earnings Surveys'.

In a 1981 consultative document the TUC emphasised the drawbacks of overtime working. 'It does have a well-known tendency to degenerate, to become systematic and self-perpetuating, to lose any simple relationship to output, and to become unresponsive to changes in demand', it argued.[3] 'Long, unsocial hours which generate fatigue, sickness, absenteeism and turnover, create gaps in the production systems which tend to be filled by even more overtime work. Once established, overtime may become the subject of competing demands for individuals and groups which may bid up the overall level.' Manual workers are likely to resist any attempts to reduce overtime if it means a cut in their pay packets and forces them to rely on a basic rate that is far from adequate to meet their needs. Moreover, the opportunities for overtime working can be a powerful attraction for many skilled manual workers who want to maximise their earning power.

On the other hand, long hours can hit morale and performance and they provide an alternative to an efficient use of labour in the productive process. There are some signs that trade union attempts to reduce overtime working have not been entirely unsuccessful. The national engineering agreement provides that no worker will be required to work more than 30 hours overtime in any four weeks, while an agreement with British Shipbuilders includes a commitment to reduce over time working to 7.5 per cent of basic hours on average in any three-month period. The agreement by the national joint council for the building industry insists that overtime in excess of one hour a day should not be worked except with the consent of the local joint overtime committee. The Post Office Engineering union has negotiated with British Telecom to restrict overtime working to 3 hours per man per week, while the government and the Inland Revenue Staff Federation have an agreement that all regular overtime should be converted into full-time jobs except for emergencies and when there are breakdowns in computer operations.

However, the rapid abolition of overtime working for manual workers is quite unrealistic. As the TUC explained in December 1980: 'In the UK overtime is correlated strongly with low pay, is used as a method of ensuring reasonable earnings for many groups of male manual workers, whose current basic rates are too low to ensure reasonable living standards, and tends to fall off as basic earnings reach more reasonable levels. Any simple blanket reduction in overtime working without compensating changes in basic rates could create considerable hardship. In Europe generally such overtime as is worked is more likely to be related to demand requirements and therefore tends to be spread more evenly and thinly over different groups'.

Union leaders condemn the widespread use of overtime among manual workers. During the seventies between 28 and 37 per cent of all operatives worked between 7.8 hours to 9.2 hours on average of overtime a week. In many manufacturing industries even the ups and downs of the economic cycle fail to make much of an impact on the amount of overtime working. Indeed, there is abundant evidence to suggest that employers provide extra hours of work to overcome serious skill shortages.

In a research paper to the Donovan Royal Commission, E. G. Whybrew explained the different attitudes towards ovetime working between trade union officials and the work group. 'To the central officials overtime appears to increase the supply of a particular type of labour with which they are concerned without bringing any compensating increase in their influence', he argued.[4] 'On the other hand, an extra employee while increasing the supply of labour is a potential recruit for the union. The individual worker, however, sees an extra employee in his department as increasing the supply of his type of labour with few compensating benefits. For him, however, an increase in overtime supplies the extra labour but raises his earnings and gives his workshop organisation the possibility of using a cheep industrial weapon – an overtime ban'.

There is little doubt that overtime working remains a highly inefficient way of using labour and its social effects on manual workers are real enough. Whybrew's detailed investigations revealed that overtime is at its highest incidence among maintenance workers and lowest among general production workers. In his view it 'encourages people to waste time at work' in order to obtain a living wage. Any future decline in overtime is more likely to refelct worsening economic prospects than any sudden improvement in labour productivity. As Whybrew explained fourteen years ago, where employers took the initiative to eradicate overtime in the Post Office, electricity supply and Esso 'trade union cooperation was readily forthcoming if asked for', but the initiative for change must come from employers since 'they alone have the power and the means to provide alternative ways of doing things.'

The holiday entitlement of manual workers has improved substantially ever the past twenty-five years. In 1955, 96 per cent of them enjoyed only a fortnight a year. Even as late as 1969 half Britain's manual workers were still only entitled to two weeks annual holiday, with a further 35 per cent enjoying from two to three weeks. The dramatic holiday breakthrough came in 1970 and 1971. In 1969 only 14 per cent of manual workers enjoyed three weeks holiday. By 1971 that proportion had shot up to 63 per cent. There was a further swift improvement in 1974, when the number of manual workers having four weeks holiday rose from 7 per cent in 1973 to 28 per cent a year later. There was also a noticeable increase in the number of collective agreements that provided additional length of service holidays to manual workers. These improvements took place independently of the reductions in the length of the basic working week for manual workers. But white-collar workers enjoyed much more holiday time. In 1970 the average totalled 3.4 weeks (compared with 2.7 weeks for full-time adult male manuals) and in 1974 4.3 weeks (compared with 4.0 weeks for the manuals), but subsequently there has been a noticeable narrowing of the gap (see Table 5.5).

A PSI study in 1980 found 95 per cent of firms with 20 days holiday for non-manuals had the same for manuals. However, differences in holiday pay remain much more stark. Most manual workers receive only their basic rate during their holiday and not average post-tax earnings. A survey in 1976 carried out by the British Institute of Management discovered that just under half the manual workers in the sample received only their basic wages, while just under a third were paid

TABLE 5.5 Basic holiday entitlement

| *Working days* | *% all employees* | *Directors* | *Senior managers* | *Middle managers* | *Clerical* | *Manual* |
|---|---|---|---|---|---|---|
| Less than 15 | – | – | – | – | 1 | 1 |
| 15 | 12 | 1 | 1 | 5 | 26 | 29 |
| 16–19 | 7 | – | 3 | 7 | 30 | 34 |
| 20 | 66 | 34 | 41 | 49 | 35 | 31 |
| 21–4 | 9 | 19 | 26 | 27 | 8 | 5 |
| 25 and more | 7 | 45 | 29 | 13 | 1 | – |

SOURCE 'Employee Benefits', British Institute of Management, 1978, p. 22.

average hourly or weekly earnings. A further quarter enjoyed a formula that gave them a figure somewhere between the basic rate and average earnings. In the engineering industry the formula was minimum time rate plus one third. Most non-manual workers enjoy their normal earnings during their holidays. However, the arrival of the holiday bonus, the so-called '13th month' in continental western Europe, remains very much the exception for both manual and non-manual workers in Britain. Over half the non-manual worker holiday agreements examined by the Labour Research Department in a survey in 1979 enjoyed an increased holiday entitlement based on the number of year's service with the company. This compared with just under 40 per cent of manual worker holiday schemes.

## SHIFT WORKING

A growing number of manual male workers are having to work more unsocial hours in continuous production processes. There are no precise figures on the extent of shiftworking in the British economy but the April 1980 New Earnings Survey revealed that 23.0 per cent of manual workers (compared with only 5.7 per cent of non-manuals) were in receipt of shift payments. A study carried out by the European Commission in 1975 estimated that 18.3 per cent of British workers were working on shifts, compared with 19.5 per cent in France, 20.2 per cent in West Germany and 22.3 per cent in Italy.

The impact of shiftworking on the health of workers is unclear. There does seem to be a process of self-selection, which must qualify any overall gloomy view that shiftworking injures health. J. M. Harrington in a study of the medical literature on the subject for the Health and Safety Executive argued that while it did not appear there was any 'excess mortality' resulting from shiftwork practices and sickness absence appeared to be lower among shiftworkers than others, 'there is no doubt that rotating shiftwork, particularly the night shift, causes disruption of biological rhythms.[5] On the other hand, Harrington found 'no concrete evidence to show that these disruptive sleeping patterns are, in the long term, harmful and permanent night workers seem to adapt better than those who only work intermittently at night'. He believed shiftwork did 'exacerbate pre-existing ulcers' and could be 'a contributory factor in initiating them', but he also thought: the pyschological consequences of shiftworking appears to be mild and reversible, if they occur at all.' Apparently 'no excess cardiovascular or neurological morbidity or mortality' had been demonstrated in the shiftwork studies. 'However, repetitive work seems more likely to cause accidents, fatigue and poor performance than does cognitive work with high motivation', wrote Harrington. 'This is especially true at night. Fatigue, leading to increased errors and diminished performance, can be offset by improved motivation and appropriate use of work breaks. Individual differences in response to fatigue can overshadow group differences. Short cycle working prevents Circadian rhythms adaptation but lessens the strain on workers of unpopular shifts which disrupt social life'.

But if the process of self-selection must qualify the medical evidence of shiftworking being harmful to the health of manual workers, there is less doubt about the belated response of society to the existence of the shiftworker in ever greater numbers. As Harrington has written:

> Community life has traditionally been geared to the light/dark cycle: work during daylight hours, recreation later in the day, sleep at night and weekends free from work. People who work out of phase with this norm suffer inconvenience, and night work is the most disruptive. There is less opportunity to eat meals with the family, the wife carries a greater responsibility for the children, visits to friends, outside entertainment such as football matches and the cinema are frequently impossible and sexual relations are strained by the two partners in the marriage living lives out of phase with each other.

It appears that 'good housing, small families and a happy marriage' are necessary prerequisites for effective night-shift working. No wonder, only 20 per cent of shiftworkers actually like working nights, most simply tolerating it while 20 per cent dislike it enough to reject it. There are signs in some areas that employers find it very difficult to recruit manual workers for jobs on double day shifts, especially in those parts of the greater London area where the labour market is still tight, despite the recession. It is perhaps not surprising therefore that black workers predominate on the night shift in the foundries and manufacturing plants of the industrial Midlands and North West.

A 1980 NEDO study suggested that 'all available evidence supports the conclusion that shiftwork has no significant effect on cardiovascular disease or on the incidence of psychological or neurotic disorders',[6] but it also did admit that shiftworking involves loss of sleep and digestive problems. There is some evidence that links shiftworking with gastro-duodenal ulceration. But the ill effects relate particularly to workers on a shift that lasts from midnight to six o' clock in the morning, who also rotate between days and nights.

The outside society is adapted to meet the needs of workers on normal day work, so that the chances of shiftworkers enjoying similar social and recreational pursuits are severely limited. Britain has a long way to go before it becomes a 24-hours society. Young single men have an intense dislike of second shift work (1430 to 2230 hours a day) and the levels of absenteeism here are much greater than on the first day shift. On the other hand, married men with children like the double day shift system, because they can finish in the early afternoon and have plenty of time at home with their families. A survey carried out in 1979 for the Equal Opportunities Commission found that, of the 113 wives of shiftworkers interviewed, 34 said they were not at all happy with the working arrangements of their husbands. In only 53 per cent of cases were the shiftworkers and his wife happy with the system.

## POOR WORKING CONDITIONS

A survey published by Peter Townsend in 1979 found that 70 per cent of manual skilled male workers spent all or nearly all of their working time standing or walking about, compared with 33 per cent of non-manual male workers in routine jobs. About a third of skilled and partly skilled and nearly two thirds of unskilled male manual workers spent all or nearly all of their working time outside in the open air.[7] Townsend estimates that as many as one in five of the employed population in Britain, more than 4½ million people, have what he describes as 'poor conditions of work', based on both indoor and outdoor criteria. He gave examples: 'Among people working indoors, 3 per cent did not have access to an indoors flush toilet, 7 per cent had no facilities for washing or changing, 11 per cent had insufficient heating in winter, 17 per cent had no place to hang a coat or keep other articles without risk of loss, 26 per cent could not make or receive a telephone call and 42 per cent were unable to control the lighting over their work'. Townsend established what he calls an index of work deprivation covering a wide range of data (how much notice of dismissal; time spent at work standing up or walking about; poor working conditions; working before 8 am or at night; no pay during illness; no entitlement to an occupational pension; no entitlement to holiday with pay). It is important to remember that most of his evidence dates mainly from the late sixties and early seventies and thus does not take account of some relative improvements described elsewhere in this chapter, but Townsend reckoned that while as many as 69 per cent of manual workers experienced deprivation, only 16 per cent of non-manuals did so.

A major inequality for manual workers derives from the nature of the jobs they have to do. At work they face much more serious health hazards than most white-collar staff. The official statistics from the HM Factory Inspectorate (see Tables 5.6 and 5.7) suggest a steady fall in the number of deaths at work and accidents, but the figures provide no grounds for complacency, especially, at a time when government spending cuts threaten to reduce the amount devoted to accident prevention.

TABLE 5.6 Deaths at work, 1974–9

| | *1974* | *1975* | *1976* | *1977* | *1978* | *1979* |
|---|---|---|---|---|---|---|
| Factory processes | 290 | 231 | 211 | 205 | 185 | 179 |
| Construction | 161 | 181 | 154 | 131 | 120 | 119 |
| Docks | 17 | 11 | 16 | 18 | 15 | 14 |
| Inland warehouses | 11 | 4 | 1 | 3 | – | 3 |
| Total | 479 | 427 | 382 | 357 | 320 | 315 |

SOURCE HM Factory Inspectorate report, 1979, p. 1.

In 1979 there were 223 997 reported accidents on all premises covered by the Factories Act. As many as 31 005 occurred on construction sites, while 16 182 were recorded in motor vehicle manufacturing; 20 087 in metal manufacture; 9789 in textiles; 9860 in electrical engineering; 24 188 in food, drink and tobacco; 20 478 in mechanical engineering and 10 351 in chemical and allied industries. Many manual workers are exposed to excessive noise, heat and danger in their jobs as well as to toxic substances such as lead and asbestos that carry with them dangers

TABLE 5.7 Accidents at work: incidence rates per 100 000 at risk of accidents in manufacturing industry

| | *1974* | *1975* | *1976* | *1977* | *1978* | *1979* |
|---|---|---|---|---|---|---|
| Incidence rate of fatal accidents | 4.5 | 3.7 | 3.4 | 3.4 | 3.1 | 2.9 |
| Incidence rate of events leading to fatal accidents | 4.0 | 3.5 | 3.2 | 3.4 | 3.0 | 2.8 |
| Incidence rate of serious accidents (based on 5 per cent random sample of reported accidents) | 580 | 540 | 560 | 580 | 530 | 540 |
| Incidence rate of all reported accidents | 3 520 | 3 490 | 3 480 | 3 590 | 3 620 | 3 350 |

SOURCE 'HM Factory Inspectorate report: manufacturing and service industries', 1978, p. 1 and 1979, p. 1.

of infection and disease. The annual reports of the Trades Union Congress on health and safety at work issues over the past ten years do not suggest that concepts such as 'job enrichment' and the 'humanisation of work' have made very much impact at all on manufacturing industry.

Current statistics suggest that around 1400 people (almost all in manual jobs) die every year as a result of occupational accidents and diseases, while at least 300 000 sustain serious injury at work. This costs an estimated £2000 million a year to the nation. The present recession is likely to weaken concern among employers, unions and workers for health and safety at work issues. The HM Chief Inspector of Factories, J. D. G. Hammer, noted in his 1978 annual report that his 900 inspectors had become aware of 'much more overt questioning of the costs and benefits of health and safety legislation'[8] among employers because of the severe economic pressures they were suffering from. Indeed, the Factory Inspector's reports in the late seventies were critical of the attitude of employers. In 1976 he found that while many major companies and employees had obviously faced up to what was involved under the new Act 'all too many still' seemed to be 'likely to be surprised by the foreseeable'[9]. 'Too often they have not yet planned ahead to set up effective systems of work for particular processes or activities or they have not thought through for themselves what the Act means for them in terms of practical action', complained Mr Hammer. The 150 000 union-based safety representatives on the shop-floor began to prove themselves more knowledgeable than supervisors and middle managers on the safety and health risks in the plant. 'One of the things which constantly surprise inspectors, and I must say also myself, is the poor quality of the information available to top management', he argued in his 1977 report.[10] 'There is still a great deal to be done in the production of safety policies by firms. Those who produced policies shortly before the 1974 Act came into force have tended to regard it as a once and for all exercise and have made little or no attempt to re-examine the policies and revise them in the light of experience'.

Many doctors believe that stress at work is becoming a major problem and it is by no means confined to busy directors in the boardroom.[11] Hypertension, peptic ulcers and heart disease are not confined to the executive or even white-collar grades. Indeed, there is considerable evidence to suggest that manual workers (especially drivers, shop stewards, shift workers) are particularly vulnerable to stress-related illnesses. Medical research, for example, has shown conclusively the correlation between vehicle driving and stress, because continued driving produces increased blood pressure and high levels of adrenalin. The coronary ward at the Charing Cross hospital was said to be full of taxi-drivers. Dr Malcolm Carruthers of St Mary's hospital medical school at London University gave evidence for the train driver's union ASLEF on the stress of the job on its members. 'Responsible jobs requiring high levels of concentration and coordination over long periods of time, do set up considerable bio-chemical stresses within the body', he explained. 'Unless these are offset by a high level of physical activity they are likely to be harmful to the heart and blood vessels'. Sickness absence research in the civil service suggests that certified absenteeism for respiratory infections is much higher among typists and clerical assistants than it is in the senior administrative grades. Research carried out by Dr L. E. Hinkle at the Bell Telephone Company in the United States suggests that managers and executives had a lower heart and coronary death rate than workers or foremen. Dr Peter Raffle of London Transport has published findings on sickness absence rates among staff over the past twenty years and these show that since the late forties and early fifties there has been a marked increase in the amount of sickness absence for short spells of under a week among younger men. Dr Bill Jones of the TUC Institute of Occupational Health asserts that 'The black death was far more stressful than any general strike could be', but he acknowledges that 'since the war the expectations of life getting less stressful has contrasted with the reality'. It is true that the magnitude of stress is relative and hard to pin down with medical precision, but the limited work that has been done does suggest that employers who take an active interest in their workers, provide sensitive supervision and group work, and disclose as much information as possible about their activities, are more liable to get a satisfactory performance out of them.

In a review of the academic literature on work stress and mental strain Professor Murrell of the University of Wales reached the conclusion that there was no 'firm evidence which suggests working on a properly designed assembly line is any better or any worse in terms of job pressure than any other kind of work. If any group of workers come out as being under the greatest pressure it is the foremen', and he added that 'in spite of the enormous volume of work which seems to have been undertaken the results are really rather inconclusive'.[12] After all, what might be seen as one 'man's intolerable pressure' might be another's 'challenge'. As in shiftwork, there is a strong element of self-selection among manual workers who decide to work in stressful jobs. Most emphasis has been on production line 'blues', the authoritarian world portrayed by Chaplin in his 'Modern Times'. Yet Murrell found little evidence to indicate that assembly workers were more liable than others to suffer from physical or psychiatric illness as a result. He commented: 'It would seem that dissatisfaction with one's work is more likely to express itself in the form of a strike than as a nervous breakdown and that the steady erosion of the workforce with age may remove men from the line before the risk of breakdown of health occurs'.

Such findings may be seen as complacent, but loose language about alienation and anomie on the shopfloor has tended to obfuscate the problem. If any broad conclusion is possible in this highly controversial area of research it must be that manual workers (particularly those in jobs that require concentrated effort) are more endangered by stress diseases than executives.

There remain wide differences in the provision of sick pay to manual and non-manual workers (see Table 5.8). The 1976 BIM survey discovered that while as many as two thirds of the companies they examined had reduced the differentials in sick pay entitlement between different kinds of worker, 36 per cent of skilled manual employees and 40 per cent of semi-skilled and unskilled employees received no sickness benefit at all other than that provided by the state, compared with only 2 per cent of foremen and supervisors and the same proportion of clerical and secretarial workers. Even where sick pay entitlement did exist there was no immediate provision for manual workers. While only 7 per cent of semi-skilled and unskilled workers had immediate sick pay entitle-

TABLE 5.8 Sick pay and social class

| | % who get paid when they are sick | |
|---|---|---|
| | *1971* | *1976* |
| Managers in large establishments | 99 | 99 |
| Managers in small establishments | 94 | 95 |
| Professional workers – employees | 100 | 98 |
| Intermediate non-manual workers | 95 | 97 |
| Junior non-manual workers | 90 | 93 |
| Personal service workers | 71 | 75 |
| Foremen and supervisors | 78 | 87 |
| Skilled manual workers | 48 | 60 |
| Semi-skilled manual workers | 50 | 60 |
| Unskilled manual workers | 57 | 63 |
| Agricultural workers | 66 | 67 |

SOURCE 'The General Household Survey', HMSO, 1978

ment, as many as 28 per cent of clerical and secretarial employees, 34 per cent of foremen and supervisors and 38 per cent of executive and technical personnel did so. Half the manual workers received pay for less than 13 weeks, whereas the majority of the non-manuals could enjoy sick pay from their employer for more than 14 weeks. In over two thirds of the firms surveyed by the BIM in 1976 giving sick pay to manual workers, the period for which it continued was less than for the non-manuals in the same companies.

Nor do manual workers enjoy anything like their full earnings when they are on sick pay, whereas the overwhelming majority of non-manuals experience no break in their earnings as a result of being ill. But a further BIM survey in 1978 found evidence for an improvement in harmonisation in sick pay. 'It is clear that an increasing number of companies ensure that payments are close to normal earnings for all employee categories once they meet the full requirements of the scheme', it reported.[13] Just under two thirds of the BIM company participants in 1978 said they made exactly the same sick pay provisions for all their workers, while nearly half of those companies ensured sick pay was equivalent to full pay/average earnings for everybody. But where sick pay schemes differed the vast majority of non-manuals had the equivalent of full pay, whereas 54 per cent of manuals received nothing beyond the basic rate and just under a third had to fall back on state provisions alone, though these were usually in small companies. The 1978 BIM survey also pointed out that no more than 18 per cent of their company sample gave any permanent disability cover to their employees. It revealed that while a third of workers in 65 subsidiaries of American companies in Britain could receive permanent disability benefit, only 15 per cent of UK-based firms did so.

Inequalities in health are seen in the mortality rates for different social classes to be found in the reports of the Registrar General. Both men and women are two and a half times more likely to face the risk of death before they reach retirement age if they come from unskilled manual worker jobs than if they are professional men and their wives. While the chances of death are still much greater among the babies of unskilled manual worker families than among the professional classes, the differences remain obvious enough during the years of working life. Among men under the age of 44 the ratio of deaths among unskilled workers compared to the professional is 2.45, while after 45 years it drops to 1.7.

Tables 5.9 and 5.10 indicate the enormous inequalities, as measured by sickness and medical consultation.

TABLE 5.9 Sickness: class differences (a) in early adulthood, 15 to 44

| *Socio-economic group* | *Long-standing illness* | | *Restricted activity* | | *Consultation* | |
|---|---|---|---|---|---|---|
| | *Men* | *Women* | *Men* | *Women* | *Men* | *Women* |
| Professional | 145.4 | 138.2 | 84.0 | 106.4 | 75.5 | 140.4 |
| Managerial | 149.7 | 141.9 | 63.1 | 93.3 | 61.3 | 133.9 |
| Intermediate | 164.0 | 145.4 | 85.1 | 105.5 | 72.3 | 130.6 |
| Skilled manual | 161.9 | 167.2 | 89.7 | 95.2 | 85.1 | 142.5 |
| Semi-skilled manual | 173.8 | 170.3 | 81.5 | 99.3 | 80.5 | 146.0 |
| Unskilled manual | 197.4 | 202.3 | 110.4 | 95.3 | 93.5 | 145.9 |

SOURCE Rates per 1000 population General Household Surveys 1974–6 from 'Inequalities in Health' DHSS, 1980, p. 52.

In the 45 to 64-year old age group as many as three out of every ten men and women on average are affected by chronic illness, while among unskilled manual households the percentage increases to 50 for men and 40 for women. As the 1980 DHSS study argued: 'Chronic disorder of the kind which resists treatment and cure but instead persists as a routine discomfort to the individual must be one of the most unfavourable dimensions of middle age to the working class.'[14]

TABLE 5.10 Sickness: class differences (b) middle age, 45 to 64

| *Social-economic group* | *Long-standing illness* | | *Restricted activity* | | *Consultation* | |
|---|---|---|---|---|---|---|
| | *Men* | *Women* | *Men* | *Women* | *Men* | *Women* |
| Professional | 228.9 | 291.3 | 71.1 | 92.2 | 75.6 | 94.7 |
| Managerial | 257.0 | 265.7 | 75.4 | 77.0 | 74.8 | 99.8 |
| Intermediate | 368.0 | 329.7 | 98.4 | 94.6 | 122.1 | 122.4 |
| Skilled manual | 357.7 | 315.1 | 102.6 | 102.7 | 112.4 | 109.2 |
| Semi-skilled manual | 387.6 | 380.8 | 101.0 | 114.9 | 124.9 | 121.5 |
| Unskilled manual | 485.5 | 401.6 | 120.0 | 111.9 | 145.5 | 122.6 |

SOURCE 1974–6 from 'Inequalities in Health', DHSS, 1980, p. 53.

Evidence from the Office of Population Censuses and Surveys suggests there was actually a deterioration in the position of the lower social classes during the sixties and early seventies, relative to more advantaged classes. 'The age standardised death rate for class IV (manual partly skilled) actually increased during the early sixties', asserted the 1980 DHSS survey. 'And the rate for class III (skilled manual and non-manual) declined only marginally'.[15] Apparently 'during the 1960s a deterioration in the rates for men aged 35 to 54 in class III, IV and V (unskilled manual) (and little or no improvement for older men in these classes) took place'. For each ten-year age group it was found that the mortality rates for men in classes III to V worsened over the sixties and seventies relative to men in classes I and II (managerial).

The 1980 DHSS survey argued: 'In 1959–63 more class V men died at every age than in 1949–53 from cancer of the lung, vascular lesions of the central nervous system, arteriosclerotic and degenerative heart disease, motor vehicle accidents, and other accidents. Some diseases like lung cancer and duodenal cancer, which showed no trend with social class or like coronary disease, an inverse trend forty to fifty years ago, were by the 1960s producing higher mortality rates among social classes IV and V than I and II'. For Registrar General reports for 1970–2 it was found that for 92 causes of death picked out for men aged 15 to 64 the mortality ratios for both classes IV and V were higher than for I and II in as many as 68. This represents a proportionate increase compared with a decade earlier.

There is no straightforward correlation between excessive mortality rates and the kinds of work people do, mainly because the 'lifetime and total effects of occupation have not been measured or are difficult to measure'. But the central finding of the 1980 DHSS survey is not easy to discount, namely that there was a 'lack of improvement, and indeed in some respects deterioration, of the health experience not merely of occupational class V but also class IV in health, relative to occupational class I, as judged by mortality indicators, during the 1960s and early 1970s'.[16]

The normal age of retirement for men remains 65 and for women 60, but lower retirement ages are mainly in the public sector (60 for men and 55 for women). An Incomes Data Study found in 1977 that 'the physical stress suffered by manual workers might suggest that they would be likely to have a lower retirement age, but in fact non-manual occupations in insurance, banking and finance are much more likely to have a lower retirement age, many employees retiring at 60.'[17] In 1977 underground miners achieved a phased move to early retirement as part of their annual pay negotiations, but the Coal Board opposed any extension of the early retirement scheme to cover miners who were working on the surface. If such a concession had been given, there would have been immediate pressure from many other groups of workers demanding similar treatment. The sheer cost of any move to earlier retirement for men has tended to make governments less than interested in the idea.

In October 1976 the Department of Health and Social Security estimated that it would cost the taxpayer £2500 million (at 1976 prices) a year to bring the male retirement age down to 60, with a drop to 64 costing as much as £350 million. Indeed, the growing cost of Britain's ageing population has become a severe burden on the Exchequer. During the seventies the state pension was able to improve its real value against the rate of inflation, but this looks more unlikely in the years ahead. Inevitably, it will be the manual workers who will suffer as a result, because they are far more dependent on the flat rate state pension to make ends meet than other workers.

There is some evidence to suggest that manual workers were more likely to be included in a company's pensions provisions for its employees during the seventies. 'Pensions is an area in which manual and white-collar trade unions have recently shown considerable interest, both in terms of negotiating improved benefits and in participating in the management of pension funds by the appointment of union-nominated trustees', observed a BIM survey in 1978.

But sharp differences in treatment over pensions remains for the manual worker. His or her position in retirement mirrors the wide disparities that existed during the years of work (see Table 5.11).

TABLE 5.11 Inequality in pensions

| | % companies (number = 391) | | |
|---|---|---|---|
| | *Contributory* | *Non-contributory* | *Total* |
| Same basis for all employees | 61 | 13 | 74 |
| Directors | 18 | 9 | 27 |
| Senior managers | 20 | 6 | 26 |
| Middle managers | 20 | 5 | 25 |
| Junior managers | 19 | 4 | 23 |
| Clerical | 17 | 2 | 19 |
| Manual | 4 | 4 | 8 |

SOURCE 'Employee Benefits', British Institute of Management, February 1978, p. 11.

A 1978 survey by the British Institute of Management (see Table 5.12) found that 52 per cent of firms made no provision to give their employees anything in excess of the statutory minimum when they lost their job. The difference is partly to do with the different methods of payment for manual and non-manual. Being paid by the month rather than the week gives greater security in employment to the non-manual, and it also enables employers to display more generosity in the provision of service-related payments to workers, depending on the length of their service with the company. Very few companies are ready to provide their employees with extra payments (based on age and service criteria) in

TABLE 5.12 Dismissal from work: inequalities persist

| *% of companies* | *Same policy for all employees* | *Directors* | *Senior managers* | *Junior managers* | *Clercial* | *Manual* |
|---|---|---|---|---|---|---|
| Regardless of length of service | 32 | 83 | 74 | 31 | 16 | 1 |
| Only after certain length of service | 11 | 16 | 16 | 17 | 13 | 4 |
| None | 52 | 1 | 10 | 52 | 71 | 95 |

SOURCE 'Employee Benefits', British Institue of Management, 1978, p. 27.

addition to their statutory redundancy entitlement. In the BIM survey, only 12 per cent of employers did so without regard to age or service, while 34 per cent did so taking those criteria into account. There is some evidence that the presence of unions in workplaces can ensure a greater willingness by companies to give extra payments to their redundant employees.

The 1978 BIM survey found that only 40 per cent of the 622 companies in the sample had any form of worker financial participation in their operations. The most common was cash-based profit sharing without restrictions, but only three out of the 90 firms that practised that kind of scheme gave an equal share of the bonus to all their employees. Just over half the firms excluded their manual workers from their cash-based profit sharing scheme, while 34 per cent did not cover their clerical or technical employees with profit sharing either. By contrast as many as 26 per cent restricted such bonus payments to their senior staff alone and 22 per cent ensured only management grades were the beneficiaries. While 28 per cent of the employers covered in the BIM survey had a share option or SAYE scheme, none extended that to either their manual or clerical staffs, preserving share ownership in two thirds of cases to executive directors. The reasons given for this remarkable degree of discrimination by companies to the BIM suggest that many employers are less than willing to recognise that all their workers (manual as well as non-manual) play a vital part in whatever success their companies can claim to have. Certainly many privately owned enterprises are quick to deplore the lack of loyalty by their own employees if economic pressures build up. The 1978 Finance Act, mainly under Liberal party insistence, did provide some tax incentive for companies to establish profit-sharing schemes for their workers, but there is little evidence to suggest that this led to any noticeable increase in the numbers in existence.

During the late seventies, mainly under the influence of government incomes policies, there was a rapid increase in the range of fringe benefits for non-manual employees, particularly at managerial level (see Table 5.13). The BIM 1978 survey found that there had been a big increase in the possession of company cars; free private medical insurance; house purchase assistance; top hat pensions and the like over the past decade. It is only fair to recognise that the growth in perkery brought unequal rewards for different groups within the non-manual grades, but there are no signs that manual workers gained any tangible benefits at all from such a trend. The annual surveys of Inbucon management consultants provide graphic evidence of what happened. In 1976 only 62.3 per cent

TABLE 5.13 The growth in executive benefits 1975–1980 (%)

| | *Proportion of the sample receiving benefits in* | | | | | |
|---|---|---|---|---|---|---|
| | *1975* | *1976* | *1977* | *1978* | *1979* | *1980* |
| Top hat pensions | 20.3 | 19.4 | 15.2 | 15.6 | 16.1 | 17.5 |
| Full use of company car | 60.6 | 62.3 | 63.8 | 67.4 | 69.0 | 72.4 |
| Allowance for regular use of own car | 12.8 | 10.7 | 8.6 | 8.3 | 7.3 | 8.9 |
| Subsidised lunches | 63.6 | 67.3 | 65.9 | 68.6 | 74.4 | 71.3 |
| Subsidised housing | 1.1 | 1.0 | 0.7 | 1.0 | 0.7 | 0.9 |
| Assistance with home purchase | 6.4 | 5.9 | 7.4 | 8.0 | 5.8 | 6.3 |
| Life assurance | | | | | | |
| – Up to and incl. 3 times salary | 57.9 | 58.8 | 61.6 | 62.4 | 65.1 | 59.0 |
| – Exceeding 3 times salary | 25.5 | 27.5 | 23.9 | 26.7 | 27.7 | 31.9 |
| Free medical insurance | 37.9 | 37.3 | 38.8 | 44.1 | 50.6 | 57.9 |
| Share option scheme | 4.3 | 5.3 | 3.7 | 6.0 | 10.5 | 9.6 |
| Share purchase scheme | 3.5 | 4.1 | 3.3 | 3.4 | 3.6 | 5.2 |
| Low interest loans | – | 7.2 | 9.7 | 9.6 | 9.0 | 7.0 |
| Bonus | 31.1 | 33.9 | 33.3 | 37.1 | 43.9 | 36.6 |

SOURCE 'Survey of Executive Salaries and Fringe Benefits', Inbucon, 1980, p. 74.

of business executives enjoyed use of a company car; by July 1980 that figure had climbed to 72.4 per cent. As many as 86 per cent earning over £10 000 a year at that time received a company car, worth around £2000. The proportion who gained access to free medical insurance for private health treatment rose from 37.3 per cent in 1976 to 57.9 per cent by 1980. The numbers enjoying subsidised meals (mainly through expense accounts) went from 71.3 per cent to 87.3 per cent over the same period. Such facts must put the grumbles of the executive class about the burdens of income tax into some perspective.

There were some moves towards greater workplace equality over the past two decades through the stimulus of legislation. During the sixties measures such as the 1963 Contract of Employment Act and the 1965 Redundancy Payments Act made a modest contribution. But Dorothy Wedderburn argued that the Labour governments between October 1964 and June 1970 'did nothing to interfere with those fundamental ideological and market mechanisms which serve' to perpetuate the division between manual and non-manual workers.[18] The record of Labour between March 1974 and May 1979 does not look very much better in retrospect. To be fair, neither Labour's programmes of 1973 and 1976, nor the innumerable policy statements issued during the heyday of the TUC-Labour party liaison committee took up the issue of workplace equality, while the unions with large manual worker memberships failed to put staff status for blue-collar workers at the forefront of their bargaining agenda.

Yet it would be wrong to conclude that the period of Labour government during the seventies was entirely barren of achievement in this area. The 1975 Employment Protection Act, described by Jack Jones of the Transport and General Workers, as a 'worker's charter', extended a wide range of basic rights to all workers, but which were of particular value to the manual grades. These covered the provision of guarantee payments for workers on short time or temporarily laid off; maternity leave and job security for pregnant women workers; entitlement to normal pay when under medical suspension; time off work for union activities, public duties and job search after receiving notice of redundancy; unfair dismissal; the payment of debts to workers by their employers when insolvent and procedures to be carried out by employers over redundancies.

A study carried out by the Policy Studies Institute in 1978 concluded that the most effective change in the law concerned unfair dismissal, a legacy from the 1971 Industrial Relations Act. This enabled workers to seek redress from their former employers through an industrial tribunal if they had been sacked from their job unfairly. The investigation discovered that the unfair dismissal requirements had encouraged 'the reform or formalisation of procedures adopted in making disciplinary action and in executing dismissals',[19] while employers were becoming much more careful in their selection of new employees and appraising the performance of existing ones. There was also some evidence that employers had reduced their rates of dismissal as a result of the 1975 Act. But the PSI study concluded that for the most part the measure – designed to strengthen worker rights on the shop floor – had been far more modest in its impact than its critics had alleged. There were no signs that industrial tribunals were being inundated with cases from workers claiming to have been unfairly dismissed. Yet the Conservative government moved in the 1980 Employment Act to ease the laws on maternity leave, redundancy warnings, and guaranteed pay for small firms employing 20 workers or less. This was taking away from many manual workers in mainly non-union firms some legal safeguards that were designed to protect them in their work.

The achievement of some form of industrial democracy could prove of immense benefit to extend equality of treatment for manual workers, but little progress was made over that issue in the seventies. There are belated signs that attitudes are starting to change. 'We are at the beginning of a change which will spread to all the countries of western Europe and is comparable with the managerial revolution earlier in this century which transferred the effective control of companies from the shareholders, to those employees who manage the business', wrote Lord Bullock in a personal statement as chairman of a committee of inquiry into industrial democracy, when it published its report in January 1977.[20] 'In a democratic society, democracy does not stop at the factory gate or the office door. We spend a large part of our lives at work and invest our skills and energies in industry. There is growing recognition that those of us who do so should be able to participate in decisions which can vitally affect our working lives and our jobs', declared the Labour government's White Paper on industrial democracy published in May 1978.[21] It saw 'industrial democracy' as a means of achieving a 'positive partnership' between management and workers to replace the 'them' and 'us' divisions, the conflict in industry that was due in part to 'poor communications, lack of information and lack of trust'. Through a sharing of responsibility between boardroom and shop-floor there would be a fresh impetus to efficiency and creativity in industry.

By the standards of continental western Europe, Britain lags far behind our competitors in moves towards industrial democracy. The Confederation of British Industry fought a bitter and successful rearguard action against any attempt to produce legislation on industrial democracy in the late seventies, while the unions were divided over whether they wanted their own employee representatives in equal number with shareholder representatives on boards of companies.

Nor was there much evidence from the shop floor that workers, whether manual or non-manual, wished to have seats in the boardroom for their shop steward representatives. The debate about industrial democracy was rather unsatisfactory, partly because the very term remained shrouded in ambiguities. Congress House and Jack Jones of the Transport and General Workers favoured a statutory right for union nominees to sit on the unitary board of companies in equal number with shareholder representatives, with a small group of independents added in case of deadlock (2x + y formula) but other union leaders wanted to see an extension of collective bargaining in companies, but falling short of any acceptance of responsibility for executive decision-making. They feared such a radical move would confuse the function of the union as a negotiator on behalf of the members with that of management supervising the enterprise.

The Labour government wrestled with the problem for over two years without reaching any firm and acceptable conclusion. The May 1978 White Paper left many thorny questions unanswered, such as methods of electing worker representatives, the rights of workers who did not belong to trade unions and the role of management in an industrial democracy system. It involved a clear retreat from the original Bullock conception. The present slump has stilled any passionate discussion of industrial democracy. Perhaps more fundamental issues are now at stake. The main danger is that an over-concentration on intricate details of company law divert attention from general principles. There are few signs that workers on boards by law in West Germany have really been the cause of that country's industrial peace in the sixties and seventies. Moreover, Britain is unlike other western industrial nations, because it has a substantial and widespread network of trade union activity in the workplace already through the shop stewards, the combine committees and the like.

Up until very recently the white collar workers and their unions were the militants on workplace inequalities, anxious to defend their pay differentials and incentives, staff privileges between the office and the shop-floor. As Dorothy Wedderburn has argued: 'Manual worker trade unions have been concerned to defend their members within managements' own rules rather than to question the assumptions upon which those rules are based'.[22] In Britain there have been few obvious signs of discontent among manual workers about these issues, a readiness to accept their unequal position in the labour force without much questioning. Such phenomenon as 'blue collar blues' have been more widespread in the United States than here and ideas covered by catch-all terms like the 'humanisation of work' and 'job enrichment' – have been treated with perhaps understandable scepticism and suspicion by many manual workers, who are more likely to see such reforms as an attempt by their employers to boost productivity at their expense rather than as altruistic gestures to make the job they are doing more stress-free and enjoyable. The annual figures provided in the General Household Survey show that the vast majority of manual workers are satisfied with the work they do, though the proportion of discontented skilled men grew during the late seventies (see Table 5.14). The undeniable fact remains, however: the terms of reference that manual workers use to assess their pay, benefits and working conditions remain narrow and mainly confined to comparisons with workers doing similar kinds of work to their own.

The persistent inequalities at work described in this chapter are not all

TABLE 5.14 Job satisfaction

| | *Very satisfied* | *Fairly satisfied* | *Neither satisfied nor dissatisfied* | *Rather dissatisfied* | *Very dissatisfied* |
|---|---|---|---|---|---|
| Managers and employers in large establishments | 46 (57.5) | 41 (34) | 4 (4) | 8 (3) | 2 (1) |
| Managers and employers in small establishments | 46 (54) | 40 (34) | 3 (6) | 9 (3) | 2 (3) |
| Professional workers | 39 (41) | 44 (45) | 4 (7) | 11 (6) | 2 (1) |
| Intermediate – non manual | 36 (51) | 46 (38) | 5 (4) | 10 (4) | 4 (1) |
| Skilled manual workers | 38 (37) | 43 (46) | 6 (9) | 9 (5) | 4 (3) |
| Semi-skilled manual workers | 38 (38) | 42 (45) | 5 (9) | 9 (4) | 6 (3) |
| Unskilled manual workers | 52 (45) | 33 (39) | 4 (10) | 7 (3) | 5 (3) |
| Junior non-manual workers | 42 (47) | 40 (40) | 5 (7) | 9 (4) | 4 (2) |

SOURCE General Household Surveys 1972 and 1978. The figures in brackets are for 1972, made up to the nearest figure in decimal points.

of a similar consequence, but cumulatively they constitute a massive barrier to social cohesion and justice as well as an incalculable obstacle to the creation of a more dynamic and prosperous society. The Confederation of British Industry is acutely aware of the urgent need for an harmonisation of benefits for manual and non-manual workers, and a growing number of manual-based trade unions have started to place a much higher bargaining priority on dealing with such issues. But if it is merely left to voluntarism, there seems very little likelihood of any dramatic improvement in many of the existing areas of inequality at the workplace. Too often workers and their unions are ready to drop wider reforming objectives in return for more cash on the table in the annual bargain, while unimaginative employers fear the costs of any concessions on their total overheads and worry that their non-manual workers will try and re-establish some relative advantage by seeking to establish new forms of social inequality at work to replace those that have been eradicated.

Legislation has an important part to play in changing workplace attitudes over the manual/non-manual worker inequalities. Even the TUC recognises the wisdom of this. Indeed, over the past twenty years some tangible and important advances have been made in this sensitive area through the benevolent intervention of the state, with the provision of legal regulation and statutory minimum rights at law.

But there are some signs that this indifference is breaking down, at least among union negotiators. The Ford motor company, for example, faced claims from the unions that began to emphasise issues such as working hours and holidays as part of a push for equality between manual and non-manual workers. Terry Duffy, president of the Amalgamated Union of Engineering Workers, made staff status for manual workers major plank in his successful election programme both in 1978 and 1981. The British Labour movement, however – for all its rhetorical commitment to greater equality – failed to give the issue a high priority during the post-war years. Social Democracy in Scandinavia, mainly under manual trade union pressure, emphasised the rights of manual workers and helped to remove the more indefensible social barriers between the shop-floor and the office. The growth in new, more humane methods of work organisation in Sweden since the late sixties and the introduction of technological innovations to reduce stress and boredom at work owe a good deal to the alliance between the unions and Social Democracy.

Any new deal for Britain's manual workers would be concerned with the distribution of power and privilege in our society and it would require a new emphasis on the politics of class. Yet a shrewd appeal to the idealism as well as self-interest of manual workers is long overdue on the Left in British politics. During the sixties and seventies the Labour party too often lost touch with the needs and aspirations of working people on the shop-floor – especially in many inner city areas where local constituency associations were too often dominated by middle class public service activists with no direct concern or interest in the realities of shop-floor life.

The inequalities described in this chapter will not be easy to remove, and occupational changes during the eighties are likely to make the position of manual workers more difficult as they decline into an embattled and insecure minority of the labour force. The interests of manual and non-manual workers do not have to be antagonistic. A new harmony in industry based on realism and justice is surely not beyond the will and imagination of employers, unions and the political parties. The removal of shop-floor inequalities in continental western European countries since the sixties does not suggest this leads necessarily to tensions between different kinds of worker.

## NOTES AND REFERENCES

1 'The causes of poverty', *Royal Commission on the Distribution of Income and Wealth*, background paper, No. 5, HMSO, 1978, p. 51.
2 'Cashless Pay', Central Policy Review Staff, HMSO, 1981.

3 'Unemployment and Working Time', Trades Union Congress, February 1981.
4 E. G. Whybrew, 'Overtime Working in Britain', Royal Commission on Trade Unions and Employers' Associations, HMSO, 1968, pp. 51–2.
5 J. M. Harrington, 'Shift Work and Health: A critical review of the literature', Health and Safety Executive, 1978, pp. 19–20.
6 'The Introduction and extension of shiftworking', National Economic Development Office, 1980, pp. 12–20.
7 P. Townsend, *Poverty in the United Kingdom* (Penguin, 1979) pp. 432–74.
8 'Health and Safety Manufacturing and Service Industries 1979', HMSO, 1981, p. v.
9 ibid., 1976, p. vi.
10 ibid., 1977, p. vi.
11 See the author's article, 'Stress at Work', *New Society*, 17 October 1974, pp. 140–3.
12 Hywel Murrell, Work Stress and Mental Strain', Work Research Unit, Department of Employment, January 1978, pp. 77–9.
13 'Employee Benefits', British Institute of Management, 1978, p. 23.
14 'Inequalities in Health', report of a research working group, Department of Health and Social Security, 1980, p. 53.
15 ibid. pp. 66–7.
16 ibid., pp. 355–6.
17 Early Retirement, Incomes Data report, 1978, p. 11.
18 *Labour and Inequality*, ed. P. Townsend and N. Bosanquet, Fabian Society, 1972 p. 184; *see also* D. Wedderburn and C. Craig, 'Relative deprivation in work' in *Poverty, Inequality and Class Structure*, ed. D. Wedderburn (Cambridge, 1974).
19 W. W. Daniel and E. Stilgoe, 'The Impact of Employment Protection Laws' Policy Studies Institute, June 1978, p. 74.
20 Personal statement issued with 'Report of the Committee of Inquiry on Industrial Democracy', HMSO, January 1977.
21 'Industrial Democracy', HMSO, May 1978, p. 1.
22 *Poverty, Inequality and Class Structure*, ed. D. Wedderburn (Cambridge, 1974) p. 155.

# 6 Britain's Strike 'Problem'

## A STRIKE-RIDDEN COUNTRY?

Britain has won a reputation during the past twenty-five years for being a strike-prone nation. The willingness of workers to take disruptive forms of industrial action in pursuit of a wage demand or to remedy a grievance is regarded by many people (including trade unionists themselves) as a manifestation of Britain's so-called 'disease'. Certainly much of our media (particularly television and the popular tabloid newspapers) spotlight stoppages and often convey the impression that the country suffers from a peculiarly virulent form of labour militancy. 'For a number of years our industrial relations image has tended to create the impression that British industry is "riddled" with strikes', argued a 1978 study carried out by the Department of Employment.[1] 'We can ill afford an exaggerated industrial relations image which would tend to impede export orders and inhibit inward investment by contributing to decisions not to trade with or invest in the United Kingdom'. Industrial disruption is seen as 'bad news', ensuring lost production and the further impoverishment of society. Yet editorial denunciations about the strike-happy British worker remain no substitute for a careful and dispassionate scrutiny of the facts. Here, as in so many other areas of our industrial relations system, mythology tends to mask a much more complex reality.

By international comparative standards, Britain's strike record does not look especially terrible. The 1978 Department of Employment study found that the country was in sixth or seventh place in a stoppage league table covering fifteen leading western industrial nations for the 1966–75 period.

The figures compiled in Tables 6.1 and 6.2 for the nineteen seventies from the International Labour Organisation in Geneva does not suggest that Britain's position had deteriorated drastically over those years. Between 1975 and 1979 as many as seven countries suffered far worse industrial conflict than Britain did per thousand workers. No doubt, the

TABLE 6.1 Britain's strike problem: an international perspective–working days lost through industrial disputes per 1000 employees in selected industries (mining; manufacture; construction and transport)

| | *1970* | *1971* | *1972* | *1973* | *1974* | *1975* | *1976* | *1977* | *1978* | *1979* | *Average 1970–9* |
|---|---|---|---|---|---|---|---|---|---|---|---|
| Canada | 2 190 | 800 | 1 420 | 1 660 | 2 550 | 2 819 | 2 550 | 830 | 1 930 | 1 060 | 1 840 |
| Italy | 1 730 | 1 060 | 1 670 | 2 470 | 1 800 | 1 730 | 2 310 | 1 560 | 890 | 2 560 | 1 778 |
| Australia | 1 040 | 1 300 | 880 | 1 080 | 2 670 | 1 390 | 1 430 | 670 | 960 | 1 560 | 1 298 |
| United States | 2 210 | 1 600 | 860 | 750 | 1 480 | 990 | 1 190 | 1 070 | 1 070 | 890 | 1 211 |
| Irish Republic | 490 | 670 | 600 | 410 | 1 240 | 810 | 840 | 1 040 | 1 610 | 3 920 | 1 163 |
| United Kingdom | 740 | 1190 | 2 160 | 570 | 1 270 | 540 | 300 | 840 | 840 | 2 430 | 1 088 |
| France | 180 | 440 | 300 | 330 | 250 | 390 | 420 | 260 | 200 | 350 | 312 |
| Japan | 200 | 310 | 270 | 210 | 450 | 390 | 150 | 70 | 60 | 40 | 215 |
| West Germany | 10 | 340 | 10 | 40 | 60 | 10 | 40 | – | 370 | 40 | 92 |
| Sweden | 40 | 240 | 10 | 10 | 30 | 20 | 20 | 20 | 10 | 20 | 42 |

SOURCE *Employment Gazette*, January 1981, p. 28.

TABLE 6.2 Britain's strike record in the seventies

| | *Stoppages starting in the year* | *Workers involved in stoppages* | | *Stoppages in progress in year* | *Working days lost in stoppages in progress in year* |
|---|---|---|---|---|---|
| | | *directly* | *indirectly* | | |
| 1970 | 3 906 | 1 460 | 333 | 1 801 | 10 980 |
| 1971 | 2 228 | 863 | 308 | 1 178 | 13 551 |
| 1972 | 2 497 | 1 448 | 274 | 1 734 | 23 909 |
| 1973 | 2 873 | 1 103 | 410 | 1 528 | 7 197 |
| 1974 | 2 922 | 1 161 | 461 | 1 626 | 14 750 |
| 1975 | 2 282 | 570 | 219 | 809 | 6 012 |
| 1976 | 2 016 | 444 | 222 | 668 | 3 284 |
| 1977 | 2 703 | 785 | 370 | 1 166 | 10 142 |
| 1978 | 2 471 | 725 | 276 | 1 041 | 9 405 |
| 1979 | 2 080 | 4 121 | 463 | 4 608 | 29 474 |

SOURCE *Employment Gazette*, August 1980, p. 874.

arrival of democracy and the right to strike in Spain after 1976 helps to explain the upsurge of labour militancy in that country, but Italy, Canada, Australia, the Republic of Ireland and the United States all suffered far more disruption than the United Kingdom during the late seventies due to industrial stoppages. On the other hand, the British strike performance looks unimpressive, when it is set alongside the conflict figures for France, West Germany, indeed most other countries in continental western Europe.

But is like really being compared with like? Our official strike figures only include disputes that involve ten workers or more and last longer than one day unless the aggregate number of working days lost amount to 100 or more. The information is derived from reports to Unemployment Benefit offices, press reports, employer and union contacts, supplemented by returns from some nationalised industries. France, Italy and Belgium include all strikes no matter how many workers are involved or how long the conflict might last. While the French compile their statistics from the investigations of labour inspectors, the Italian provincial police send in reports on stoppages to the Central Institute of Statistics and the Belgians use their National Conciliation Service. Only in West Germany is there a legal obligation on employers to report disputes to the relevant authorities.[2] The official British strike statistics also do not include the impact of a dispute beyond the place were it takes place. Nor are disputes over political matters. For example, the 1980 stoppage figures do not include protests by aerospace workers against the denationalisation of their industry; the disruption caused by the TUC's day of action on May 14 and strikes by fishermen protesting about low fish prices. On the basis of the official statistics the Department of Employment study concluded that in an average year only 2 per cent of UK manufacturing plants which employ 20 per cent of manufacturing workers experience strikes long enough to be recorded. Less than 20 per cent of manufacturing workers are involved in strikes during the year. A mere five industries are responsible for a substantial part of the industrial disruption. Between them – coal, port and inland water transport, motor car production, shipbuilding, iron and steel – they accounted for more than a quarter of stoppages and a third of the lost working days between 1966 and 1976, although only 6 per cent of the labour force worked in those sectors.

At the time of the Donovan Royal Commission thirteen years ago the typical British strike was seen as an unofficial, short-lived disruption in manufacturing, which led to the lay-off of thousands although only a handful of workers were actually in direct conflict. During the seventies the nature of stoppages appeared to change (see Table 6.3), with more hitherto peaceful groups becoming involved in industrial conflict (for example the public services and white-collar groups). The national, big set piece strike became much more frequent.

It is true that large industrial strikes, which involve 200 000 or more lost working days remain relatively few in number in Britain.[3] Between 1960 and 1979 there were only 64 of them, but they did account for as many as 46 per cent of all lost working days during that period. In particular, they explain the sharp jump between the sixties and the

TABLE 6.3 Where the strikes broke out: working days lost due to stoppages in progress per 1000 workers

| | *1970* | *1971* | *1972* | *1973* | *1974* | *1975* | *1976* | *1977* | *1978* | *1979* |
|---|---|---|---|---|---|---|---|---|---|---|
| Motor vehicles | 2171 | 6 151 | 2 768 | 4 082 | 3 534 | 1 814 | 1 751 | 5 611 | 7 527 | 6 673 |
| All transport and communications | 835 | 4 170 | 568 | 218 | 469 | 278 | 90 | 204 | 245 | 984 |
| Mechanical engineering | 792 | 560 | 1 410 | 837 | 642 | 763 | 324 | 958 | 751 | 8 124 |
| Food, drink and tobacco | 564 | 214 | 328 | 154 | 753 | 219 | 134 | 1 140 | 958 | 1 190 |
| Textiles | 282 | 95 | 395 | 236 | 403 | 485 | 263 | 408 | 254 | 160 |
| Railways | 223 | 21 | 111 | 214 | 172 | 39 | 59 | 2 | 14 | 500 |
| Construction | 181 | 202 | 3 222 | 128 | 190 | 188 | 436 | 234 | 328 | 645 |
| Public utilities (gas, water and electricity) | 54 | 13 | 48 | 910 | 164 | 28 | 147 | 235 | 184 | 107 |
| Distribution | 15 | 13 | 3 | 7 | 41 | 24 | 5 | 34 | 23 | 27 |

SOURCE *Employment Gazette*, February 1980.

seventies in the total working days lost from strikes that rose from an average of 3.6 million a year to 12.9 million. During the sixties Britain suffered from around two big strikes a year averaging 1.1 million lost working days, but during the next decade the number rose on average to four to five a year and accounted for 6.5 million working days lost annualy.

The Department of Employment has revealed that as many as two thirds of the big disputes and 80 per cent of the working days lost by those stoppages occur in only four broad industrial sectors – mining, engineering and shipbuilding, transport and communications, and vehicles manufacturing. These figures can give a distorted impression. It needs to be remembered that as many as 16 million of the 24 million working days lost in the engineering industry in 1979 occurred in the national dispute over hours. The big strikes tend to be longer than those stoppages involving fewer workers directly. The average length of the 64 large strikes during the past twenty years was nearly nine weeks or 45 days. This compares with an average of 6.1 days for all other UK strikes over the period. As many as 42 per cent of the major stoppages lasted between five and ten weeks and a further 47 per cent were less than five or from 10 to 15 weeks.

Over the 1966–73 period it was found that 85 per cent of recorded strikes involved only manual workers, but this proportion declined during the period from 87 per cent between 1966 and 1970 and 82 per cent for the early seventies. But this is not particularly significant, because of the decline in the size of the manual labour force during those years. Indeed, there was an increased strike frequency among manual workers in the late sixties and early seventies. But more white-collar staff were also ready to take strike action than in the past. Manual disputes tend to be unofficial and involve a substantial number of workers being laid off who are not directly involved in the strike. In 1973 as many as 33 per cent of manual workers were laid off because of industrial disruption, while the remaining 67 per cent were direcly involved in the strikes. This compares with a mere 8 per cent of the non-manuals who were laid off in a dispute not of their direct concern. Dockers and stevedores were the most strike prone occupational group of workers in the late sixties and early seventies, followed by drivers, fitters and labourers. But there was much less industrial conflict in dockland during the late seventies. The researchers at the Department of Employment found that stoppage frequency was 'positively related to the proportion of male workers, the proportion of employees covered by collective agreements and the proportion of short service employees'.[4]

A clear correlation also exists between plant size and the incidence of industrial stoppages (see Table 6.4). The 1978 Department of Employment study concluded that

> both industries and regions which have relatively high average plant size tend to experience relatively high rates of strike incidence and relatively high rates of strike frequency as well. This does not mean that strikes are inevitable in United Kingdom plants over a certain

TABLE 6.4 Big is strike-prone, 1971–5: percentage of establishments and of employment in establishments that were not affected by stoppages (manufacturing industry) 1971–3 UK

| *Establishments not affected by stoppages* | *1971* | *1972* | *1973* | *1971–3* | *1974* | *1975* |
|---|---|---|---|---|---|---|
| | 98.1 | 97.5 | 97.7 | 97.8 | 97.2 | 98.1 |
| *Employment in unaffected establishments by plant size* | *1971* | *1972* | *1973* | *1971–3* | *1974* | *1975* |
| 11–24 employees | 99.9 | 99.8 | 99.9 | 99.9 | 99.5 | 99.7 |
| 25–99 employees | 99.0 | 98.9 | 98.9 | 98.9 | | |
| 100–199 employees | 97.3 | 96.3 | 96.7 | 96.7 | 96.2 | 97.6 |
| 200–499 employees | 94.8 | 92.0 | 92.5 | 93.1 | 92.6 | 94.6 |
| 500–999 employees | 86.5 | 82.1 | 82.4 | 83.7 | 79.6 | 87.1 |
| 1000 or more employees | 59.7 | 54.1 | 54.4 | 56.1 | 59.3 | 69.7 |
| All establishments | 83.1 | 80.0 | 80.3 | 81.1 | – | – |

SOURCES 'Strikes in Britain', HMSO, 1978, p. 55, and *Department of Employment Gazette*, January 1978, p. 9.

size; indeed, a number of large strike-free plants exist. But serious loss of time through strikes becomes much more likely as plant size increases.[5]

During the 1971–3 period a quarter of one per cent of all manufacturing plants employing 11 workers or more (only 150) accounted for two thirds of all days lost in recorded strikes.

The official figures of strikers help to convey a misleading picture, if they suggest grounds for complacency. The Warwick University industrial relations research unit discovered much wider disruption occurred in manufacturing plants than showed up in the statistics.[6] Their study revealed that in 1976–7 (years of relative industrial peace) as many as 45.7 per cent of manual workers and 9.4 per cent of non-manual workers had taken some form of industrial action such as work to rules, overtime bans, go slows or work ins (32.8 per cent of manual workers had taken part in a strike). A total of 71 per cent of manual workers in the motor car industry had been involved in industrial action, but only 65.3 per cent of them had been in any strike. The Warwick study estimates that the official statistics of stoppages record only 62 per cent of eligible strikes but 96 per cent of working days lost, so the under-recording may not be so serious a problem.

BL's own strike statistics, for example, suggest that the vast majority of small short-lived stoppages simply fail to show up in the official figures (see Table 6.5), even if they do not constitute the main headache for the company. Without the 1979 national engineering strike, which

TABLE 6.5 BL disputes

| | *1977* | *1978* | *1979* | *1980* |
|---|---|---|---|---|
| Man-hours lost through disputes (millions) | | | | |
| internal | 14.8 | 10.0 | 13.5 | 3.5 |
| external | 12.2 | 0.5 | 1.3 | – |
| total | 27.0 | 10.5 | 14.8 | 3.5 |
| Man-hours lost as a percentage of available time (%) | 5.9 | 3.5 | 5.1 | 1.4 |
| Vehicles lost through strikes (000) | | | | |
| internal | 192.9 | 117.9 | 113.0 | 48.7 |
| external | 58.6 | 13.4 | 10.8 | 0.7 |
| Stoppages of one hour or more | 582 | 584 | 548 | 252 |

SOURCE 'Finance for BL', Commons Industry and Trade Committee report, HMSO, April 1981, p. 28.

had nothing uniquely to do with the company, only 2.1 per cent of available time (6.1 million man-hours) would have been lost because of industrial conflict. It is perhaps not surprising that BL decided to leave the Engineering Employers Federation shortly after that shattering experience.

There can be no denying there was a significant upturn in industrial militancy in the late sixties and early seventies, As Tim Sweet and Dudley Jackson have observed: 'During the 1950s and for most of the 1960s, the average number of working days lost through disputes in the industrial sector per 1000 workers moved up and down between 300 and 400 days lost a year. But in 1969 the average of working days lost rose to 752 per 1000 workers. After falling slighlty in 1970 and 1972 the average rose to an incredible peak of 932 working days lost per 1000 workers in 1973'.[7] Indeed, between 1969 and 1975 the strike wave in the western industrialised world brought the loss of an annual average total of 100.8 million working days in all countries put together, almost double the annual average for the 1953–68 period.

## WHY STRIKES?

What were the reasons for the growth of industrial conflict over the past twenty-five years? Many commentators have drawn some comfort from the labour militancy. Cronin, for example, sees 'the persistent function' of the strike as 'the fundamental statement of the humanity and intelligence of the working class',[8] while Barkin discovered a 'humanistic Socialism' in the resurgence of conflict in the late sixties and early seventies.[9] A symposium organised under the auspices of the Ford Foundation tended to suggest that the phenomenon marked a clear break with the labour consensus and apathy of the post-war era, promising the return of a more aggressive class conflict in 'late' capitalism.[10] Ernest Mandel, one of the more perceptive of Marxist economists, believed he could see a refreshing new dimension to the militancy. 'The emphasis of class struggle increasingly shifts from the issue of the division of the values newly created by labour between wages and surplus value, to the issue of the right of control over machines and labour power', he asserted. 'The number of immediate labour disputes detonated by revolts against the structure of the enterprise is constantly growing; workers today are increasingly rejecting the right of employers to reduce the number of employees, to shift machines and orders, to set the rythmn of the assembly belt, to alter the organisation of labour, to revise the system of wage payment, to widen the span between the highest and the lowest (or average) earnings in the factory or to close factories'.[11] Italy's long hot autumn in 1969, the events of May 1968 in France and a sudden, unexpected outbreak of unofficial shop-floor strikes in that haven of industrial peace – West Germany in 1969 – all seemed to herald a more militant age, full of revolutionary potential.

A shop-floor revolt against the speed of the assembly line in January 1972 at the General Motors plant in Lordstown, Ohio, appeared to show that the new spirit of labour militancy had actually crossed the Atlantic to reach the politically quiescent American working class. The great British strike wave of 1968–72 was even given an ideological dimension by some observers. 'Strikes about wages are becoming equally political', argued Glyn and Sutcliffe. 'Given that the Tory government's wages policy is part of a programme to rescue British capitalism, a strike against that wages policy is a strike against capitalism, and hence is really political'.[12]

It is certainly true that Britain's overall strike statistics tend to depoliticise industrial militancy, because no figures are given for what constitutes a 'political' strike. Yet we have seen a number of stoppages since 1969 that have been sparked off by trade union action against the government of the day. On 1 May 1969 an estimated quarter of a million workers struck in protest at 'In Place of Strife'. In 1971 and 1972 there were nation-wide strikes, mainly against the Industrial Relations Act. On 1 March and 12 March 1971 as many as one and a half million are believed to have struck for the day, following an official call from the Amalgamated Union of Engineering Workers. On 1 May 1973 two million went on strike for the day against the Conservative pay policy and the decisions of the National Industrial Relations Court, while on 8 May 1974 half a million struck, again mainly from the AUEW, in protest at the seizure of trade union funds because of the refusal of the AUEW to honour the court in a case coverning Con Mech, a small Surrey engineering firm. More recently, on 14 May 1979 the TUC itself called a one-day strike against the government when around half a million workers joined in.

A major explanation for the greater instability of the industrial relations system both in Britain and elsewhere in the western world during the late sixties and seventies, at least up until the severe impact of the economic recession, lies in the reaction of workers to the phenomenon of inflation and rising taxation. Soskice has argued that frustrations built up among workers, because of a slowing down in the rate of increase in money wages; a squeeze on pay differentials between skilled and semi-skilled workers; and changes in the ownership of production because of rationalisation and/or increased workloads.[13] It was the response of governments to temper the post-war boom through deflation of demand and wages policies combined with employer offensives that detonated an upsurge in industrial militancy.

For their part, Sweet and Jackson point out that in 11 out of the 15 western industrialised countries which experienced a strike wave between 1969 and 1975 the upsurge in labour militancy preceded the upturn in price inflation. Turner and his colleagues found the explanation for the explosion of industrial conflict in Britain during the period in the 'combined effect of inflation and increased wage taxation' which brought an 'increasing distortion of perceived differentials between wage-earners' living standards so that many workers were also involved in attempts to restore their relative position'. Such explanations look far away from the rather romanticised view that workers were striking here or in western Europe for wider aims beyond the pay packet. Shalev in a study of 11 countries for the Organisation for Economic Co-operation and Development concluded that while disputes over the social and physical working environment had become more common in the late sixties[14] 'in hardly any instance' had 'their rate of increase exceeded the rise in the frequency of strikes revolving round more conventional issues'.

Indeed, the evidence suggests Britain experienced fewer strikes about non-money issues than in the past during the period. 'Pay' was found to be the dominant reason for striking in the seventies. As many as 82.3 per cent of the working days lost because of disputes between 1965 and 1974 were due to conflicts over wages. This compared with 70.9 per cent in the 1955–64 period and 49.7 per cent during 1945–54. A larger proportion of the number of stoppages were also caused by differences over pay during the 1965–74 period (56.1 per cent) than at any other time-span since 1915–24. Of all the strikes in Britain between 1966 and 1976, 38.5 per cent were concerned with 'straight pay rises', accounting for 69.4 per cent of working days lost, followed by 11.3 per cent over reductions in earnings (5.4 per cent working days lost) and 9.4 per cent over the operation of wages systems (4.4 per cent working days lost) and 7.1 per cent concerned with pay differentials (4.9 per cent working days lost).

The two main non-pay issues that provoke contemporary strikes are dismissal and other disciplinary problems and manning levels. Together they explain nearly a quarter of stoppages, though accounting for only 9 per cent of working days lost. Despite the publicity attached to inter-union disputes and conflicts over demarcation they are less frequent than you might suppose. While disputes between unions were responsible for 9.5 per cent of the non-pay strikes, demarcation accounted for no more than 1 per cent of all stoppages in 1965–74. The closed shop provoked less than one per cent of disputes. Around a third of those strikes involving trade union matters concerned the status of worker representatives, many of these involving the dismissal of a shop steward.

The picture looked no different in the late seventies during the upsurge of labour militancy that helped to humiliate the Labour government. In 1979 as many as 3 804 700 of the 4 120 800 workers involved in strikes were fighting over pay issues, compared with 117 200 who struck about dismissal and other disciplinary measures; 71 200 on trade union matters; 50 300 over redundancies; 44 700 over manning and work allocation; 25 700 on working conditions and supervision; and 6900 over working hours. This was the worst year for strikes in Britain since the early twenties, with nearly 29.5 million working days lost as a result. There were 2045 separate stoppages in a wide range of industries.

It was hard to discover any political perspective in the huge explosion. This was not due to any sudden outburst of class war or solidarity between workers. The bitterness and frustration of car workers, lorry drivers, low paid public service workers and the rest arose from an acquistive desire for 'more money now' after three years of voluntary wage restraint. The strikers were not attacking the power of the employers. Nor were wider issues of work control being raised in the stoppages. The self-regarding sectionalism of the industrial actions was clear enough. This was no heroic struggle of the forces of downtrodden labour against overmighty capital. Indeed, often the main thrust of the militant activity was aimed at other workers and the community as a whole, not the rich and the powerful. Those who suffered from the siege of schools, hospitals and graveyards in the low pay dispute of January–February 1979 were children, the old, the sick and the bereaved.

As Hobsbawm observed – some months before those terrible events that inflicted severe moral damage on the trade union movement –

> We now see a growing division of workers into sections and groups, each pursuing its own economic interest irrespective of the rest. What is new here is that their ability to do so is no longer related to traditional criteria such as their technical qualifications and standing on, as it were, the social ladder. In fact it now often happensn not only (as sometimes occurred even a hundred years ago) that groups of workers strike, not minding the effect on the rest – skilled men on

> labourers, for example – but in the inconvenience they can cause to the public.[15]

In Hobsbawm's view 'this is a natural consequence of a state monopoly capitalist system in which the basic target of pressure is not the bank account of private employers but, directly or indirectly, the political will of the government'. But the strikes of the seventies were about economism, not changing the world or making Britain a more humane and just society.

Indeed, the strike is rarely so straightforward nowadays as a 'supreme example of working class solidarity'. In Kahn-Freund's words, it has become 'dialectically transmuted into its opposite; action of groups of workers seeking advantages at the expense of others'.[16] Increasingly, the consumer has replaced the employer as the primary target for disruption, even though the consumer is invariably a fellow trade unionist. Both the expansion of employment in public services during the past twenty-five years and the growth of trade unionism among white-collar workers have accentuated the problem. Inflation has helped to remove some of the traditional inhibitions, the sense of public obligation, that used to hold back many public service workers from taking disruptive action at the expense of the people they were paid to care for. The creation of enormous bureaucracies in the public services has added to a widening sense of frustration and helplessness among many workers, who fear their viewpoint can only achieve recognition through militant behaviour. The new generation of young workers coming into the public services are less reverential of authority, more impatient with stuffy rules and procedures and unlikely to practice collective self-restraint for any supposed national interest. At the same time there has been a greater subdivision of labour and a growing interdependence in the administration of the public services. The installation of computers have provided wider opportunities for small handfuls of workers to wreak maximum havoc. As a result there is a new awareness among thousands of the collective power they possess to paralyse society by hitting its most vulnerable members – the sick, old, the poor.

When air traffic controllers disrupt holiday plans for the consumer by causing chaos at airports the main victims are the community and not the employer. By turning the screw on the general public, service workers hope to compel their employer to back down and give in to their strike demands. This is no longer a classic struggle between organised labour and capital but part of an internecine war within the working class itself. Striking has become a dangerous zero-sum game in the monopoly public services, for which nobody has found a satisfactory answer. The position is even more difficult when it involves workers in the monopoly public utilities – water, gas and electricity. During the past decade all three groups have become much more conscious of their collective muscle power to maximise their demands against the community as a whole and they are now quite ready to use disruptive tactics when they believe it necessary to achieve their aim of fatter wage packets. Such self-regarding sectionalism helps successfully to insulate a large number of key groups of workers in the core of the labour market from the harsh realities of the recession.

'The strike weapon has had a serious impact on the nationalised industries', confessed Sir William Barlow, former chairman of the Post Office in a lecture to the Royal Institute of Public Administration (26 January 1981).

> When management of a nationalised industry decide to withstand a strike they are at first supported if they are seen to be resisting unreasonable demands but within a very short time complaints about lack of service become strident and the management is then criticised for allowing the strike to develop in the first place. In any case, the damage done to the economy is clear to management and is a limiting feature on their conduct of the dispute if it is in a monopoly situation.

During the late seventies the men of muscle were able to ensure that their annual wage increases kept well ahead of the inflation rate. The mere threat of disruption tended to concentrate 'official' minds. In the 1980–1 wage season the public monopoly utility workers and the miners enjoyed rises which were twice as high as the figure the government sought to establish in its cash limits incomes policy for the public services. Such money improvements had nothing to do with genuine productivity increases (except partly for the miners) but they were the price the government believed it had to pay in order to ensure industrial peace. But the result was an attempt to tighten up on other areas of public sector expenditure, with resulting unemployment, and low wage settlements for more disadvantaged groups in the labour market. It is very hard in any sense to interpret such exactions under the threat of strikes as demonstrative of working class solidarity.

## THE CONDUCT OF STRIKES

Responsible union leaders are well aware of the frightening ability of some work groups to bring society to a stand still. The TUC recognised the difficulties in its voluntary code of conduct published early in 1979. Its TUC advice was sensible, clear and forthright. The code suggested that strikes should only be 'a measure of the last resort, one which should be used responsibly'.[17] The document continued: 'Industrial action causes interruptions to production or to the provision of services. It has to be recognised that these can damage the ability of the employing establishment to provide subsequent growth in earnings and to maintain employment. More immediately industrial action, particularly strikes, cause loss of earnings and a sharp drop in workers' living standards.' And it added: 'Regard needs to be paid to the effects of the action on other workers, the movement generally and the community at large'. Although the TUC code accepted that these were not sufficient reasons to avoid industrial disruption when necessary, it did argue that acts of labour militancy should not be undertaken unless there was both 'care' and 'regard' for other factors. It was not good enough to cause disruption 'simply on an immediate issue about which there are strong feelings'.

The TUC suggested that unions ought to hold secret ballots before calling strikes, with a 'strictly defined procedure' for their conduct, with 'sanctions for any breach of such procedure'. It also recommended that unions should protect 'emergency or essential services' and maintain plant and equipment during a dispute. As the code advised: unions should, 'where necessary, make arrangements in advance and with due notice, in consultation and preferably in agreement with the employer, for the maintenance by their members of supplies and services essential to the health or safety of the community or otherwise required to avoid causing exceptional hardship or serious pollution'.

Some of the most enlightening words in the TUC code concerned the use of picketing in strikes. It suggested that 'unions should in general, and save in exceptional circumstances, confine picketing to the premises of the parties to the dispute or the premises of suppliers and customers of those parties'. The TUC pointed out that there is in fact no 'legal right to picket as such', but it is lawful for workers 'in contemplation and furtherance of a trade dispute' to picket 'at or near a workplace or any other place (except a person's home) providing they do no more than peacefully obtain or communicate information or peacefully persuade workers to abstain from work'. The 1980 Employment Act has made some fundamental changes in the picketing laws, so that workers can only picket 'at or near' their own place of work, but they may pursue secondary action such as blacking of the employer's supplies to his first supplier and customer. Yet Jim Prior's picketing code bears close resemblance to the commonsense advice contained in the TUC's own manual, which was particularly concerned to ensure authorised pickets were clearly identified with armbands or badges and exercised a disciplined control over what occurred on the picket line. Although the TUC did not suggest that there should be a clear limit on the number of people on a picket line, its code pointed out that the larger the size of the picket presence, the more difficult it would be to ensure they picketed and did not obstruct. Again, the TUC code put it well:

> The effect of a large body of trade unionists outside a workplace demonstrates the depth of feeling that exists among the strikers and also may constitute an effective appeal for solidarity. However, the police may regard a large body of workers as obstructing entry to premises or as intimidation towards those who wish to enter. In any situation where large numbers of people with strong feelings are involved, there is a danger that things can get out of control particularly in a confined area such as access to a factory. It is therefore particularly important for any such demonstrations to be conducted in a well-organised and disciplined manner. It is also important that demonstrations of this kind do not convey the impression that the object is to blockade a workplace.

Under the pressure of events in 1979 the TUC gave belated recognition to the importance of constructing a civilised but effective code of conduct for industrial disputes. But there were precious few signs that affiliate unions bothered to take much notice of the movement's own code. With a return of a Conservative government in May 1979 and the passage of the 1980 Employment Act, which has come under bitter attack from the TUC, the substance of the TUC's own advice was either conveniently overlooked or forgotten. No doubt, it is seldom easy to keep tempers down in strikes or to exercise restraint among workers who wish to see their disruptive action bring quick results. Any self-denying ordinance that weakens the effectiveness of a strike is always going to be hard to enforce. What sounds sensible and practical in Congress House may look rather different down on the ground in the messy, unpredictable realities of an industrial conflict. As so often, the work group determines the character of the militancy and not the trade union to which they belong.

## THE COST OF STRIKES

Workers do not strike for fun. They withdraw their labour through a sense of collective grievance, a belief that they can achieve their usually limited aims more quicly by a short, sharp stoppage than painstaking negotiations. Often workers have been provoked into action by their employer, who tends to set the climate of industrial relations at the workplace. Yet there is a widely held belief that people who strike do not suffer any real financial hardship for doing so.

A striker can expect to bring together financial aid from a variety of sources. Back pay from the employer is often helpful. Manual workers usually have one week's pay packet in hand and many employers agree to pay out the full arrears due to an employee on the first Friday pay day after the start of the strike. Then there are tax rebates to be paid, although these are not begun until the end of the second week of a strike. Strike pay from the union is not often paid out because most strikes are never made official. In the 1970–5 period only 5.5 per cent of all stoppages were recognised as such by the unions, while from 1976–80 the proportion was only 4.2 per cent. Very few unions have specific strike funds. In 1978 the average amount of dispute benefit per member added up to the princely sum of 70 pence under 2 per cent of their income.

Many wives of strikers are also likely to go to work and their earnings can help to cushion the setback of a dispute, though more women tend to work part-time so that the sums of money involved are unlikely to be very substantial. Many strikers and their families survive to a limited extent to extended credit facilities during the period of the dispute. Local councils are likely to be willing to remit rents of strikers homes during a dispute, on the condition that the accumulated arrears are settled with the return to work. Private landlords are usually ready to act in the same way. A similar flexibility can also be expected for charges on water, gas, electricity and telephone. Rate deferrals are accepted by councils as well. It is often forgotten that hire purchase firms need to obtain a court order before they can repossess goods on which there are arrears in payments, and they are almost always ready to offer bridging concessions rather than seek a form of legal redress against a striker, particularly if he or she has not proved to be a difficult customer in the past. Many strikers are ready to borrow money from their relatives or friends to see them through the dispute. Banks are also usually willing to help out for high paid workers, though most manual workers do not have bank accounts. The payment of social security benefits to the dependants of strikers has aroused considerable anger among many Conservatives, but it is nothing new. The practice first began under the Poor Law towards the end of the last century and it was confirmed by a test case in the High Court as long ago as 1900. The general picture does not give substance to the widely held view that strikers can draw substantial benefits for their families. As the 1979 annual report of the Supplementary Benefits Commission argued:

> Over 80 per cent of strikes last less than a fortnight, and because final earnings are regarded as covering an equivalent period at the start of a strike, benefit seldom becomes payable. In those strikes which last long enough for benefit to begin, the proportion of strikers claiming is never more than 50 per cent and is usually much less. At the height of the 13 week steel workers' strike in the early part of 1980, for example, the proportion claiming was 30 per cent.[18]

The commission was quite clear that any blanket restriction on payment of benefit to strikers families would involve considerable suffering for those on low incomes. As the commission pointed out: 'To remove the capacity to protect them (strikers' families) would be a break in the long-standing tradition of social assistance in this country to meet pressing need, regardless of cause, and without forming judgements about the merits of the individual case. Most western European countries find it impracticable to exclude the families of strikers entirely from social assistance'.

The figures in Table 6.6 belie the popular view that the benefits system encourages industrial militancy. In their study of strikes during the sixties Durcan and McCarthy concluded that: 'less than 2.4 per cent of strikers received any form of supplementary benefit in any one year' and they added: 'The overwhelming majority of strikers involved in both long and short strikes suffered substantial monetary loss – some 80 per cent or more of normal earnings. Because of this fact and because the incidence of state subsidy was so unevenly spread within the average group of strikers, we suggest that it is implausible to believe that state payments can have been regarded as much more than gratuitous windfalls.'[19] While they recognised some workers might have calculated that they would qualify for some benefits, few have realised that the real value of those benefits had been rising 'to the great majority the prospect or receipt of state payments was not sufficiently stable, or at high enough a level, to operate as a decisive factor'. Developments during the seventies may have added to the passion and ignorance of the public debate on this controversial issue, but they did nothing to detract from the force of that earlier conclusion.

TABLE 6.6 Benefits for strikers' families since 1975

| | *Number of claims to supplementary benefit* | *Number of people involved in trade disputes* | *Those involved in disputes and receiving supplementary benefit* | | |
|---|---|---|---|---|---|
| | | | *With dependants* | *Without dependants* | *Expenditure (£m)* |
| 1975 | 5 200 000 | 800 000 | 26 000 | 200 | 0.8 |
| 1976 | 5 700 000 | 700 000 | 10 000 | 100 | 0.4 |
| 1977 | 5 700 000 | 1 100 000 | 54 000 | 400 | 2.5 |
| 1978 | 5 600 000 | 1 000 000 | 45 000 | 200 | 3.3 |
| 1979 | 5 200 000 | 4 400 000 | 50 000 | 300 | 2.5 |

SOURCE *Supplementary Benefits Commission Annual Report, 1979*, p. 95.

Yet in their May 1979 general election manifesto the Conservatives promised that they would review the position of the financial treatment of workers, in order to 'ensure that unions bear their fair share of the cost of supporting those of their members who are on strike'. After initial hesitation, the government decided to calculate that a striker would be deemed to have received £12 a week in strike benefit from his union, so that the sum would be deducted from the welfare benefits to which his family was entitled. Ministers also agreed to move against the instant tax rebate to a striker. But whether such steps would make any real difference to the propensity for workers to take industrial action is highly debatable. Such modest steps are more likely to enflame than coerce workers. In practice they look an irrelevance, because it is not often clear that aggrieved and angry workers make any hard-headed cash calculation before going on strike.

There is little doubt that most strikes mean belt-tightening for the vast majority of workers. A striker is estimated to suffer a loss of between a quarter and a half of what he normally earns. The longer the dispute continues, the more losses the worker will suffer and therefore the bigger the wage increase necessary in the final settlement in order to make the whole disruption worthwhile financially. Of course, workers rarely sit down and work out in a dispassionate way the arithmetic of striking. The emotions, the feelings of anger and frustration combined with a sense of comradeship in common adversity with the other workers in dispute count for far more.

But strikers ought also to be aware of the balance of risks involved before they withdraw their labour. Gennard estimated that the average net loss of the Chrysler electricians who struck in 1973 amounted to £292, while the striking postmen in 1971 lost £73 net.[20] It is quite true that victories in some disputes can produce massive rises, and a change in the balance of power and climate of bargaining in an industry will often determine the outlook for pay for a number of years. The recent classic example of this is the miners who struck in 1972 and 1974 and moved as a consequence to the head of the manual earnings league table, where they have remained ever since, the one outstanding group to have improved their relative position during the seventies. Moreover, many manual workers are able to recoup money losses during a dispute by working more overtime when they go back to work. These incalculables must be thrown onto the strikers' balance sheet of profit and loss. But the losses calculated by Gennard, on the basis of the additional earnings accruing to the workers between the end of their strike and their next pay settlement cannot be easily dismissed as atypical. An internal study carried out by the Department of Employment confirms the point. An analysis of the nine-week long 1971 Ford strike discovered that workers lost earnings of £235 for an unskilled manual worker to £264 for a similar worker with four year's experience. The period needed to recoup lossed earnings during the strike was as long as a year and seven months for an ordinary grade C manual worker and two years two months for his colleague with four years service. In the 1978 nine-week Ford strike the production worker lost £635 as a result. The final pay settlement meant that he needed a year and a month to recoup the lost earnings. The firemen during their 1977–8 dispute lost money which required eight months to make up.

Yet perhaps far too much 'official' attention is being misdirected to this issue. It is worth remembering for what a short length of time most strikes actually last. In 1979, for example, 32.1 per cent were over within two days, while only just over a quarter lasted longer than 10 working days. We must not be misled by the more spectacular disputes that hit the headlines into assuming that most workers are involved in marathon conflicts.

## STRIKES IN THE SLUMP

An economic slump is hardly the best moment for any major worker offensive. There has been a dramatic decline in strike activity in Britain, as the statistics in Table 6.7 reveal.

In 1980 there were the lowest number of strikes since 1941 and less than half the annual average for the previous decade, but with a total of 11 910 000 lost working days, the highest number (excepting 1979) for

TABLE 6.7 Strikes and the depression, January 1980 – December 1981

| | *Number –* | *– of which known official* | *No. of workers involved* | *Working days lost* |
|---|---|---|---|---|
| *1980* | | | | |
| January | 155 | 10 | 227 000 | 2 774 000 |
| February | 117 | 7 | 42 000 | 3 250 000 |
| March | 149 | 12 | 79 000 | 3 260 000 |
| April | 156 | 10 | 139 000 | 960 000 |
| May | 128 | 5 | 70 000 | 457 000 |
| June | 136 | 10 | 44 000 | 319 000 |
| July | 67 | 3 | 35 000 | 680 000 |
| August | 63 | 4 | 17 000 | 118 000 |
| September | 99 | 11 | 31 000 | 206 000 |
| October | 99 | 8 | 29 000 | 191 000 |
| November | 73 | 10 | 56 000 | 165 000 |
| December | 20 | 2 | 16 000 | 42 000 |
| *1981* | | | | |
| January | 119 | | 71 000 | 237 000 |
| February | 97 | | 76 000 | 437 000 |
| March | 114 | | 458 000 | 599 000 |
| April | 130 | | 328 000 | 375 000 |
| May | 93 | | 62 000 | 375 000 |
| June | 108 | | 50 000 | 353 000 |
| July | 74 | | 38 000 | 300 000 |
| August | 69 | | 21 000 | 107 000 |
| September | 116 | | 80 000 | 161 000 |
| October | 127 | | 46 000 | 330 000 |
| November | 113 | | 134 000 | 493 000 |
| December | 54 | | 43 000 | 172 000 |

SOURCE *Employment Gazette*, April 1982, p. 4.2.

any year since 1974. As many as 8 954 000 of the lost working days were in the metal manufacture sector, due almost entirely to the bitter and protracted national steel strike, but a former trouble-spot like motor car manufacture was almost a haven of peace (427 000 lost days compared with 3 071 000 in the previous year). Indeed, the steel strike gives a rather distorted picture of stoppage activity in 1980, accounting for 74 per cent of all the lost working days in the year.

The sudden arrival of relative industrial peace in 1980–2 should give no body the mistaken belief that a new sense of 'realism' entered our industrial relations system. It was far more due to the fear of losing one's job than a recognition of the wisdom of the government's efforts at pay restraint through cash limits. In any economic upturn, however modest it might be, we can expect an upsurge of militancy on the shop-floor to restore lost ground. Workers did not resist (at least not in important enough numbers) the cascade of plant closures and redundancies that hit the labour market with furious rapidity from early in 1980 onwards. Union negotiators found themselves in the invidious position of having to bargain in high redundancy terms under rank and file pressure for their members rather than mobilising them for a rearguard action to protect their jobs through factory sit-ins and the like. But the fundamental weaknesses in our pay bargaining system remain and the frustrations and resentments, which are never far from at least some group of workers at any one time, will accumulate. The 1980 and 1982 Employment Acts are unlikely to make much difference in preventing any future wages explosion.

The right to strike remains a fundamental freedom in any democratic society. Workers in Poland and South Africa have demonstrated recently how powerful the strike weapon can be in any confrontation with a political tyranny. Yet there are severe limitations to the potentiality of such displays of collective worker solidarity in Britain. To a large extent, most of our strikes mirror a self-regarding sectionalism, with narrow aims, offering no direct challenge to the existing economic and social system. While more and more workers during the seventies were ready to strike for their demands, particularly among white-collar groups and in the public services, this has done little (if anything) to highten their own critical awareness about the realities of power in our unequal and divided society. Strikes might thrill revolutionary Socialists and incense established authority, but these are ephemeral, limited actions, conditioned by time, circumstance, and the amount of muscle workers can use to get what they want. Once a dispute is settled, workers go back to their jobs with a rare questioning of the pattern of authority that remains intact at the workplace.

For the moment, the balance of power has shifted in industry from the workgroups to the management. The slump has enabled employers to recoup former controls and take back other worker gains made during the years of affluence. We have sullen acquiescence, fear and bewilderment among workers, but no stable system of industrial relations in Britain can be established on the basis of suspicion and mistrust.

## NOTES AND REFERENCES

1 C. T. B. Smith, R. Clifton, P. Makeham, S. W. Creigh, and R. V. Burn 'Strikes in Britain', HMSO, 1978, p. 87.

2 S. Creigh, N. Donaldson and E. Hawthorn, 'Stoppage Activity in OECD countries' *Employment Gazette*, November 1980, pp. 1174–80.

3 'Large industrial disputes 1960–1979', *Employment Gazette*, September 1980, pp. 994–9.

4 Department of Employment, HMSO, 1978, p. 36.

5 *Strikes in Britain* op. cit., pp. 60–2.

6 *The Changing Contours of British Industrial Relations*, ed. W. Brown (Basil Blackwell, 1981) pp. 80–101.

7 T. Sweet and D. Jackson, 'Le Disease Anglo-Saxon', *New Society*, 9 June 1977, p. 510.

8 J. E. Cronin, *Industrial Conflict in Modern Britain* (Croom Helm, 1979) p. 195.

9 *Worker Militancy and Its Consequences 1965–1975*, ed. Solomon Barkin (Praeger Publishers, 1976) p. 365.

10 *The Resurgence of Class Conflict in Western Europe since 1968*, two volumes, ed. C. Crouch and A. Pizzorno, (Macmillan, 1978) pp. 571–2.

11 E. Mandel, *Late Capitalism* (New Left Books, 1975).

12 A. Glyn and R. Sutcliffe, *British Capitalism, Workers and the Profits Squeeze* (Penguin, 1972) pp. 21–2.

13 *Resurgence of Class Conflict*, Vol. 2, ibid., p. 245.

14 ibid., Vol 1 p. 10.

15 E. Hobsbawm, *The Onward March of Labour Halted?*, (New Left Books, 1981) p. 14.

16 O. Kahn-Freund, *Labour Relations: Heritage and Adjustment* (Oxford, 1979) p. 78.

17 'TUC codes of conduct', 1979, p. 14.

18 'Supplementary Benefits Commission annual report 1979', HMSO, p. 44.

19 J. W. Durcan and W. E. J. McCarthy, 'The State Subsidy Theory of Strikes: An examination of statistical data for the period 1956–1970', *British Journal of Industrial Relations*, March 1974, p. 43.

20 J. Gennard, *Financing Strikers* (Macmillan, 1977) and his article with R. Lasko, 'Supplementary Benefit and Strikers', *British Journal of Industrial Relations*, March 1974.

# 7 The Myths of Trade Union Power

There is a widespread belief in Britain that the trade unions are overmighty subjects with enormous power and privileges that they use irresponsibly. In a poll carried out by Market Opinion and Research International in August 1977 as many as 79 per cent of the sample agreed that the unions had too much power (54 per cent thought so 'strongly' and the others 'tended' to agree). Three years later (July 1980) the same survey organisation found there had been a drop in the proportion who thought the unions were too powerful. Now 72 per cent of the sample believed this (42 per cent thought so 'strongly' and 30 per cent said they tended to agree). No doubt, the change of government in May 1979 and the loss of direct influence by the TUC on Mrs Thatcher's Downing Street, and the retirement of major union leaders – Jack Jones of the Transport and General Workers and Hugh Scanlon of the Engineering Workers – must account for this small decline. Maybe the deepening recession began to make people aware that the unions had no power to ensure job security or determine overall economic policy.

Those poll figures mirror a common assumption, one that is even shared by large numbers of workers who are actually trade union members. In 1977 the MORI survey discovered that as many as 68 per cent of trade unionists thought the organisations to which they belonged enjoyed too much power, with 41 per cent 'strongly' agreeing with that belief. Three years the proportion, who still believed in the power of the unions, had fallen to 58 per cent (28 per cent only saying they 'strongly' agreed) but even at that time more than half continued to see the unions as powerful organisations.

These poll findings suggest that the unions remained unpopular institutions, even with many of their own members. In August 1977, 66 per cent of the MORI sample thought that 'most trade unions are controlled by a few extremists and militants' (58 per cent of the trade union rank and file agreed with that statement), while three years later as many as 70 per cent of the sample supported that view, with 55 per cent of trade unionists doing so. Even less than half the trade unionists in both surveys thought that unions helped to improve the efficiency of British industry. In August 1980 a Gallup poll found that 66 per cent of the public said that the union leaderships did not represent the views of ordinary rank and file members. Yet if people in general are hostile to the unions, they also accept that unions 'are essential to protect workers' interests'. In the 1977 MORI poll as many as 76 per cent of the sample believed this was true (86 per cent of trade unionists did), while in July 1980 the proportion was still as high as 72 per cent for the entire sample and 90 per cent for trade unionists themselves. This suggests that union bashing is more likely to arouse ambiguous responses from many people.

Yet the idea that the unions as organisations wield massive power and influence is a myth, conveniently propagated by much of the media, aided and abetted by employers, and union leaders themselves. For too long, unions and the workers they are supposed to represent have been viewed in a narrow and confining context. It is when we examine their role in the wider circumstances of a divided, unequal and economically depressed society that we can recognise the severe limitations under which the unions must function. Indeed, during the eighties they will be fighting for their very lives.

It is the legal framework (or lack of it) under which unions operate that most arouses the animosity of their enemies. Professor F. A. Hayek has suggested that 'the legalised powers of the unions have become the biggest obstacle to raising the living standards of the working class as a whole.' 'They are the chief cause of the unnecessarily big differences between the best and worst-paid workers. They are the prime source of unemployment. They are the main reason for the decline of the British economy in general', he claims.[1] In his opinion, the fault lies with the 1906 Trade Disputes Act, passed by a Liberal government under pressure from the recently formed Labour party. Professor A. V. Dicey suggested in the second edition of his highly influential *Law and Public Opinion in England* (1914) that the measure was dangerous because it had made 'a trade union a privileged body exempt from the ordinary law of the land'. 'An enactment which frees trade unions from the rule of equal law stimulates among workmen the fatal delusion that workmen should aim at the attainment, not of equality, but of privilege', he wrote.[2] From the 1906 Act grew the delusion that Britain's unions are somehow either above or beyond the law of the land. In 1977 the Confederation of British Industry suggested that the balance of power had moved away from employers to the unions because of the 'uniquely favourable' framework of law, which the CBI argued enabled the unions to 'organise and cause industrial disruption with wide immunity'.[3]

What is the truth of the matter? The most effectively concise answer lies in the Thatcher Government's own consultative document on trade union immunities published in January 1981. The 1906 Act gave unions protection from liability for criminal offences and civil wrongs in the courts if individuals called and organise industrial actions that were 'in contemplation or furtherance of a trade dispute'. 'The immunities do not abolish the offences and wrongs against which they provide protection', pointed out the Green Paper. 'Rather they remove liability in the circumstance of a trade dispute. To the extent to which these immunities are reduced, therefore, the common law liabilities are immediately restored. If they were repealed altogether, then trade unions and individuals would be at risk of legal action every time they organised a strike'.[4] The existing law does not protect individual workers who break their contract of employment by taking part in an industrial action. 'It is a singular feature of the British system that, though the immunities protect the organisers of strikes for inducing a breach of contract, they do not protect the individual striker, who in going on strike without due notice, breaks his contract of employment', explains the Green Paper. An employer, faced by a stoppage or other form of industrial disruption, has always enjoyed the legal power to sue each individual employee for having broken his or her contract, but this happens rarely because it is simply not worth the time, cost or effort for an employer to go to such lengths, which would inevitably poison future industrial relations in his workplace.

It is also wrong to see the legal immunities of 1906 as providing trade unions with unique privileges that ensured their eventual domination of the labour market. 'While common law immunities gave certain limited protection to workers and unions, they provided no legal basis for a trade union challenge to the right of the employer to manage in his own workplace' argue England and Weekes. 'The common law employment contract which, in the guise of "freedom of contract" masked the subjection of the individual worker to the power of management, remained unaffected. Immunities were consequently for the employer a lesser evil than the alternative of a code which bestowed positive legal rights upon the unions or which allowed forms of state intervention'.[5]

Indeed, the original preference for trade union immunities rather than positive rights stemmed from a commitment to the liberal free market economy of pre-1914 Britain. It was also a grudging recognition by

Parliament that unions should be tolerated within clear limits in an unequal society where the power of capital was far superior to that of labour. 'It is quite false to see the present negative statutory immunities as some sort of privilege', argued the TUC in evidence to the Commons employment committee in April 1980. 'Immunity' in this context is a legal term, and statutory 'immunities' from common law liabilities for those who act in furtherance of a trade dispute is simply the British method of affording workers in a modern democratic society the ability to take lawful industrial action which is in other countries expressed in terms of positive rights'.[6] In short, if our unions did not enjoy immunities from actions under the common law in a trade dispute, they would face the real danger of extinction at the hands of unsympathetic judges who often still appear to regard combination as little short of conspiracy. Time and time again, Parliament has been compelled to intervene to rescue the unions from a weakening of their complex position under the law because of the sporadic attack on them from a legal system that has too often managed to demonstrate its lack of understanding and knowledge of industrial relations in practice, as well as hostility to the purposes of trade unionism.

The former TUC general secretary, George Woodcock, summarised the peculiar legal position of the unions in a lecture at Leicester University in 1968. 'Strictly the trade unions have no legal existence whatsoever', he argued.

> They are not criminal bodies but they have no legal rights. The state does not require an employer to recognise trade unions or to negotiate with trade unions and if he does recognise and negotiate with the trade unions and make an agreement, that agreement is not legally forcible. No union can use the courts of this country to enforce on employers negotiated wages or conditions of employment even though the employer, as a member of his federation, has willingly and voluntarily agreed that they are the right terms of employment. The unions are, in fact, not allowed to use the civil courts at all. The position is really that trade unions are bodies to which the state gives no rights and from which the state has consequently removed most of the legal restrictions which unions came up against in the course of their normal activities. Trade unions today have no legal existence except for such purposes as owning land, the relief of income tax on their expenditure on provident benefits and various things of that kind; activities which are not peculiarly trade union activities or which are essential to trade unions.[7]

It was in this unique legal context that Woodcock's phrase – 'unions are outlaws' – must be placed.

But this has never given trade unions special privileges. As Wedderburn argues, there is a real danger of giving a misleading view of the legal position of the unions by the use of such phrases as 'collective *laissez-faire*' and 'abstention' from the law. Indeed, during the sixties and seventies the judges made severe inroads into the immunities enjoyed by the unions in trade disputes. 'The legal form of the "immunities" in Britain frequently confuses discussion of trade union law because many people – including eminent lawyers – never reach beyond the form', Wedderburn explained to the Commons employment committee in May 1980.

> They forget that without statutory protection trade unions would, under the general or 'common' law created by judges over the last three centuries, have no lawful status; that most, if not all industrial action would suffer criminal and civil liability; and that the stream of 'labour injunctions' issued by the courts to stop workers' industrial action in the 1960s and 1970s could grow into a flood which would submerge the rights of trade unions in Britain altogether.[8]

We need to demystify the language that governs the legal relations of the trade unions in order to understand the limited and unstable, narrow ground on which those organisations are allowed to pursue their legitimate objectives. In the post-war years, there was an unmistakable tendency in the courts for judges to interpret the common law in such a way as to make industrial actions more restrictive, by challenging whether unions were entitled to induce breaches of commercial contract and practice 'intimidation' in 'contemplation and furtherance of a trade dispute'.

During the period of Labour rule in the seventies three major pieces of legislation were placed on the statute book to clarify and strengthen the legal immunities of unions after a number of adverse judgements in the courts had appeared to undermine their position. In the case of the *BBC* v. *Hearn* (1977). Lord Denning, Master of the Rolls, suggested that the Trade Union and Labour Relations Act 1974, the Employment Protection Act 1975 and the Trade Union and Labour Relations (Amendment) Act 1976 had 'conferred more freedom from restraint on trade unions than has ever been known to the law before'. 'All legal restraints have been lifted so that they can now do as they will', he claimed.[9]

But the changes in statute law did not provide unions with irresponsible privileges that somehow placed them above the rest of society. The 1974 Act sought to re-enact the intended effects of the 1906 Act. As the TUC explained to the Commons employment committee: 'It was the Labour government's aim that protection should extend to an act done 'in contemplation or furtherance of a trade dispute' if it induced a person to break any contract or interfered with or induced another person to interfere with its performance. Similar protection was to be provided for threats and neither interference with a contract nor a breach of contract itself should, in a trade dispute, constitute 'unlawful means'.[10] Opposition in the House of Lords and the resistance of the Conservatives compelled the Wilson government to restrict Section 13 of the 1974 Act giving immunities to the breach of contracts of employment alone. Two years later liberty of action was extended to enable interference with commercial contracts as well. Lord Scarman suggested that this put the law back to what Parliament had intended in 1906 'but stronger and clearer than it was then'.

The changes in labour law of 1974 and 1976 over immunities did not confer on the unions new and wider privileges.

Nevertheless, the judges began to unravel the statutory protections through the issuing of interim labour injunctions against trade unions. The Court of Appeal was particularly adept at raising doubts about whether certain planned actions by unions were covered by the immunities for being in 'contemplation or furtherance of a trade dispute'. Judges began to apply certain tests of 'motive', 'objective capability' or 'remoteness', which began to severely limit the application of statutory safeguards from civil liability to those involved in industrial action. Wedderburn explained to the Commons employment committee why the Court of Appeal was able to acquire such power to disqualify acts as 'furtherance' of a dispute.

> These cases like most trade dispute cases – were applications for 'interlocutory injunctions' to stop industrial actions. Theoretically, such actions are for 'interim' injunctions until a full trial of the action. Therefore evidence is given by written affidavits and is rarely open to cross-examination. The affidavits have to be put together quickly – especially by trade union defendants who rarely have more than a few days (sometimes only a few hours) to put their evidence together, a task not made any easier by the fact that the union officers who know about the dispute of which the plaintiff has suddenly complained are often spread over the country on union business.[11]

The 'interim' character of such injunctions was unreal because the plaintiff in an industrial disputes case never goes on to a full trial.

One of the most blatant examples of judicial hostility to union immunities came in the case of *Duport Steels* v. *Sirs* early in 1980. The Iron and Steel Trades Confederation, a moderate union, decided to call out its members on strike in the private sector of the steel industry to intensify the pressure that was being applied on the British Steel Corporation during an official, national strike. Sixteen private firms led by Duport Steels sought an injunction in the High Court to restrain the union from doing so. Although the employers lost their case in the lower court, Lord Denning and his Court obliged on appeal. Indeed, an unprecedented hearing occurred on a Saturday morning in the Court of Appeal to adjudicate on the case. The employers were granted an injunction on the grounds that such an extension of the national steel strike to the private sector was not judged by Lord Denning and his colleagues as falling within their understanding of the words 'in furtherance or contemplation of a trade dispute'. The union took the matter to the House of Lords where the Court of Appeal was overruled, not for the first time over trade disputes. The intervention of the judges, particularly Lord Denning and his colleagues in the Court of Appeal, appeared to the unions as yet further confirmation of the bias and hostility against their activities from the legal profession. Lord Scarman displayed characteristic sensitivity in his comments in *Express Newspapers* v. *McShane* (1980) when he observed: that it would be 'a strange and embarrassing task for a judge to be called upon to review the tactics of a party to a trade dispute and to determine whether in the view of the court the tactic employed was likely to further or advance that party's side in the dispute. It would need very clear language to persuade me that Parliament intended to allow the courts to act as some sort of backseat driver in trade disputes'.[12]

The messy realities of industrial relations seem far away from the orderly authority of the courtroom. As Len Murray explained in his 1980 Granada lecture:

> Governments tend to deal in absolutes. Their typical instrument is the law; the typical instrument of unions is the agreement, sometimes written, often verbal, which can be applied and interpreted by custom and practice to accommodate the constantly changing needs of industry and used to solve problems on an agreed and therefore mutually acceptable basis. We see the law itself as summing up and generalising practices which are generally accepted as good and

> relying not on the use of sanctions – though sanctions may exceptionally be needed to deal with deviations – but on acceptability.[13]

No doubt the judges left the state of legal immunities for unions in a confused condition during the late seventies, but it would be hard to conclude that unions were enjoying enormous new powers as a result. Yet the Conservatives, back in office after their May 1979 election victory, were determined to clarify the position, while at the same time a new piece of legislation was carried through Parliament to curb some of the alleged powers of the unions. The Employment Act 1980 was strongly condemned by the TUC, who saw the measure as an attempt 'to diminish the negotiating strength of trade unions in modern society'.[14] On the other hand, employment minister, Jim Prior, was criticised by many right-wing Conservative MPs who argued that the Act was far too modest and failed to deal with alleged union privileges in a fundamental way.

The main thrust of the Act was certainly designed to limit the ability of trade unions to take effective industrial action. The legal immunities are restricted in three vital ways. No picket can enjoy immunity from action unless the picketing is carried out at the picket's own place of work. The immunity is also not to apply to any secondary industrial action (such as blacking and sympathetic action) unless it is undertaken by employees of the first suppliers and first customers of the employer in dispute, the principal purpose is directly to disrupt the supplies of goods and services to and from that employer, and the action is likely to achieve that aim. And finally the immunity does not cover instances where a worker induces an employee of one employer to break his contract of employment in order to force workers of another employer to join a particular union unless they are working at the same place. Contrary to Prior's innumerable right-wing critics, these restrictions on trade union immunities are considerable, and they could bring about serious confrontations between unions and the law in the future. Indeed, there are those who argue that the 1980 Act has gone some way to make even so-called 'primary' strikes unlawful. Wedderburn argues that the measure has 'diminished trade union rights in Britain to a point where it can properly be said that organised workers have never had fewer rights to take industrial action (including picketing) since 1906.'[15]

But the Act went much further than this. Its provisions make it very difficult indeed for workers to achieve future closed shop agreements. The measure allows any worker to opt out of a closed shop and claim unfair dismissal if they are fired as a result if he or she 'genuinely objects on grounds of conscience or other deeply held personal conviction to being a member of any trade union whatsoever or of a particular trade union'. It will be up to the courts to determine what these imprecise phrases actually mean in practice. In any case brought against an employer by a worker who feels he has been unfairly dismissed because of an objection to the closed shop, the employer can now require the union or any other worker whom the dismissed worker alleges exerted pressure on the company to be 'joined' in the proceedings as a party to them. The government's own code argues: 'If the industrial tribunal finds the dismissal unfair and the employer's claim well-founded it may make an order requiring that union or other person to pay the employer any contribution which it considers to be just and equitable up to the full amount of any compensation it has awarded'.[16]

In any future union membership agreement it is now necessary under the 1980 Act for at least 80 per cent of the workers entitled to vote in a secret ballot to say they wish to be covered by such an arrangement. This looks an impossibly high 'yes' figure to be acquired and it seems that few new closed shops stand much chance of satisfying the law. At the same time the code of practice calls for a 'periodic review' of existing agreements and lays down specific circumstances when such reviews should take place, including 'when there is evidence that the support of the employees for the closed shop has declined': 'when there is a change in the parties to the agreement'; where 'there is evidence that the agreement or parts of it, are not working satisfactorily; or 'where there is a change in the law affecting the closed shop', such as the 1980 Act itself.[17]

To many people the closed shop remains the unacceptable face of British trade unionism, a tyrannical system that threatens the freedom of the individual. Nothing seemed more outrageous to them during Labour's last period of office than the legitimisation of the closed shop in the Trade Union and Labour Relations Act 1974. Under that law dismissal for non-membership of a trade union in a closed shop was stated to be fair unless the worker genuinely objected to membership on' religious or any other reasonable grounds'. The 1976 amending Act narrowed exclusion to workers who could demonstrate they had a 'religious' objection alone to a closed shop arrangement they were being asked to join. The TUC established their own Independent Review Committee as a result to deal with sensitive cases. Its members urged flexibility on unions in their handling of closed shops and the need to stress the positive advantages of why a worker should become a trade union member. A number of closed shop cases have aroused some public concern in recent years. In 1976 a British Rail worker lost his job because he refused to join a union after the introduction of a new closed shop agreement in the industry. He and two other colleagues who had also been fired for the same reason took their cases to the European Commission on Human Rights. That august body decided that the 1976 Act (now repealed) was in breach of the European Convention on Human Rights and the issue was referred to the European Court for their adjudication. In August 1981 the Court upheld the case of the three sacked British Rail workers. Joanna Harris, a poultry inspector with Sandwell Council in the West Midlands was dismissed in 1981 by her employers for refusing to join the National and Local Government Officers' Association (NALGO) under a closed shop agreement. The Harris case became something of a *cause célèbre*, although the union's own members in Sandwell agreed to scrap the agreement. There was also the case of the dismissed cleaning ladies of Walsall who refused to join a closed shop. Widespread victories by the Labour party in the May 1981 local government elections raised the prospect of further sackings as Labour-controlled councils in alliance with public service unions sought to tighten up the closed shop in the Town Halls.

Prior's critics were able to capitalise on such individual cases. 'Closed shops have no place in our society', thundered Walter Goldsmith of the Institute of Directors.[18]

> Quite apart from human rights considerations, the closed shop has a damaging effect on productivity. It encourages overmanning. It makes it more difficult to remove rigid demarcations and restrictive practices. It impedes the introduction of new technology. The closed shop leads managements to abrogate their responsibilities and allows shop stewards to usurp their role. In effect, in a closed shop employees are encouraged to think of the trade union as the employer, armed with the right of hiring and firing.

But such a forthright attitude was not held by all employer organisations. Indeed, although the closed shop has been seen as evidence of the power of the trade union, it is proving perhaps more advantageous to employers. A survey by John Gennard and others at the London School of Economics in 1978–9 found that at least 5.2 million workers, or under one in four workers were covered by a closed shop arrangement. It is no longer confined to older industries like coal-mining, metal manufacture, engineering, shipbuilding and printing. Over the past fourteen years there was an expansion of the closed shop into the food, drink and tobacco industries. clothing and footwear, gas, water and electricity and transport and communications. Gennard and his colleagues also discovered that the closed shop has spread into white-collar areas of employment. They reckon at least 1.1 million non-manual workers (22 per cent of the closed shop population) were covered by such arrangements, compared to only 8 per cent back in 1964. But manual workers are far more likely to be in a closed shop – at least a third of them, compared with 10 per cent of white-collar staff. Only a small minority of the closed shop workers are in what is known as a pre-entry closed shop, where entry to the job is contingent on entry to the union, giving the union control over the supply of labour. Around 16 per cent (837 000) were in that position, mainly in paper, printing and publishing, transport and communications, mechanical engineering, shipbuilding and motor manufacture. It should be noted, as Gennard and his colleagues observe: 'Only 14 per cent of workers covered by pre-entry closed shop arrangements work under a collective arrangement reached between the union and the management. The vast majority of pre-entry arrangements are long standing, appearing well before 1970 and almost always unwritten'.[19]

During the late sixties and early seventies there was a growth in more formalised closed shops to cover post-entry, which laid down in considerable detail how the union membership agreement should operate. But Gennard's research suggests that both employers and unions have gone some way to avoid embarrassing cases by enabling existing employees in a workplace to remain outside a union, while at the same time union membership is a condition for any new worker joining the company. 'Almost two thirds of the agreements place no obligation upon existing non-members to join the union', argues Gennard.

> The remaining third state that union membership becomes compulsory for all employees, again with exceptions, whether or not they are already in the union. Just over half these 'tight' agreements are formalisations of closed shop practices stretching back at least to the 1960s and in some cases to before the war and the absence of protection for existing non-members is because 100 per cent membership was already established when the agreement was negotiated.

Only four out of the 136 closed shop agreements examined by Gennard and his colleagues were 'full blooded 100 per cent formal post entry closed shops' insofar as they allow no exemptions from membership of a signatory union on any grounds whatsoever. In their 1978 survey of

970 manufacturing establishments the Warwick University industrial relations research unit estimated that 37 per cent of the entire full-time workforce outside managerial grades in manufacturing establishments of at least 50 workers were covered by closed shops (46 per cent of the manual workers and 10 per cent of the white-collar staff). In three quarters of the closed shops management gave the practice their open support. The most important development that reinforced the existence of the closed shop during the seventies was the rapid growth of the check-off system, whereby union dues are paid by the employer to the union as a deduction from the worker's wage packet. As the Warwick industrial relations unit argue: 'the check off shifts the burden of administering the closed shop more than ever to management'.[20] Many employers do not disguise their warm support for closed shops covering their own workers, contrary to belief. First and foremost, they bring order, cohesion and a sense of authority to the workplace. It means management knows whom it has to deal with as representative of the views of the entire workforce. Secondly, the existence of pockets of non-unionists in a workplace can threaten stability and good industrial relations. It means fragmentation and conflict, something that employers would like to avoid whenever possible. Indeed, Moira Hart has raised the interesting question of whether workers should be so keen on closed shops, if they are now seen as being in the interests of management.[21] In recent years, mainly as a result of the 1971 Industrial Relations Act, there is some evidence to suggest that the operation of closed shops has become more rigid and less easygoing.

Mrs Thatcher's government has made it clear that 'it is opposed to the principles underlying' the closed shop. 'That people should be required to join a union as a condition of getting or holding a job runs contrary to the general traditions of personal liberty in this country', maintained the Green Paper. 'It is acceptable for a union to seek to increase its membership by voluntary means. What is objectionable, however, is to enforce membership by means of a closed shop as a condition of employment. Individual employees should have the right to decide for themselves whether or not to join a trade union'.[22] The TUC takes an opposite view. 'The position of individual workers is normally weak relative to the employer', it noted in its guide to union organisation, published in February 1979.

> It is only by collective action through trade unions that individual workers can help determine their terms and conditions of employment through negotiating procedures and to generally make known

> their point of view on the operation of the workplace. This is the motive force behind trade unionism and trade union organisation. Therefore the logical objective of a trade union in terms of organisation is clearly 100 per cent organisation, in other words to bring about a situation in which all workers in the relevant trade or unit of employment belong to the union.[23]

Unions argue – with some persuasion – that the benefits negotiated by them apply to all workers whether they belong to the union or not. 'People who object to trade union membership on "principle" are not known to refuse to accept the gains made by trade union negotiation and settlements and indeed many trade unionists strongly resent working alongside non-unionists because the non-unionist or "free-rider" receives the benefits of trade unionism without paying for them.'

In the summer of 1981 a number of business organisations responded to the Government's Green Paper on legal union immunities with a wide range of demands that promised a further change in the labour laws to weaken the alleged power of the unions. These included:

1) The loss of legal immunity for organisers of industrial action which is in breach of a precedure agreement between an employer and unions.
2) Making unions legally liable for the unlawful actions of their members unless they can show they have made reasonable efforts to prevent a dispute from breaking out. This will be determined by the courts.
3) Punitive levels of cash compensation (maximum £30 000) to any worker who loses his or her job for refusing to join a closed shop, if there is a failure to reinstate.
4) A much narrower definition of what a 'trade dispute' means in order to outlaw political strikes, disputes between workers or acts of international labour solidarity. There would be threats of injunction and damages to an employer where an industrial action was not covered by the term 'trade dispute'.
5) The abolition of union labour only clauses in commercial contracts.
6) The abolition of forms of secondary action by a union unless a secret ballot of members concerned agreed with this.
7) The abolition of the pre-entry closed shop.
8) A move to 'buy out' workers in essential services, like gas, water supply and electricity, from taking strike action, by giving them some form of wage protection against inflation.

The mobilisation of bodies like the Aims of Industry, the Institute of Directors, the Chambers of Commerce, and the Centre for Policy Studies (established by Sir Keith Joseph and Margaret Thatcher in 1975) in the pressure for more labour law against the unions was carried through under the eager stimulus of Downing Street itself. John Hoskyns, head of Mrs Thatcher's policy unit, was a regular attender at private lunch meetings of a new group of business organisations that acted as a kind of alternative (known as the Argonauts) influence to the Confederation of British Industry on government itself. The tougher coordinated business line against the Prior 'softly softly' approach helped to force the CBI itself into a more hardened position than first seemed likely. But not all employer organisations subscribed to the need for yet more extensive legislative change in the immediate future.

The Engineering Employers Federation – hardly a Tory 'wet' body – made some shrewd observations about the danger of bringing in more law to curb the unions. 'Unions will not willingly acquiesce in any significant reduction in their immunities', argued the EEF in June 1981.

> Under the British political system it is virtually certain that immunities taken away by a government of one complexion will be at least restored by another government more sympathetic to the cause of union power. There is no merit therefore in initiating this kind of debilitating struggle in industry merely to make use of a temporary political advantage. However desirable in principle the wholesale radical reform of union immunities may seem to be, there is no advantage in attempting it unless the British political system can deliver the prospect of its durability.[24]

But Mrs Thatcher's government ignored the advice. In September 1981 the emollient Prior was moved away from the Department of Employment and replaced by the more abrasive Norman Tebbit with the clear remit to make further legislative changes in reducing the so-called power of the unions. In an address to the Commons, Tebbit argued that the aims of his set of proposals were two-fold: 'to safeguard the liberty of the individual from the abuse of industrial power and improve the operation of the labour market by providing a balanced framework of industrial relations law'.

The government proposed more stringent provisions for closed-shop agreements. In future such arrangements, it would require 80 per cent of the workers concerned to give their approval in a secret ballot. Massive cash compensation (up to around £20 000 for workers) would be paid out to any worker who was found by an industrial tribunal to have been dismissed unfairly and his employer thought it was not practicable to reinstate him. Periodic reviews of existing closed shops were also proposed, so that workers would decide by secret ballot within a year of the new provision becoming law whether they wished the closed shop to continue. It was suggested that further ballots on the existence of each closed shop should be held every three to five years thereafter. Even more controversially Tebbit suggested that unions as well as employers should be made accountable for closed-shop dismissals and therefore liable to pay a share of any compensation awarded by a tribunal to the worker. The government argued that union pressure on an employer lies behind most cases of workers forced into a closed shop against their deeply held personal convictions. The Tebbit proposals also favoured that union-labour-only requirements in contracts tendered by local authorities and nationalised industries in particular should be outlawed.

The new Employment Secretary also decided to move against the legal immunities for unions in industrial disputes. His proposals argued that 'under section 14 of the Trade Union and Labour Relations Act 1974 trade unions as such have virtually unlimited immunity from actions in tort, even where they organise industrial actions outside a trade dispute. This means that trade unions cannot be sued for their unlawful acts or for unlawful acts done on their behalf by their officials'. In Tebbit's view this 'is unfair and anomalous' because 'while trade union officials may be sued for organising unlawful industrial action on behalf of a trade union, the union itself can escape liability altogether'. The new law was to make unions themselves liable to be sued in tort when they were responsible for unlawful acts which were not in 'contemplation or furtherance of a trade dispute'. This opens corporate union funds to damages which could add up to £250 000 for any union with more than 250 000 members in a sliding scale of proposed fines to be exacted by the courts on behalf of an employer damaged by a strike. The government was anxious to lay down when unions would be held 'vicariously liable for unlawful acts committed by their officials'.

Apparently union funds will only be at risk if the disputed action has been specifically authorised by a union executive or ratified by one or, in the words of the consultative paper: 'the subordinate body or official of the union whose action was complained of had authority for the action under the rules of the union or was acting on instructions from a body or officials who had such authority and its or his action had not been repudiated by a more senior authoritative body or official of the union'. However, because of the ambiguities in some union rule books about the authority conferred on different levels of officialdom in disputes, Tebbit also suggested that the unions should be liable unless a senior union leader or body had repudiated the action under threat.

At the same time it was proposed to narrow the definition of a trade dispute so that inter-union strikes, actions expressing international labour solidarity and strikes of a political or personal character would no longer be covered by the legal immunities. Trade disputes that took place between an employer and a union where the employer was not in conflict with workers would also become unlawful. In effect, such a step made forms of secondary action in strikes illegal. On top of this, the Tebbit proposals also enabled an employer to pick and choose which workers he rehired after an industrial dispute without facing a charge of unfair dismissal before an industrial tribunal. Such a change appeared to strengthen a company's position in handling militants.

The unions reacted predictably to the proposals that represented a great leap forward in the government's step-by-step approach to curbing union power by the use of legal regulation. Their leaders believed the Tebbit proposals were a provocation and a clear threat to what they saw as their hard-won freedoms. A major campaign of resistance from the TUC was threatened from the spring of 1982.

Yet it is arguable that the union 'problem' does not stem from the legal strength of the unions, their immunities or monopoly control through closed shops. The trouble lies in the acute *weaknesses* of the unions, something that even the Confederation of British Industry began to recognise early in 1980. In a discussion document at that time, the CBI argued that unions suffered from a genuine paradox. On the one hand, it was alleged unions were too powerful *vis-à-vis* employers, but 'too often weak and ineffectual' when it came to relations with their members. 'There is a diminishing influence and leadership exerted by the unions over their members', claimed the CBI. 'The result is that the relationship between an employer and a union, based as it is on reconciling genuine differences through an agreed framework of procedures and agreements, cannot function effectively'[25]. The CBI document went on to portray a picture of virtual anarchy on the shop-floor where full-time union officials found their words and actions treated with contempt or derision by their own members, which undermined their moral authority or their capacity to speak as the representative voice of the rank and file. For the first time in more than twenty-five years employers wanted to see much more power and control moving away from the workplace, where it had devolved to the shop steward and combine committee, back to the trade union bureaucracy outside the plant. 'The combination of shop-floor power and management neglect has led to a diminishing respect for officials and their function – and unions have encouraged this over the years', wrote the CBI.

> The authority of officials now depends mainly on their personality; but those who seek to exercise judgement or make binding agreements increasingly risk conflict with their members. It is not surprising therefore that many officials now prefer to act as delegates who are mandated by their membership – leaving management negotiators frustrated and the negotiating process a lengthy and uncertain one. With the decline of the official, the most stable element in a union's dealings with management has been seriously eroded'.

What the CBI sees is a crisis of authority within a divided, competitive trade union movement where unions operate with very limited resources. 'The growth in independence of the individual workgroup, the competition between unions for membership and above all the pattern of union growth with the extension of unionisation into white-collar, professional and managerial areas have all contributed to a reduction in the instinctive solidarity of the wider trade union movement'.

What the CBI did not address itself to was the fact that the developments the organisation so much deplored – the weakening of the union and the strengthening of the workplace organisation – were stimulated by many employers. It is true that the existence of multi-unionism in a workplace was a major influence on the growth of shop steward organisation and the emergence of the combine committee. But the Warwick University industrial relations research unit discovered in 1978 that as many as 3500 manual stewards in 1800 manufacturing establishments and 300 non-manual stewards in 160 manufacturing establishments were working full-time on trade union business in the plant, being paid for doing so by their employer. The numbers are far higher than the size of the full-time union bureaucracy. Once employers and unions alike tended to see the shop steward as an unpredictable menace. During the seventies many companies found a *modus vivendi*, and even went out of their way to cultivate and strengthen shop steward organisation in the spread of single employer wage bargaining.

The Warwick industrial relations unit also found evidence of a big increase in employer interest in a more professional response to workplace industrial relations. Under the stimulus of government action and the Donovan Royal Commission recommendations to improve industrial relations practices, many larger sized companies began to formalise agreements, encourage job evaluation, and carry through extensive improvements in procedures governing shop-floor behaviour. All of this has tended to boost the position of the shop steward and his colleagues. However, it is by no means clear that this trend, which became predominant in manufacturing during the seventies, has intensified the conflict between the lay activitists in the union and the full-time union officials. On the contrary, that complex relationship seems to have grown more into one of assistance by the union bureaucracy for the shop steward in single employer bargaining than domination.

It is very difficult to marry the realities of the shop-floor in manufacturing with the analysis of the CBI and the rhetoric of other employer organisations that wish to weaken the supposed power of the unions in the workplace in as many ways as they can. Such a concerted class conscious employer offensive still looks most unlikely, in part because it simply does not fit the facts. Most employers most of the time recognise the value of trade unionism for the peace and well-being of their own business activities. In general terms they may regret that they cannot behave like a Victorian robber baron, but in practice most companies are far too sensible to wish for naked class conflict in their own establishments. The present slump has helped strengthen the hand of employers to push through unilateral change that means the assertion of management strength over workers and unions. But an all-out attack on the highly complex and sophisticated shop-floor arrangements, which have grown up so rapidly over the past decade, seems unlikely to succeed, even if it were tried in earnest.

The power of workers or unions is conditioned by the corresponding lack of strength to be found among employers. We tend to overlook the undeniable fact that the terms of the industrial relations debate are determined first and foremost by the economic circumstances of the individual enterprise. If unions lack solidarity and face enormous difficulties in reconciling the views of their full-time officials, the activist union minority and the rank and file in the workplace, the same problem is also just as true of employers. In the post-war period British industry has lacked strong and united bosses who were ready to stand together for what they believed to be right, no matter what the business consequences. The absence of solidarity between companies in their conduct of industrial relations stimulated workplace bargaining and resulting fragmentation. The weakness stems from the top.

Like the Trades Union Congress, the CBI is a loose confederation of divergent interests that lacks any sanctions to ensure unity behind a firm, agreed strategy. Sir Terence Beckett, the CBI's director general and his council must argue and persuade, lobby and pressurise, but they lack powers of compulsion to make companies do what they oppose. In 1979 the idea of a strike mutual insurance fund was floated by CBI leaders as a way for companies to create a solid stand against what they saw as excessive workplace muscle. The aim was to help protect firms from losses if they decided to resist inflationary pay demands. But most CBI members doubted the practicality of such a step and the suggestion was dropped quietly. Large and influential industry-based employer organisations like the Engineering Employers' Federation also experience genuine difficulties in forging a common purpose between their affiliates. In 1979 the EEF failed to stick together against the industrial disruption that sought a reduction in the length of the basic working week.

The highly competitive and fragmented labour market makes it hard for employers as well as unions and workers to display much sense of solidarity, either in the same industry or locality. The use of the lock-out may not be unknown in Britain, but it remains far more commonplace in continental western Europe. One firm's problems are seen, after all, as another's opportunity in the market place. Certainly union negotiators in many sectors of the economy can play off one firm against another to ensure they maximise the bargaining strength of workers. As long as the *laissez-faire* principles of individualism thrive in our industrial relations there seem little prospect of any concerted employer counter-offensive designed to humble the shop-floor, let alone the unions.

But it would be wrong to go on from this observation to assume that either unions or workers exert muscle because employers find it hard to stand together. The present slump has done much to underline the illusory nature of so-called union and worker power. The balance in industry has moved decisively towards the forces of capital. Fear of the dole is now a sobering calculation for most workers, who are battling to defend their living standards from the corrosive effects of inflation. Yet even during better times, the employment relationship between company and worker is an unequal one. Workers have acquired very few rights in the workplace. The ultimate decisions over investment, manpower planning, the distribution of profits, and product development remain firmly in the hands of the boardroom. The work disciplines on the shop-floor are still considerable and in many companies recently there has been either an abolition or reduction in mutuality (joint union-management control) over the speeds of production, manpower depolyment and the rest.

When you scrape away all the managerial talk about better communications and participation, the reality of the power structure of the enterprise (whether private or state-run) remains virtually intact. Workers are subordinate to the demands of capital. There is not much evidence that many question this inequality. Nor are many opposed to the fruits of the social market economy. Alienation is a convenient catch-all word that provides a misleading impression of shop-floor realities. The battle over the 'frontiers of control' remains an endless one in industry. Employers, unions and workers have an obvious common interest in the success of an enterprise, but they also have divided loyalties.

In a free society where the ideas of *laissez-faire* are still very strong, company paternalism is the exception rather than the rule. Our unions have tended to buttress an underlying individualism through their attachment to the voluntarist dogmas and the unique system of legal immunities from the actions of the common law. It might make more sense for unions and workers to press for positive legal rights in the workplace to cover fundamental issues like the right to work, the right to strike, the right to a 'just' wage, but there are few signs that the Labour 'movement' is interested in taking up such a potentially revolutionary course of action. For the moment, workers and unions are very much on the defensive, battling to hold their own in the face of the slump and technological change that threatens to transform the nature of the workforce in our society by the end of the century. The economic power of the unions has been much exaggerated, and so has the suggestion that immunities equal privileges, rather than being the necessary prerequisite for unions to function at all in our democracy, without the threat of the sequestration of their funds and the imprisonment of their officials.

It is also questionable how much political power the unions really enjoy. At the level of officialdom and the small handful of rank and file activists there remains a tenacious and instinctive bond of loyalty between many (though *not* the majority) trade unions and the Labour party. They provide its bulk of finances. They dominate its policy-making annual conference and they make up the largest share of the electoral college now used to choose Labour's leader and deputy leader. But it remains very doubtful whether most workers in the unions support such a close identification between their union and one political party. The results of polls of the general public and rank and file trade unionists carried out by Market and Opinion Research International both in 1977 and 1980 found widespread disapproval of the link between Labour and the unions (see Table 7.1).

TABLE 7.1 Rank and file opposition to the labour/union connection
'The Labour party should not be so closely linked to the trade unions'.

| | *24–5 August 1977* | | *24–7 July 1980* | | *Change %* | |
|---|---|---|---|---|---|---|
| | *All sample* | *Trade unionists* | *All sample* | *Trade unionists* | *All sample* | *Trade unionists* |
| Strongly agree | 36 | 28 | 28 | 22 | −8 | −6 |
| Tend to agree | 31 | 29 | 31 | 24 | 0 | −5 |
| Neither agree nor disagree | 8 | 7 | 12 | 11 | +4 | +4 |
| Tend to disagree | 12 | 15 | 15 | 21 | +3 | +6 |
| Strongly disagree | 10 | 19 | 9 | 17 | −1 | −2 |
| No opinion | 4 | 2 | 5 | 4 | +1 | +2 |
| Agree | 67 | 57 | 59 | 46 | −8 | −11 |
| Disgree | 22 | 34 | 24 | 38 | +2 | +4 |

SOURCE Market and Opinion Research International poll.

Behind the rhetoric lies a rather different reality. Most of the rank and file in the unions are not dedicated Labour party voters. An increasing number of trade unionists have been supporting other political parties over the past twenty years. Butler and Stokes concluded in 1969 that

> there is remarkably little evidence that the ethos of the workplace, and still less the persuasive efforts of the unions themselves, have much impact on the direction of the worker's party allegiance. On the contrary, the evidence strongly implies that much of the difference of Labour support between union and non-union families in the country as a whole results from the tendency of workers already disposed towards Labour to join unions where membership is optional. Indeed, among workers for whom membership is optional but fairly routine Labour support is no higher than its average among non-union families over the whole of Britain.[26]

In their survey, Butler and Stokes found widespread support among rank and file trade unionists for the separation of the unions from the Labour party (see Table 7.2).

The world outside the Labour 'movement' changed significantly during the sixties and seventies. There was evidence of a marked decline in the number of voters identifying themselves with the major political parties between 1970 and February 1974. Labour suffered in particular as a gap opened up in the sixties between its official party policy and the

TABLE 7.2 Views as to proper relationship of trade unions to Labour party (%)

| *Believes the trade unions . . .* | *1963 union members* | *1964 full sample* | *1964 union members* | *1966 full sample* | *1970 full sample* |
|---|---|---|---|---|---|
| . . . should have close ties to Labour | 25 | 19 | 31 | 16 | 17 |
| . . . should stay out of politics | 60 | 69 | 65 | 74 | 72 |
| Don't know | 15 | 12 | 4 | 10 | 11 |

SOURCE D. Butter and D. Stokes, *Political Change in Britain*, first edition (Macmillan, 1969) pp. 168–9, second edition (Macmillan, 1974) p. 199.

views of those voters who identified with the Labour cause. Hostility towards the trade unions grew appreciably between 1964 and 1970 among Labour identifiers, though it was already underway before the sharp disillusionment with Labour rule following the party's electoral triumph in April 1966. As Crewe, Sarlvik and Alt argued, 'Endorsement of the traditional links between the Labour party and the trade unions trickled down from 38 to 32 per cent', while 'a near 60 per cent rejection of the idea that trade unions were too powerful in 1964 turned into a 60 per cent agreement six years later; and declarations of general sympathy towards strikers were more than halved, from 37 per cent down to a miniscule 16 per cent.'[27] During the early seventies there was no recovery in support for the unions among Labour identifiers. The Essex University research discovered the 'most serious loss of faith in Labour principles' occurred 'amongst those who should be its firmest adherents: solid Labour supporters amongst the organised (manual) working class' and they concluded that it was a measure of Labour's failure 'that it was unable to generate enthusiasm amongst its erstwhile strongest partisans in an election marked by an unusual class and ideological polarisation'.

The sixties and seventies saw the spread of a self-regarding sectionalism among trade unionists and an erosion of older notions of solidarity. Goldthorpe and his colleagues discovered the new calculative form of trade unionism among manual workers in Luton. 'Neither as a way to greater worker participation in the affairs of the enterprise nor as a political force is unionism greatly valued', they argued. 'Rather, one would say, the significance that unionism has for these workers is very largely confined to issues arising from their employment which are economic in nature and which are local in their origins and scope'.[28]

Trade union membership was valued not so much as an expression of a collective or class interest, but a meal ticket to a better life. This did not mean that workers were becoming more middle class in their life styles and ambitions. The embourgeoisement theory that worried revisionists in the Labour party during the early sixties proved to be an over-simplification. Goldthorpe coined the phrase 'instrumental collectivism' to describe the outlook of the Luton manual workers. They sought self-fulfillment outside the workplace in their families and the networks of friendship within the community, not among fellow workers in the shop-floor. No doubt, it remains something of an exaggeration to suggest that trade unionism before post-war affluence was an idealistic expression of a collective solidarity. Sectionalist attitudes have deep roots in our labour history, even if Socialists tend to play down their significance. The temptation to construct a mythical golden age of ethical Socialism must be resisted. Nor would it be sensible to jump to the conclusion that workers in Britain think and act entirely as self-regarding individualists, who come together in collective groups for limited, tangible aims. A sense of class consciousness, rather than class conflict, is firmly embedded in working class culture. But there remains no straightforward relationship between trade union membership and an unquestioning loyalty to the Labour 'movement'.

This underlines the primary weakness of the unions. Their leaders cannot deliver restraint as part of a wider social and economic programme to Labour governments, whether they want to do so or not, if this means they must come into conflict with the aspirations of the shop-floor. Frank Cousins, general secretary of the Transport and General Workers union, put his finger on the genuine dilemma, when he wrote in his union journal in October 1963: 'If we do not fulfil the purposes for which members join unions, to protect and raise their real standard of living, then the unions will wither and finally die. We can give leadership, we can persuade, but basically we must serve trade union purposes'.[29]

The trade union rank and file are not revolutionary proletariat nor paid up members of the Labour party. Those in the unions who claim to speak for them cannot do so on wider political questions. The difficulties of reconciling shop-floor realities with the aims of Labour have grown more acute over the past fifteen years. The devolution of bargaining to plant and company level in private manufacturing and the new recognition of the central role of the shop steward and the combine committee exacerbated sectionalism. 'Our success – and indeed the success of industry itself is going to be determined by the extent to which we can decentralise – spread decision-making amongst the work people, and above all get industrial agreements settled where they are going to be operated', declared Jack Jones, general secretary of the Transport and General Workers in October 1969.[30] 'I am working for a system where not a few trade union officials control the situation but a dedicated, well-trained and intelligent body of trade union members represented by hundreds of thousands of lay representatives – every one of whom is capable of helping to resolve industrial problems and assist in collective bargaining and the conclusion of agreements'. But was it really possible to reconcile the inevitable parochialism of shop-floor bargainers with the wider needs and aspirations of trade unionism? The optimistic assumption that harmony and well-being could be achieved through the sum of diverse, often conflicting worker self-interests was not borne out by the virulent sectionalism of the sixties and seventies. Far from being a liberation for a thwarted idealism and sense of moral purpose on the shop-floor, decentralisation enflamed the underlying tendencies for fragmentation. Certainly it failed to generate much solidarity between workers or a political perspective of even a remotely Socialist hue for the endless, unedifying scramble for higher and higher money wages.

Unions serve a limited purpose for most workers. They do not shape or dictate opinion they are often accused of doing. 'Trade unions cannot determine the greater part of the experience to which their members react', wrote Flanders over twenty years ago. 'They react very closely to their members and their members in the main react to their everyday industrial experience. They can only be changed by different experience that teaches different lessons'.[31]

Over the past two decades trade unionists did not constitute a formidable political block. Indeed, there was a noticeable and steady decline in the proportion of trade unionists who voted Labour in general elections (see Table 7.3).

During periods of rank and file discontent with Labour (between 1967 and 1970 and again from 1977 to 1979) trade unionists – like other

TABLE 7.3 How trade unionists voted (%)

| | *1964* | *1966* | *1970* | *1974* | *1974* | *1979* |
|---|---|---|---|---|---|---|
| Labour | 73 | 71 | 66 | 55 | 55 | 51 |
| Conservative | 22 | 25 | 28 | 30 | 23 | 33 |
| Others | 5 | 4 | 6 | 15 | 16 | 13 |

SOURCE Market and Opinion Research International.

disillusioned voters – turned to the Conservatives or the parties of the political centre. No grouping to the left of Labour made any electoral impact at all. Over the general elections of the sixties and seventies the Communist party's share of the poll fell from an already derisory 0.2 per cent in 1964 to a mere 0.1 per cent in 1979. Shop-floor anger and frustration were never translated into a radical left political mood among workers.

It is perhaps therefore unsurprising that the main beneficiary of the breakdown of Labour's incomes policy in 1978–9 was the Conservative party under Margaret Thatcher. The appeal of her acquistive brand of economic liberalism in the May 1979 general election evoked a sympathetic response from many trade unionists. The Conservatives won significant support from skilled manual workers in the industrial Midlands and South East who wanted to restore lost pay differentials. They believed in the benefits that would come to them from promised Conservative cuts in income tax and they liked the self-reliant language of the Conservative party.

But the identification of many workers with Conservative policies went much deeper than this in 1979. A survey carried out by Research Services Ltd in April 1979 discovered widespread sympathy among Labour voters for Conservative causes like cuts in social benefits for strikers' families; an end to secondary picketing; the sale of council houses and a reduction in the size of the civil service. 'Seldom can a major party have penetrated the political thinking of the other side's staunchest supporters', claimed Anthony King.[32]

No doubt, the slump since 1980 has changed political loyalties among many trade unionists, but it seems unlikely to have altered the basic problem: the so-called people's party no longer speaks the language of the people. Labour has become dominated by a powerful alliance of public sector unions and middle class constituency activists. It fails to articulate the views of the poor, the old, the ethnic community, manual workers. Socialism is a convenient word used to cover over the all-pervasive demands of strong producer interests at the expense of our society as a whole. Perhaps this will change in time, but the outlook is unpromising. The tensions between free collective bargaining, worker power, self-regarding sectionalism and the aspiration to social justice, economic growth and solidarity are real and they will not be spirited away by rhetorical gestures or fudges.

We have come full circle. The planned economy and the shop-floor free-for-all are obvious incompatibles, but the Labour 'movement' has failed during the past eighty or so years to change the basic social attitudes on which people act. The virtues of mid-Victorian England – of thrift, self-reliance, individualism – coexist with harsher feelings about personal failure, scroungers and the work-shy.

The electoral appeal of a cut in personal taxation makes much more impression on working class voters than talk of the 'social wage'. It is true our society has vague ideas about fairness and equity. The welfare state – in the form of the National Health Service – remains a highly respected institution. But most gut feelings are Tory not Socialist. This is why those who speak so sweepingly about the power of the trade unions miss the whole intractable problem of the so-called British 'disease'. It lies with people themselves, not the institutions that claim to speak for their conflicting interests in the wider society. The social stability and cohesion of this country are now at risk because of a long period of relative economic decline. Our politicians have no obvious, painless panaceas to solve deep-rooted troubles. The search for scapegoats has become a national pastime. Blaming the unions is a convenient way of avoiding an attack on workers themselves. It also remains a sad, but obvious diversion for many, who cannot see the ills of our society stretch far beyond the shop-floor. Indeed, unions and workers are often the victims – far more than the aggressors. Like almost everybody else, they remain trapped by attitudes of mind, complacency and inertia inherited long ago, when Britain was the first industrial nation and the workshop of the world.

## NOTES AND REFERENCES

1 F. A. Hayek, *1980s Unemployment and the Unions* (Institute of Economic Affairs, 1980) p. 52.
2 A. V. Dicey, *Law and Public Opinion in England*, second edition (Macmillan, 1914) pp. xlv–xlvii.
3 'The Future of Pay Determination', Confederation of British Industry, 1977, p. 20.
4 'Trade Union Immunities', HMSO, January 1981, p. 24.
5 J. England and B. Weekes, 'Trade Unions and the State: A review of the crisis', *Industrial Relations Journal*, Vol. 12, No. 1, January/February 1981.
6 'The Legal Immunities of Trade Unions', TUC, April 1980, p. 11.
7 G. Woodcock, *The Trade Union Movement and the Government* (Leicester University Press, 1968) pp. 7–8.
8 'The Legal Immunities of Trade Unions and Related Matters', evidence from Lord Wedderburn of Charlton to the Commons Employment Committee, May 1980, pp. 2–3; *see also* his article, 'Industrial Relations and The Courts', *The Industrial Law Journal*, June 1980.

9 Lord Denning, *The Discipline of Law* (Butterworths, 1979) p. 191.
10 TUC, April 1980, p. 3.
11 Wedderburn evidence, p. 39.
12 TUC, April 1980, pp. 5–6.
13 'The Role of the Trade Unions', Granada Guildhall lectures, 1980 (Granada, 1980) p. 85.
14 TUC, April 1980, p. 7.
15 Wedderburn evidence, p. 46.
16 'Code of Practice on Closed Shop Agreements and Arrangements', Department of Employment, 1980, p. 3.
17 'Code of practice', ibid., pp. 11–12.
18 Institute of Directors press release, February 1980.
19 *Employment Gazette*, Vol. 88, No. 1, January 1980, pp. 16–22.
20 *The Changing Contours of British Industrial Relations*, ed. W. Brown (Basil Blackwell, 1981) p. 73.
21 *New Society*, 15 February 1979.
22 'Trade Union Immunities', Department of Employment, 1981, p. 66.
23 'TUC Guides', February 1979, p. 7.
24 'Response to Green Paper on Trade Union Immunities', Engineering Employers' Federation, June 1981, p. 2.
25 'Trade Unions In a Changing World: the challenge for management', Confederation of British Industry, 1980, p. 11.
26 D. Butler and D. Stokes, *Political Change in Britain* (Macmillan, 1974) p. 199.
27 I. Crewe, B. Sarlvik and J. Alt, 'Partisan Dealignment in Britain 1964–1974', *British Journal of Political Science*, Vol. 7, Part 2, April 1977, pp. 179–80.
28 *The Affluent Worker: Industrial attitudes and behaviour* (Cambridge University Press, 1978) 1st reprint, pp. 176–7.
29 G. Goodman, *The Awkward Warrior: Frank Cousins – His Life and Times*, (Davis-Poynter, 1979), p. 355.
30 Transport and General Workers union pamphlet, 1969, p. 6.
31 A. Flanders, *Management and Unions* (Faber & Faber, 1975) p. 293.
32 *Observer*, 6 May 1979, p. 12.

# Postscript
# In the Depths of the Slump

By the spring of 1982 Britain's slump was accelerating the contraction of the manual working class. Its sheer ferocity has cut a swath through the ranks of manufacturing industry. Between June 1979 and January 1982 as many as 1 300 000 jobs were lost in manufacturing, nearly 19 per cent of the entire labour force in that sector. In just two and a half years one third of all workers in metal manufacturing and a quarter of textile workers lost their jobs. In mechanical engineering just under 200 000 jobs disappeared, over one in five of the workforce. Nearly 20 per cent of building workers went as well. By contrast, a mere 45 000 jobs went in public administration and defence over the same period from a workforce of 1 566 000 and only 6 000 jobs out of 335 000 in the public sector monopolies of gas, water and electricity.

For the first time since the onset of the Great Depression in Britain in 1921 the unions (at least the vast majority) have lost members, many of them have done so heavily. At least a million trade unionists joined the dole queues in Mrs Thatcher's first two and a half years in office and the haemorrhaging looks like going on. The giants of the TUC – the Transport and General Workers, the Engineering Workers, and the General and Municipal Workers – suffered particularly heavy losses, but even the white-collar conglomerate – the Association of Scientific, Technical and Managerial Staffs found its endless growth brought to a standstill. Only the big public service unions – the National and Local Government Officers' Association (NALGO) and the National Union of Public Employees – continued to expand through the slump.

There are growing fears in the TUC that we may have reached the high watermark of trade union penetration of the workforce. In 1979 around 56 per cent of workers belonged to a union, but the proportion has begun to fall (Table 8.1). The more rapid disappearance of manual workers from industry is hastening the change of balance within the trade union movement towards the public service and white-collar unions.

TABLE 8.1 How the slump has hit Britain's top ten unions

| *Union* | *Leader* | *Members, end of 1979* | *Members, end of 1981* | +/− | % |
|---|---|---|---|---|---|
| TGWU | Moss Evans | 2 087 000 | 1 676 000 | −411 000 | −20 |
| AUEW | Terry Duffy | 1 250 000 | 1 024 000 | −226 000 | −17 |
| GMWU | David Basnett | 967 000 | 866 000 | −101 000 | −8 |
| NALGO | Geoffrey Drain | 753 000 | 796 000 | +43 000 | +6 |
| NUPE | Rodney Bickerstaffe | 691 700 | 704 000 | +13 000 | +2 |
| ASTMS | Clive Jenkins | 480 000 | 441 000 | −39 000 | −8 |
| USDAW | Bill Whatley | 450 000 | 438 000 | −12 000 | −3 |
| EETPU | Frank Chapple | 420 000 | 405 000 | −15 000 | −4 |
| UCATT | Les Wood | 349 000 | 299 000 | −50 000 | −14 |
| NUM | Arthur Scargill | 253 000 | 245 000 | −8 000 | −3 |

This will exacerbate the sectionalism of the unions and make it even harder for them to achieve any sense of solidarity that would help to establish a national understanding on the management of the economy with any government. It will also add to the difficulties of manual workers in exercising any direct influence on both the political and economic system. The new emerging Social Democratic/Liberal Alliance looks an unlikely vehicle to concern itself with the interests of manual workers and their families, while equally the Labour party continues to abandon any commitment to an ethical Socialism. It is not too much of an exaggeration to suggest that manual workers face the grim prospect of their virtual disenfranchisement from the political system. Manual workers look like becoming an embattled, insecure minority of the labour force by the late eighties.

The first industrial proletariat in the world is fast disappearing with hardly a whimper. During the best of times, ideas of fellowship, probity, self-respect, existed alongside a moralistic individualism, an intolerance, a basic acceptance of the values of the market society. 'The most repulsive thing here is the bourgeois 'respectability' bred into the bones of the workers,' wrote Engels to F. A. Sorge in December 1889. 'The social division of society into innumerable gradations, each recognised without question, each with its own pride but also its inborn respect for its 'betters' and 'superiors', is so old and firmly established that the bourgeois still find it pretty easy to get their bait accepted.'[1] Workers in a trade found it easier to combine to strengthen their individual labour power than establish a sense of common self-interest with other workers in the same industry, let alone workers in general. The primary struggle of workers was not for the establishment of Socialism but for control of authority in the workplace.[2]

Even in Labour's golden age of the forties it is doubtful whether most manual workers who supported the party did so because of their commitment to democratic Socialism. Patriotic emotions have always been strong among manual workers, with contempt for foreigners and love of royalty. The Conservative party, with its belief in 'one nation', has been the most successful political organisation in any democratic, industrial society. The present slump provides no sign that people are voting in line with their supposed class interests. We ought to remember that Labour failed to make much of a political recovery in the thirties after the 1931 débâcle, *despite* the Great Depression.

On past experience, there is no evidence to suggest that manual workers will act as a unified and powerful force in the pursuit of their own interests. Indeed, the practice of 'free' collective bargaining in a depressed labour market is tending to fragment and divide workers more effectively than ever. But the slump of the eighties also looks like widening the already-large gap between workers in work and workers who are unemployed. In its spring 1982 policy review the Department of Applied Economics at Cambridge University warned that aggregate wages and salaries were going to rise in real terms in line with national income by an average of 1 per cent, with increases of 2 per cent in real take-home pay for workers, so that continued stagflation would not damage their living standards, whereas the unemployed would bear most of the burden in the slump. 'With such a widening divergence in living standards between two sections of the community it is hard to see how increasing conflict and social unrest could be avoided,' argued the economists.[3]

Yet unemployment forecasts for the rest of the eighties provide a bleak picture. There seems no prospect at all of returning to the levels of worklessness we knew a decade ago. On the contrary, even if we were to have a massive reflation, import controls, devaluation and an incomes policy more than two million workers in Britain would still be without a job after five years of expansionist demand management policies.

It looks as though Britain under any government during the eighties will have to learn to live with some of the longest dole queues in the western world. This must threaten social cohesion, but widespread inertia, complacency and lack of vision seem likely to inhibit much radical action. The sad truth is that the return of mass unemployment has failed to revive any sense of community. Those without work have been privatised. Their personal tragedies remain hidden away from public view. The harsh moral and social climate of 'official opinion' has worsened the stigma of being without a job.[4]

For manual workers the pain is especially acute. Their world is passing away. The labour market has less and less need for unskilled or semi-skilled men and women without educational qualifications. The jobs of the future will require higher levels of numeracy and literacy than in the past. Workers will have to become more flexible, mobile, responsive to the bewildering impact of technological change, if they hope to survive and compete. There are some parts of Britain (the so-called 'sunrise strip' between London and Bristol, East Anglia, Hertfordshire) which can look forward to a prosperous, relatively trouble-free future as the beneficiaries of the Micro-chip revolution, but for the old industrial heartlands there is nothing but further structural decay and worker despair to look forward to during the rest of this century.

The new depression has brought the days of our economic reckoning nearer. By the nineties North Sea oil and gas will be running out. Britain and its workers then face the prospect of a savage decline in living standards. Whether the labour market will have become more dynamic and competitive by then is highly questionable.

In the spring of 1982 there were a few belated signs of government readiness to take industrial training more seriously. Measures to improve the mobility of the labour market seem likely. Output per head began to shoot up in 1981–2, leading some over-optimists to suggest Britain – with Japan – would lead the western world out of depression. But none of these hopeful signs could really divert attention away from the crisis of mass unemployment.

On the shopfloor 'free' collective bargaining continued to hold sway and apparently tough government cash limits in the public sector were expected to reduce pay expectations for many workers. But in the spring of 1982 there was a wide scattering of wage settlements and some evidence to suggest that rises were moving up towards 8–9 per cent. While a pay explosion on the scale of 1974–5 or 1979–80 seems improbable in the middle eighties, because of the ferocity of the deflation, the inner core of the labour market is still set to keep up with the rate of inflation or beyond. Fear has frozen pay expectations for the moment, but the so-called new 'realism' on the shopfloor will not survive a thaw, no matter how high the registered unemployment figure might still be in 1983–4.

Can workers stage a militant comeback in a trade union offensive against the 1982 Employment Act? In the early eighties the TUC enjoyed none of the élan and self-confidence of the early seventies, when it neutered the Heath Industrial Relations Act. In 1981 there were the lowest number of working days lost because of industrial stoppages since 1976 (4 196 000) and the lowest number recorded since 1941. It would be a mistake for anybody to assume that the unions and the workers they represent have been bashed into oblivion by the slump and government policy. Unlike in the United States, Britain has experienced no year of the employer take-back.

At a one-day conference in London that coincided with the departure of a naval task force to deal with the Falkland Islands crisis in April 1982, the TUC declared all-out war on the new Employment Bill. Union leaders feel threatened and their old sense of insecurity has returned. Norman Tebbit was seen by the TUC as the most anti-union Employment Secretary they have ever had to deal with. Most of his Conservative predecessors were more ready to preach sweetness and light towards the unions. The TUC believes that only the return of a majority Labour government to office can change the climate of industrial relations and lift the depression, but the more unions seek to defy the new laws on industrial relations the greater is likely to be the already widespread anti-union feeling in the country, even on the shopfloor. If unions through the pursuit of self-regarding sectionalism helped to ensure the triumph of Margaret Thatcher, they would have only themselves to blame for the resulting further diminution in their powers and influence.

## NOTES AND REFERENCES

1 Karl Marx and Frederick Engels, *On Britain* (Moscow Foreign Languages Publishing House, 1962) p. 568.
2 A brilliant exposition of this long-neglected theme of labour history can be found in R. Price, *Masters Unions and Men-Work Control in Building and the Rise of Labour 1830–1914* (Cambridge University Press, 1980). H. Pelling, *Popular Politics and Society in Late Victorian Britain* (Macmillan, second edition, 1979) represents a refreshing revision of familiar themes in labour history. But for labour historians, there is still much to be done.
3 *Cambridge Economic Policy Review*, April 1982, Vol. 1, p. 8.
4 J. Seabrook, *Unemployment* (Quarter Books, 1982).

# Index


Absenteeism, among railway workers, 94
Accidents at work, 133, 134
Age, characteristic of long-term unemployed, 13
Apprenticeships
affected by business cycle fluctuations, 104
as restriction on trade entry, 83
decline in numbers (1968–80), 104, 105
drawbacks of system, 101–2
EITB proposals, 106–7
inflexibility, 102
UK figures lowest in EEC, 100
*see also* Training

Bakery workers, overtime worked by, 125
Banking system, use in wage payments, 124
Bill payment problems, 39
Bonuses, 120, 121
*see also* Payment by results
British Leyland Ltd
effect of disputes, 155
Ryder report, 91
short-time stoppages, 155
working practice changes (1980), 97

Career structure, non-existent in manual jobs, 121–2
Central Policy Review Staff, criticism of industrial training system, 102–3
Chemical industry
accidents, 133
in UK compared with W. Germany and Holland, 89–90
Children, number in family related to father's occupational status, 40
Civil service
Inland Revenue's overtime converted to full-time jobs, 128
occurrence of respiratory infections, 135
pay, 58
Clegg commission pay awards, 59, 73
Closed shop agreements, 86
advantages for employers, 180–1, 182
ambiguous attitudes to, 179–80
cases brought against, 180
effect of 1980 Employment Act, 178–9
extent in manufacturing industry, 182
post-entry problem, 181
spread to non-manual workers, 181
Commission earnings, 120, 121
Community enterprise programmes, 17
Community industry, 21, 22
Company cars, 142, 143
Computer-related skills, shortfall in, 108
Conservative Party
attitudes to incomes policy, 70–3
support among union members, 195
Construction industry
accidents, 133
agreement on overtime working, 128
days lost through strikes, 153

Construction industry – *continued*
in UK compared with USA, 92
NEDO report on productivity, 92
Coronary heart disease, 135

Deaths at work, 133, 134
class differences in occurrence before retiring age, 138, 139
not related to occupation, 139–40
Debt repayment problems, 39
during strikes, 164
Demarcation
disputes less frequent, 95
in steel industry, 89
provocation for few disputes, 158–9
Demonstrations against unemployment, 3
Disabled people
permanent disability cover, 138
*see also* Handicapped people
Dismissal
for failure to join union, 179
strike-provoking, 158
unfair, 144: compensation for, 184–5
Distribution industry, days lost through strikes, 153
Dock workers, reduction in industrial action, 154
Donovan Commission (1968), 50–1
on drawbacks of apprenticeship system, 101–2
on restrictive labour practices, 83

Earnings-related benefit, 36
of decreasing value, 39
Economy, cost of unemployment to, 33–43
Electoral aspects of wage increases, 66
Electricity supply industry, improvement in productivity in, 84–5
Employers
lack of cohesion against strikes, 189
wage-inflation tax, 56
Employment Act (1980), 178–9
Employment protection legislation, 143
Employment Transfer scheme, 28–9
Energy price increases, effect on inflation, 46–7
Engineering industry
accidents, 133
agreement on overtime working, 127–8
days lost through strikes, 153
loss of apprenticeships, 106
low productivity, 92
overtime, 125
skilled trades entered through apprenticeships, 102
Training Board attempts at reforms, 105–6
Engineering Industry Training Board (EITB)
criticism of schools, 106
module approach to training, 106
Ethnic minorities
attitudes to unemployment, 25
on night work, 132
unemployment among, 24–5
young unemployed, 20

Financial hardship, 35–9
Flexible shift system, 126
Fringe benefits, for non-manual workers, 142–3

Handicapped people
and long-term unemployment, 14, 24
number unemployed 10, 24
*see also* Disabled people
Health and safety
class inequalities, 138
costs to employers, 134
lack of management information, 135
shop-floor representatives, 135
manual workers' jobs more hazardous, 133
Health insurance, as fringe benefit, 142, 143
Holiday entitlement
length-of-service additions, 129
of manual workers, 129, 130
of non-manual workers, 129–30

Holiday pay, differences between manual and non-manual workers, 129–30
Hours of work
  flexible shift system, 126
  manual/non-manual distinction, 125–30
  reduction in 1979/80 wage round, 126
  UK compared with continent, 126
Housing, as obstacle to mobility, 30–1

Illness
  and long-term unemployment, 14
  class differences, 138–9
  pay under medical suspension, 144
Income
  distribution, 61–5: not an electoral issue, 196
  losses from unemployment, 37–8
  of unemployed, 35, 36
  *see also* Wages
Incomes policies
  against public sector employees, 57–8
  as emergency measures, 68
  bedevilled by fragmented bargaining, 50
  Conservative attitudes, 70–3
  effect on higher paid workers, 63
  failure, 65–8
  for social justice, 62–3
  Layard's proposals, 56
  Meade's proposals, 54–6
  related to market forces, 77
  support from workers, 48
  *see also* Wage bargaining
Industrial action
  demonstrating employers' weaknesses, 188
  economic consequences, 162
  incidence in manufacturing industry, 155
  increasing militancy from late 1960s, 156
  inter-union disputes, 158–9
  involving breach of employment or commercial contracts, 176
  labour injunctions against, 176
  legal position, 173
  proposals to remove union immunities, 185
  *see also* Strikes
Industrial democracy, 144–5
  CNI against legislation, 145
  issues lost in recession, 146, 189
  lack of shop-floor interest, 145
  strike as way of demanding, 156
Industrial relations
  employers' initiative, 164
  shaky basis in UK, 169
  use of agreements rather than law, 177
Industrial training boards (ITBs), 108–9
  finance from MSC, 110
  number abolished (1981), 109
  reforms in early 1970s, 109
  *see also* Engineering Industry Training Board
Industry
  impact of strikes, 152–3
  reasons for failure, 80–1
  *see also* Manufacturing industry
Inflation
  caused by excessive wage awards, 47: and fragmentation of bargaining, 52–3
  encouraging workers' militancy, 157
Inner city areas, high unemployment in, 28

Job creation programme, 20–1
Job searching
  by long-term unemployed, 14–15
  disincentive effect of benefit payments, 40
  time off work for, 144
Job security
  threatened by productivity deals, 96–7
  threatened by strikes, 168
Job vacancies
  decline since 1979, 8
  reductions for young people, 18

Judiciary, hostility to union immunities, 174, 175, 176–7

Labour injunctions, 176
Labour Party
  electoral support from union members diminishing, 194–5
  link with unions, 56, 190–1
  no longer 'people's party', 195
  not supported by many union members, 191, 192
  suffering from change in popular attitudes, 191–2
Law and order, problems arising from unemployment, 43
Layard, Richard, 56
Living standards
  as main aim of unions, 193
  effect of industrial action, 162
  eroded in electoral mid-cycle, 67
  expectation of steady improvement, 48
  rise under Thatcher government, 73
  unaffected by wage rises in inflation, 67
London weighting, 59
Low-paid workers
  demands for legal minimum wage, 76
  high percentage made jobless, 38–9
  not helped by incomes policy, 66
  pay expectations from future jobs, 39–40

McGregor Commission on the newspaper industry, 87
Manning levels
  strike-provoking, 158
  *see also* Overmanning
Manpower Services Commission (MSC)
  community enterprise programme, 17
  cutbacks in staff, 42–3
  protests against cutbacks, 16
  STEP for long-term unemployed, 15–16
  work experience schemes, 20–1
Manual workers
  fall in total hours worked, 31
  main victims of recession, 11, 31
  *see also* Workers
Manufacturing industry, 182
  fall in employment, 28, 31–3
  incidence of industrial action, 155
  rapid drop in output (1980), 73
  small firms' problems, 32
  use of overtime, 128
Maternity leave, 144
Meade, James, 54–6
Meals, subsidised, 143
Microtechnology, TUC attitudes to, 103
Midlands
  low wage levels, 65
  unemployment, 26–7
Mining
  days lost through strikes, 153
  NUM cooperation with productivity plans, 85
  wages as result of strikes, 167
Mobility of workers, 28–9
  obstacles to, 30
Monetarist policies
  affecting unemployment levels, 35, 43
  effects on wage bargaining, 71
Moonlighting, 41
Motor vehicle industry
  accidents, 133
  days lost through strikes, 153
  few strikes in 1980s, 168
  Ford union moves towards greater workplace equality, 147–8
  in UK, compared with continent, 90–1: compared with Japan, 91
  industrial action, 155
  payment systems, 122
  slow work pace, 90–1
  union fragmentation, 91
  working practices at BL reformed, 97

National insurance surcharge, 56
National joint industrial council (NJIC) agreements, 51

Nationalised industries
 dilemma of strikes, 161
 *see also* Public sector
Newspaper industry
 management's lack of resistance to chapels, 86–7
 restrictive practices, 86
 unions' lack of control over chapels, 87
Night work
 attitudes to, 131
 health implications, 131
North of England, unemployment in, 27
North Sea oil industry, 28
Northern Ireland, unemployment in, 28

Organisation for Economic Cooperation and Development (OECD), unemployment levels, 1
Overmanning, 82
 in car industry, 90
 on railways, 92
 *see also* Manning levels
Overtime
 adverse effects on efficiency, 127
 cutback in recession, 126
 hours worked, 125
 manual/non-manual differences, 125–6
 to recoup strike losses in wages, 167
 TUC on disadvantages, 127, 128
Overtime pay
 of manual staff, 120
 of non-manual staff, 121

Part-time workers, not included in statistics, 10
Pay, *see* Wages
Pay Research Unit, 58
Payment by results, 120, 121
 favoured system, 122
Pension schemes, inequalities between manual and non-manual workers, 140–1
Pensions, state, unlikely to remain ahead of inflation, 140
People's March (1981), 3
Picketing
 Employment Act (1980) provisions, 162–3, 178
 TUC suggestions, 162, 163
Post Office
 agreement on overtime working, 128
 conflict between union and workers, 95
Printing, paper and publishing industry, union power over employment, 86
 *see also* Newspaper industry
Productivity
 changes imposed as result of economic conditions, 97
 EEC performance, 79
 in coalmining, 85
 in electricity supply industry, 84–5
 in shipbuilding, 88
 need for involvement of workers by management, 97
 output per head, 80
 seen as conflicting with job security, 96–7
 trade unions blamed for drop, 81–2
 UK performance, 79
Profit sharing schemes, 142
Promotion, not common in manual jobs, 121–2
Psychological problems
 of long-term unemployment, 14
 posed by insecure wage expectations, 124
Public sector
 Conservative policy on pay bargaining, 72
 employment as percentage of total workforce, 57
 involvement in strikes, 152, 160
 measures to outlaw 'union labour only' contracts, 185
 ministerial interference in pay matters, 58–9
 pay awards from Clegg commission, 73
 problems of wage bargaining, 57

Public sector – *continued*
  *see also* Nationalised industries
Public sector borrowing requirement (PSBR), 34
Public utilities, days lost through strikes, 153

Qualifications
  lack of, among long-term unemployed, 14
  lacked by young people, 18
  not sufficient for industry's needs, 100

Railway system
  absenteeism, 94
  causes of low productivity, 93–4
  inflexible shift pattern, 93
  lowest productivity in Europe, 92–3
  NUR agreement with BR (1980), 93
  overtime, 125
  report on London and Southeast commuter services, 93
  strength of local work groups, 94–5
  stress-related illness, 135
Rayner report, 41
Recruitment subsidy, 21
Redundancies
  combatted by short-time working compensation, 123
  increase in 1980, 32
  leading to long-term unemployment, 13
  minimum payments from employer, 141
  period of notice, 33
  procedures, 144
Regional differences
  in earnings, 64, 65
  in unemployment, 25–31
Respiratory infections, 135
Restrictive labour practices, 82
  at all occupational levels, 83
  by work groups, 83–4
  difficulties to be overcome, 96
Retirement age, 140
  cost of lowering to 60, 140
Riots (1981), 2, 25

Salaries, *see* Wages
Savings of unemployed, 38
Schools, needs for closer links with industry, 106
Scotland, unemployment in, 27–8
Secret ballots
  before industrial action, 162
  on closed shop agreements, 179, 184, 185
Shift premia, 120, 121
Shift working, 130–2
  health implications, 130
  social problems, 132
Shipbuilding industry
  joint management-union initiatives, 88
  payment schemes, 122
  strength of work group, 87–8
  union power over employment, 86
Shop stewards, 187
  power boosted by management, 188
Short-time working, 123
  government compensation scheme, 123
  guarantee payments, 144
Sick pay
  manual and non-manual workers compared, 136–8
  permanent disability benefits, 138
  state benefit entitlement, 136
Skillcentres, 111
Social security payments
  not an encouragement to militancy, 165
  to strikers' dependants, 164–5, 166
  *see also* Earnings-related benefit; Sick pay; Unemployment benefit
Southern England, employment advantages, 28
Special temporary employment programme (STEP), 15–16
  expenditure on young unemployed, 22

STEP – *continued*
superseded by community enterprise programme, 17
Steel industry
demarcation, 89
in UK: compared with continent, 89; compared with Japan and USA, 89
labour injunction granted against union, 177
locally agreed productivity deals, 97
national strike, 168
union agreement with BSC (1976), 88–9
Stress-related illnesses, 135
not confined to managerial staff, 136
Strike pay, sources of, 164
Strikes
against consumers and not employers, 160–1
among non-manual and public service workers, 160
as actions of opposing groups of workers, 160
as 'British disease', 150
as manifestations of class struggle, 156
by key workers, 161
causing lay-offs elsewhere, 154
changing nature in 1970s, 152
conduct, 161–3
correlation between incidence and plant size, 154–5
during recession, 167–9
economic consequences, 164–7
effect on 1970s, 151
in UK compared with other industrial nations, 150–1
increasing politicisation, 157
involving non-manual workers, 153–4
issues causing 1979 disputes, 159
large-scale, average length, 153
media exaggeration, 150
monthly figures (1980–1), 167–8
reduction in non-money issue strikes, 158
secondary action, 186
statistical inaccuracies, 152
TUC code of conduct, 162
Students, exclusion from statistics of unemployed, 10
Subsidies, employers', 21

Tax system
effect on lowest paid, 120
electoral appeal of changes, 195, 196
encouraging workers' militancy, 157
incentives for profit-sharing schemes, 142
rebates payable to strikers, 164, 166
reforms to equalise earnings, 66
Technological change, requiring new training approach, 107
Textile industry, days lost through strikes, 153
Trade unions
advantages of obtaining legal rights, 190
against dilution from TOPS trainees, 111
and elements of class consciousness, 193
and wage inflation, 59–60
attacks by judiciary, 174, 175, 176–7
attempts to gain workplace equality, 147
blamed for poor productivity, 81–2
CBI call for greater control by leaders over shop-floor representatives, 186–7
confronting government over pay bargaining, 55
Conservative document on immunities, 173
degrees of local power, 85–6
demands from business aimed at weakening powers, 183–4
direct control of labour, 86
distinguished from workers, 83
dues paid by direct deduction, 182

Trade unions – *continued*
effect of membership on wage levels, 60
effect on redundancy payments, 142
extension to white-collar workers, 63
funds threatened by legal action, 157, 185
immunities preferred to rights, 173–4
inter-union disputes, 158–9
labour injunctions against, 176
Labour Party links, 56, 190–1
lack of legal framework, 172–3
legislation giving greater immunity (1970s), 175–6
limited influence over members' lives, 194
little consistent interest in productivity, 85
little observance of TUC's guidelines on picketing, 163
lose unemployed members, 3–4
loss of tradition of solidarity, 192–3
members' view of power, 171
multiple unions within plants, 95–6
objection to 'free-riders', 183
opposed to widespread overtime, 127, 128
opposition to Employment Act, 178
opposition to Youth Training Scheme, 116
popular view of leaders as militants, 171–2
popular view of power, 171
powerful groups of workers, 74
representatives paid by employers, 187
secret ballots: before strikes, 162; on closed shop agreements, 179
slow response to unemployment, 3
strike pay, 164, 166
Tebbit proposals (1981), 184
time off work for activities, 144
TUC views on craft and technician training, 103
Victorian attitudes to, 83
view on incomes policy, 68
weakness of relations with members, 186–7
welcoming increased efficiency, 84
*see also* Workers

Training
barriers at workplace, 114
by mobile instructors, 112
changes to meet new technology, 107
collective funding scheme, 110
company-oriented, 105
CPRS criticism, 102–3
employers' lack of knowledge of government schemes, 112
firms' inability to plan ahead, 114–15
for unqualified school leavers, 113
French system, 117
in UK, compared with EEC, 100–1
lack of, among long-term unemployed, 14
lack of incentive, 114
limit of financial incentives to employers, 109
MSC's 'new initiative', 115
need for greater employer involvement, 117
of adults, 115
resistance to change, 103–4
role of ITBs, 108–9
state intervention, 108
unable to respond to new requirements, 103
West German system, 117
*see also* Apprenticeships

Training Opportunities Scheme (TOPS), 110–11
seen as diluting crafts, 111
structure and usefulness of scheme, 111
waiting lists, 112

Transport industry
days lost through strikes, 153
*see also* Railway system

Unemployed people
changing force, 5–8
characteristics, 11
cost to Exchequer, 34
financial hardship, 35–9
groups excluded from statistics, 10
lack of cohesion, 5, 10–11
little impact
long-term, 12–17
main categories, 11
mainly non-union people, 3–4
many previously low-paid workers, 38–9
objections to voluntary registration, 42–3
official definition, 8, 10
TUC-sponsored centres for, 4
with previous periods of unemployment, 38
Unemployment
changing composition, 5–8
cost per family, 35
cost to economy, 33–43
estimated loss in national production, 34
frictional, 7
government response, 43
in European countries (1980), 2
lack of revolt against, 2–5
psychological aspects, 10
regional variations, 25–31
world levels, 1
Unemployment benefit
dependent on previous stable employment, 36
disincentive aspects, 40
earnings related, 36, 39
failures to take up entitlement, 42
fraud cases, 41
groups debarred, 36
need for reform, 4
withdrawals and refusals, 42
Unemployment Review Officers, 41, 42
Unfair dismissal, 144, 184–5
United Kingdom, unemployment in, 1
growing problem through 1960s and 1970s, 2
post Second World War, 1
Unsocial hours, *see* Shift working

Vocational preparation programme, 113

Wage bargaining
affected by unemployment fears, 73–4
at plant or corporate level, 51–2
bidding-up practice, 50
CBI views, 52–4
collective, 50
concept of 'fairness', 63–4
Conservative approach, 71–3
in private sector, 49–52, 75
in public sector, 57–9
in West Germany, 68, 70
increasing living standards by reducing inflation, 55
industry-wide agreements, 49–50: used as base only, 51
lack of will to change system, 75–6
limitations of free collective bargaining, 68, 76
need for cohesion among private employers, 53
power shifted to trade unions, 60
proposed centralisation, 55
round related to national Budget, 53–4
system faults, 46, 48: potential for strikes, 169
Welsh TUC's Social Plan, 69–70
*see also* Incomes policy
Wages
affected by overtime cuts, 127
as basis of 1970s strikes, 158
as main reason for union membership, 193
as major factor in job flexibility, 41
comparability within social classes, 64–5
effect of industrial action, 162
factors influencing demands, 48–9
fluctuations in pay packets, 122–3
holiday pay, 129–30

Wages – *continued*
importance of differentials, 61–2
incremental stages, 121–2
inequalities, 75, 119–25
losses suffered by strikers, 165, 166
methods of payment, 124–5
non-manual earnings unaffected by illness, 137
occupational variations, 120
of manual workers, relative to age group, 121
of non-manual workers, relative to age group, 121
period of payment, 125
public/private sector comparability, 57
related to electoral cycles, 66
rises during 1970s, 46, 47
rises related to inflation, 46
structural changes encouraging militancy, 157–8
supplements earned by manual workers, 120
unrelated to firm's profits, 62
wage-inflation tax, 56
*see also* Income; Sick pay; Strike pay; Unemployment benefit
Welsh TUC, Social Plan, 69–70
Women
increases in number employed, 23
possibility of discrimination against, 24
unregistered jobless, 10, 24
*see also* Working wives
Work experience schemes, 20–1
*see also* Vocational preparation programme
Workers
changing attitudes to wages, 48–9
craft association mentality, 82–3
financial participation schemes, 142
independent power of work groups, 86
inflexibility imposed by training system, 102
little concern over manual/non-manual differences, 146
loss of power in recession, 189
manual tasks likely to become less numerous, 148
need for cooperation in productivity aims, 97
not protected against breach of contract while striking, 173
self-inflicted wounds of 1979 strikes, 159–60
status differences of manual and non-manual, 119
subordination to demands of capital, 190
trade unions distinct from, 83
*see also* Trade unions
Working conditions
manual/non-manual compared, 132–48
negotiated through closed shop, 182
Working wives
cushioning economic effects of strikes, 164
of unemployed men, 38
period of child-rearing, 121
related to husbands' periods of employment, 40
Workplace
defects in facilities, 132–3
little concern over inequalities, 146
moves towards manual/non-manual equality, 143–4

Young people
apprenticeship shortages, 104, 105
attitudes to jobs, 23
employers' dissatisfaction, 20
high percentage of unemployed, 17–18, 19, 20
long-term unemployed, 13
MSC proposals for better training provision, 115
problems of increased pay rates, 18
Youth employment subsidy, 21
Youth Opportunities Programme (YOP), 21
abuse by employers, 22
expansion, 22
replaced by Youth Training Scheme, 116
Youth Training Scheme, 116